Wallington's World

Wallington's World

A Puritan Artisan in Seventeenth-Century London

PAUL S. SEAVER

Stanford University Press, Stanford, California

Stanford University Press
Stanford, California
© 1985 by the Board of Trustees of the
Leland Stanford Junior University
Printed in the United States of America

Original printing 1985
Last figure below indicates year of this printing:
03   02   01   00   99   98   97   96   95   94

The illustration facing the title page
is a wood engraving of a turner at his
lathe done by Thomas Bewick or one of
his pupils, probably around the end of
the eighteenth century.

Stanford University Press publications are dis-
tributed exclusively by Stanford University
Press within the United States, Canada, and
Mexico; they are distributed exclusively by
Cambridge University Press throughout the rest
of the world.

Library of Congress Cataloging in Publication Data

Seaver, Paul S.
    Wallington's world.

    Bibliography:p.
    Includes index.
    1. Wallington, Nehemiah. 2. Puritans—England—Biography. 3. Artisans—
England—Biography. I. Title.
BX9339. W26S4 1985   285′.9′0924 [B]   84-40447
ISBN 0-8047-1267-0 (cl) ISBN 0-8047-1432-0 (pbk)

For My Parents

Preface

This study arose out of an effort to answer two questions: first, what did ordinary Englishmen make of the particular kind of Protestantism preached by the godly ministers, the Puritan clergy, in the decades during which Puritanism was a vital impulse; and second, in particular what did the urban Londoner make of their message? The thought and even the personalities of the clerical intelligentsia are comparatively well documented and well studied, beginning almost in their own time in the collective biographies of Samuel Clarke and Edmund Calamy, and ranging down to our own time in Patrick Collinson's illuminating studies of Edward Dering and John Field and in the apparently inexhaustible series of works on the Mather dynasty in Old and New England. Their powerful lay patrons among the titled aristocracy—the great Leicester and the Earl of Huntington, or in a later generation the Earl of Warwick and Lord Brooke—are more than insubstantial shades, names once to be conjured with but now no more than empty titles. And their gentry adherents, the Barringtons of Essex or the Lewkenors of Suffolk, are, thanks to the preservation of family papers, known to some degree in their hopes and inward thoughts. Even the commonalty have not been neglected. If little is known about particular individuals beyond their names attached to wills and depositions, vestry minutes and protestations, the collective mentality of the godly of Keith Wrightson's and David Levine's Terling or of Peter Clark's Kent has been brought to light. Nevertheless, whereas these studies have been multiplied until they number far more than can be mentioned in the brief compass of a Preface, the urban artisan remains largely unknown. We know far more about Margaret Spufford's Cambridgeshire husbandmen than we do about the godly London artisans, and yet it is hard to imagine English Puritanism without London and in particular to imagine that part of the "Great Rebellion" that can in some sense be called the Puritan revolution without the London crowds, the London trainbands, and the London godly.

The study of the obscure London artisan that follows is justified in part, then, because it illuminates that most unlikely "dark corner" of English Puritanism, London itself. And yet to such a justification, it is only fair to append a caveat. For all that Nehemiah Wallington's life and writings reveal much that was obscure in the absence of such a glimpse inside an articulate artisan's mental world, the fact remains that one does not emerge from such a study with a clear picture of "popular religion" in early Stuart England or even in early Stuart London. At least not a picture of popular religion and popular beliefs analogous to that Carlo Ginzburg has uncovered among the peasant *benandanti* of Friuli. Wallington's mental world is not separated by a gulf of incomprehension from the mental world of the Protestant intelligentsia; on the contrary, his categories of thought and angle of vision were profoundly shaped by their preached and written words, their sermons, guidebooks, and catechisms. At the very moment when lay literacy was opening a gulf between the high culture of the lettered and the popular culture of the illiterate masses, Puritanism created for a brief moment a minority religious culture that joined artisan and husbandman, minister and gentleman. It was a culture that could be deliberately learned and studied by the godly; once internalized it left the godly blind to much of traditional culture and largely immune to its attractions. So at least seems to be one of the apparent lessons of this study. But if the traditional world of the urban artisan had vanished along with the public pageantry, the ceremony, and the pious observances of the urban guilds and confraternities, the post-Reformation godly set out to explore a new mental world that brought under intense scrutiny not only the outward actions of the moral man, but even his most vagrant thoughts and errant feelings. The monuments to this new culture are not the Corpus Christi pageants or guild chapels of an earlier generation, not public artifacts at all, but the new diaries, letters, memoirs, and autobiographies that testify to the extraordinary vitality of the inner lives of these ordinary Englishmen who chose the path of unremitting self-examination, as though constantly before the throne of judgment. This study owes more to others than I can easily acknowledge, and the Notes cite only my more obvious scholarly debts. I am particularly obliged to the archivists of the Guildhall Library in London and of the British Library, who made both the originals and the microfilm copies of the Wallington papers accessible, and who remain so patiently helpful in the face of the importunities of the Americans and Canadians whose annual pilgrimage disturbs the quiet of their reading rooms every summer. I am particularly grateful to the archivist of the Folger Library in Washington, D.C., who brought to my attention the existence of the one Wallington notebook that seems to have found its way to this side of the Atlantic and who then made a microfilm copy available. I owe much to the indulgence of Stanford colleagues and graduate students who have listened patiently to my Wallington stories for a number of years now and in particular want to acknowledge the helpful suggestions of David Riggs, Paul Robinson, Judith Brown, and Lewis Spitz. I have obviously learned much from the transatlantic community of scholars who write on early modern topics; in particular I have benefited much from the conversations and friendships of Sears McGee and Richard Greaves on this side of the Atlantic and Felicity Heal and Nicholas Tyacke on the other. Finally, I want to thank Conrad Russell, whose careful reading caught some of my more egregious blunders and tamed some of my wilder enthusiasms.

Wallington's hand is an exceptionally clear schoolboy italic, but his spelling and punctuation, like those of most of his contemporaries, are haphazard at best. In the quoted material I have modernized spelling and punctuation; his meaning and feeling do not, I think, suffer from appearing in modern dress. Days, months, and years remain in Old Style, but dates falling between January 1 and March 25 are expressed as follows: January 5, 1639/40.

P.S.S.

Contents

Wallington's World

*Not out of a vain affectation of my own glory, which I know how
little it can avail me, when I am gone hence; but out of a sincere
desire to give glory to my God, (whose wonderful Providence I have
noted in all my ways) have I recorded some remarkable passages of
my forepast life: what I have done is worthy of nothing, but silence
and forgetfulness; but what God hath done for me, is worthy of
everlasting and thankful Memory.*

—Joseph Hall

1. The Examined Life

Nehemiah Wallington was a London Puritan artisan whose long
life (1598–1658) left almost no discernible impact on his time. Yet he
was nevertheless in almost every respect an exceptional Englishman. In an era of high mobility when many Englishmen moved,
sometimes great distances, in search of work, of better economic
prospects, or of means to escape from religious persecution, Wallington lived out his life in the tiny parish of St. Leonard's Eastcheap
a few dozen yards north of London Bridge.[1] At a time when most
ordinary Englishmen in the course of adolescence sought appren-
ticeships or went into service in another household, Wallington remained in the house of his birth, where he learned his father's trade
as a turner and became free of the Company of Turners by patrimony.[2] Jacobean Englishmen ordinarily married late, when time and
economic opportunity permitted the formation of a new household;
Wallington was married in his twenty-third year to an exceptional
woman who, despite numerous births and miscarriages, nevertheless outlived her long-lived husband.[3] Wallington was a Puritan and
as such a member of a religious minority. He was literate at a time
when literacy was not yet commonplace even among Londoners,
artisans, and Puritans.[4] Finally, the sheer quantity of writing he left
behind makes him not merely exceptional but virtually unique.

Although a number of seventeenth-century Puritans have left records of their lives—diaries, spiritual autobiographies, and letters—
such written remains are usually from the pens of Puritan clergy,

gentry, or (occasionally) merchants.[5] The lives of most artisans can be glimpsed only fleetingly through the appearance of their names in parish and guild records, and in court depositions and wills. Nehemiah Wallington left no signed will and testament, and the churchwardens' accounts and vestry minutes for his parish have long since vanished. However, more than 2,600 pages of personal papers—memoirs, religious reflections, political reportage, letters, and a spiritual diary—have survived, and these make his life, and even more his thought and attitudes, more accessible than those of any other artisan of his time.[6]

The survival of such a quantity of private writings was not entirely accidental, for what we have today are not rough notes or miscellaneous bundles of family papers but rather works carefully copied in a schoolboy's italic, sometimes indexed, and explicitly intended for posterity. The surviving notebooks are, in fact, but part of a much larger corpus that once existed. Late in life Wallington wrote the last of his notebooks that have come down to us, a long volume to which he attached the running title, "An Extract of the Passages of My Life and A Collection of Several of My Written Treatises," a work completed at the end of December 1654. Spurred on to the writing by some "earnestly importuning me to print some of my books," Wallington finally resolved not to publish any "while I live"—"so many works continually come forth so excellent, far surpassing my capacity"—but in the process he determined, "if God spare life, to look over all the works my hands had written and give a little hint of the chief things what the books contain with some of the frailties of my life and God's mercies in his Christ unto me."[7] His brief apologia is preceded by a catalogue of 47 titles, to which he later added three more that he had initially overlooked.[8] Given such an extraordinary corpus of work—it is hard to think of any more prolific writer even in that wordy generation—it is no wonder that Wallington confessed at one point that some "say I have lost much time and neglected my calling and so brought myself to some want" by so much writing, "and I say so too, for I will not willingly excuse my sin."[9]

These 50 volumes—some 20,000 pages at least—were written between 1618, when the first was begun, and 1654, when Wallington decided on December 30 "to buy no more [books] to write in," resolving instead "to begin the New Year better . . . in holiness of life and conversation."[10] Sixteen of the notebooks were begun before 1640; 34 followed in the next fourteen years. Four of the books he gave away, three to his wife (a collection of sermons, a collection of Psalms, and a book entitled "The Mighty Works of the Lord which is a Prop to Faith" in 1646), and one to his half-sister Patience, appropriately enough on the grace of patience (it is typical of Wallington to see virtues, such as patience, as the consequence of unmerited grace). The largest number of notebooks, eleven, were accounts of God's mercies and what Wallington termed "returns of prayer," descriptions of how God answered prayers either inwardly in giving him a measure of spiritual peace or outwardly in the circumstances of his life. Three other notebooks on his sins and on the remedies for them prescribed by Scripture, as well as a fourth entitled "The Cry of Conscience," are all largely self-disciplinary in intent. He wrote two treatises on God's judgments and two more on the woeful state of the wicked and the happy state of the godly that provided reassurance of ultimate justice and of God's providential interference to obtain it. There are two on the benefits of faith and a third on God's promises—apparently works of practical divinity rather than of formal theology—and two on the Sacrament of the Lord's Supper and the benefits to be obtained by it. Similar to the last named are two notebooks on the benefits to be obtained by public fasts. Related to these were two collections of meditations, a volume in which he examined "the marks" that proved he was "a child of God," and three volumes of his various covenants, protestations, and engagements, both public and private.

There are six volumes, beginning with the account of the sufferings of Burton, Bastwick, and Prynne in 1637, which record political and military events. These seem to fit into a distinctive category of public, rather than personal, history, although that was a distinction Wallington would not have entirely subscribed to. He called a typical notebook of such news, begun in 1643, "The Wonder-Working God, or the God that Worketh Wonders," in which, along with accounts of "Coventry's victories over the Cavaliers" and of the "great store of ammunition taken from Sir John Heydon's house in the Minories," are accounts of "God's providence in guiding of bullets" and "God's mercies in discovering a hellish plot against the City of London."[11] Not only were God's providence and His mercy as evident in historical events as they were in Wallington's private life, but the two intersected in public and private prayer, for the volume begins with a description of how "God heareth and answereth our prayers"—sometimes providentially, sometimes more mercifully than we deserve—and ends with a warning "not to rest in our prayers," for providence frequently works through the instrument of human action.

Finally Wallington wrote a volume of exemplary history, two volumes of favorite Psalms, four volumes of sermons that he heard and thought worth preserving (notes on sermons are found in other volumes as well), a volume of collected letters, both Wallington's and those of others, and a catalogue of his books, both manuscript and printed, which also contained an exhortation to his wife and child and his will and testament written in 1643. There is little formal, systematic theology, although the table of contents of the work entitled "The Mighty Works of the Lord, which is a Prop to Faith," written in 1646, suggests that that work was a compendium of theological commonplaces, for there were sections on the power of God, the providence of God, the eternity of God, and then again on Christ's incarnation, on election and redemption, justification, the imputation of righteousness, and sanctification.[12] Much more typical in its focus on practical divinity and on the development of his own spiritual life are the contents of the book Wallington called "Great Sorrow Turned into Great Rejoicing," written in 1650 in the light not of what he had come to understand "by human learning but that which I sensibly feel and know by my experience." Besides 74 pages of autobiographical material (entitled "an extract of some of the passages of my life"), it contained an account of the final sickness and death of Wallington's parson, Mr. Henry Roborough, as well as "judgments upon those that did take this new Engagement," a substantial section on how "sins of commission and sins of omission are great troubles to [the] spirit," and finally nine rules or "means to keep me from falling."[13] In fact, Wallington was an inveterate cataloguer and list-maker. His book "A Touchstone of Comfort," written in 1646, contained a list of "Six Sins that Trouble Me" and eighteen "Remedies against Discontent." A book of articles to guide the reformation of his life, which he wrote in 1640, contained "30 directions on how to hear well, and 30 directions on how to pray well, and two directions on how to sanctify the sabbath, and 28 directions on how to go to the Lord's Table well."[14] Nowhere in this vast collection of autobiographical, spiritual, and historical work is there any volume of poetry—although Wallington copied verse occasionally into his notebooks, and the psalms that he sang as part of family worship were undoubtedly a metrical version.[15] Nor is there an account book, or any systematic record of the profits and losses of his shop. How much of this huge corpus was Wallington's original work is not easy to determine. In 1650 he noted that he had not only written "above forty books and read over the Bible many times," but had also read "above two hundred other books."[16] His father had given him a Bible in 1615, when he was seventeen, and his brother John had given him a copy of John Brinsley's *The True Watch and Rule of Life* in the same year—the beginning of what was to become a very substantial library of Puritan writings, to which Wallington added in the 1640's another substantial collection of current newsbooks.[17] Although the first book that he notes buying, *The Bearbaiting of Women*, was soon got rid of "because it was contrary to God's word," book buying became something of an addiction, and Wallington lamented late in life that he was prone to buy "more than I need, having enough already, saying 'if thou gettest but a word for thy soul, it is money well laid out.'"[18] It is not possible to reconstruct his library in the absence of any surviving catalogue, but he does continually allude to books he has read, ranging from John Dodd's *A Plaine and Familiar Exposition upon the Ten Commandments* and Edward Elton's *A Plaine and Easie Exposition of Six of the Commandments*, both purchased in 1620, to John Preston's *Two Godly and Learned Treatises upon Mortification and Humiliation*, which Wallington mentions in a letter written on December 25, 1638.[19] Sometimes he includes the name of the author and title he is quoting from or summarizing, as he does in the table of contents to his notebook called "the Bitter Cries and Complaints of Good and Bad at the Terrible Grim Looks of Sin," a book that includes, along with a number of "doleful complaints" of various people, a half-dozen pages on "Mr. Perkins's Dialogue and State of a Christian."[20] At other times he notes the author in the text itself, as he does on June 13, 1654, when he mentions that he did "meet with so much sweetness and profit in living an holy life" in reading Jeremiah Burroughs's works that he felt "constrained to write a little of that which is most useful," after which follows 45 pages of reflections on "the right manner of sanctifying the name of God," pages otherwise indistinguishable from other reflections or meditations except that at the end he concludes, "Thus I have written a few broken scraps what was most liking to my mind out [of] that man of God, Mr. Burroughs his book."[21] Finally, there are occasions—it is impossible to tell how many—when he quotes and paraphrases without attribution, as he does for several pages on the proper use of God's afflictions by God's children, which is taken from Arthur Dent's *Plaine Mans Path-Way to Heaven*.[22] What is evident is that Wallington was not a passive reader who simply copied memorable passages into a commonplace book. Rather, if his handling of the material from Dent's *Plaine Mans Path-Way* is typical, quoted material is interspersed with his own thoughts and observations, and his own reflections are expressed in a manner indistinguishable from that of the sources quoted, creating a unity of style and content characteristic of all of Wallington's excursuses into questions of practical divinity.

The six notebooks that have survived, and presumably the whole corpus, were intended as a legacy for his children. If he were too poor to leave them much in the way of worldly goods—"for I may say, as Peter said to the lame man, 'silver and gold have I none'"—he did nevertheless want to leave them "such precepts . . . as myself have received of the Lord" in a long and troubled life, "small quittance," as he himself admitted in the only will and testament that has survived.[23] At the time of his death only his daughter Sarah among his children yet lived, but Wallington had made it clear long before that the writings should go to her and her husband. Between November 1647 and January of the following year, Wallington notes that he and his son-in-law had read over "The Mercies of God" together early each morning.[24] All the extant volumes are endorsed by the son-in-law, Jonathan Houghton, and dated September 9, 1658, apparently the day on which Wallington's widow turned them over to him.

More generally, the impulse behind this vast quantity of writing was evidently a desire, on the one hand, to provide a means to help in leading a disciplined, examined life, and, on the other, to glorify God. In fact these ends were to be achieved by the same process. "I glorify God by self-examination and judgment of myself. As it is also God's command to examine myself, so also in examining myself I see much of God, which doth abound much to the glory of God."[25] For Wallington the real problem lay not in finding an adequate justification for self-scrutiny—that was easily done—but rather "in discovering my sin," in leaving written evidence for posterity of the failures of a godly man. With some bravado Wallington confronted the problem head on: "Did not David, a holy man, pen down his own abominable sins of adultery and murder, and so shame and condemn himself that God may have the glory of all?"[26] Shame was the inevitable consequence of an honest revelation of the details of one's life. Nevertheless, he saw that the real justification for autobiography lay precisely in its particularity, for "in the naming of particulars . . . it may be for the good of others when it hits upon the same particular sorrow or affliction which they may be in."[27] In any case, the ultimate danger lay not in self-disclosure and the disgrace that might follow, but in the scrutiny of that final judge, "for although the matter be good that I have written, yet if my life and conversation be not answerable, Oh then what an heavy account have I to give at the great and dreadful day of judgment when all books shall be open and these my own handwriting shall be brought against me."[28] After all, in the final analysis it was "the assurance of Jesus Christ," not the "applause and praise of men" that was needed, and if his books directed him and others "in the way that was holy," they had fulfilled their function.[29]

Wallington tried schemes of self-discipline with all the faith of a modern American trying the latest dietary fad, and with a good deal more persistence: "one while I did write down my sins every day"; earlier he had tried the discipline of New Year's resolutions; "after this I kept a diary of my life, the comings and goings of the Spirit." "Oh, how many ways," he admitted ruefully, "have I taken to live a holy life"; but what is significant is that they all involved a written record.[30] As he notes of letters he copied, "some are to instruct and advise, some to reprove and admonish, some are sweet and comfortable, and some are to stir up to praise and thankfulness."[31] An unexamined life was a life not worth living—"Oh, let not one night pass over my poor head in which I examine not how I have spent the day"[32]—but such an examined and painfully introspective existence was never seen as an end in itself, as a work of art or an effort to create meaning in a meaningless world. Rather, what scrupulous self-examination revealed was at once a record of human failure and of God's mercy in accepting and loving his fallen creation nonetheless. It was this latter aspect, the attention of a divinity who noted even the fall of a sparrow, that gave shape and dignity to the small triumphs and failures of an ordinary life, that elevated such a life, in fact, into a part of a cosmic drama. It was his determination to convey this central fact to his posterity—that even the life of an insignificant London artisan was of consequence in the eyes of God—that led

Wallington, sometimes with a desperate urgency, to labor harder at his writing desk than at his turner's lathe. "But shall these mercies of the Lord rest in silence? No! No! I thought good rather to take notice of them, that the generation to come might stand up and praise the name of the Lord."[33] Each mercy must be noted, examined, analyzed, and understood, for to fail to do so was an act of criminal folly as well as of gross ingratitude. In particular it was necessary to take "notice of God's great mercies in pulling me out, as a firebrand from the burning," for his election was not only the central fact of his life but also the miracle that made that life so important to record. Wallington knew himself to be a sinner, and for a sinner such as he to be saved seemed such a gratuitous act of grace and unmerited favor that showing the account of it "in this my book to some poor distressed soul, it did comfort and revive them."[34] "Godly and Christian letters" in turn, if sanctified by God to our use, served like "the Apostles' Epistles . . . to reprove, admonish, instruct, and comfort the Church of God."[35] What "fruit and benefit" Wallington gained by the sacrament worth recording in his diary "The Growth of a Christian," so that "all others might be encouraged to go to it preparedly as often as occasion is offered."[36]

In a world in which goodness seemed rewarded by poverty and obscurity Wallington might have noted God's heavy judgments on sabbath-breakers and drunkards simply as evidence that the world was ultimately just and that the enemies of the saints and of their godly ways were manifestly punished, even in this world, by their ghastly deaths. In fact Wallington knew all men to be sinners, even the saints, and he recorded these terrible judgments to reveal God's righteousness, but even more to show the ultimate mystery of a life in which some sinners were struck down "in the very act of their sins, having neither the time, power, nor heart to repent."[37] Accounts of sudden death were not only a warning that "God will not be mocked," but also served as "a little emblem of the great day of judgment," for all sinners sinned in the face of judgment, and the fact that any person escaped immediate judgment and lived to pray for mercy was in itself proof of God's ultimate love and good will toward disobedient men.[38]

All history, collective as well as personal, taught lessons, and Wallington kept his journals of political events essentially to record the public life of God's children and God's dealings with his latter-day

Israelites, for "Christ will have care of his own children and cause: at this very time the delivery of his Church and the ruin of his enemies is in working."[39] Nowhere in these notebooks is there any sense of detached curiosity, or of the recording of personal or political events for their inherent interest. The didactic purpose is everywhere controlling.

If the surviving notebooks do not provide a coherent autobiography, it is due in part to Wallington's lack of interest in his life as such. What was important, what had to be recorded, was his life *sub specie aeternitatis*. Hence, much of his writings has an almost sermonic structure: theological truths illustrated and offering practical lessons for the discerning eye. Thus, Wallington's substantial and circumstantial account of the robbing of his house on August 1, 1641, concludes with an expression of gratitude for "God's goodness" that more was not stolen; and he then immediately asks "why doth the Lord permit this thief to steal from me his poor child that have some care to get it honestly?" Reflection immediately suggests the answer: "because the Lord doth see the world is ready to steal away my heart; therefore, He doth it in love to wean me from the world and to cause me to set my heart on that which no thief can steal away." The robbery became a lesson in the proper object of one's affections, and once the theological truth is discerned, it is necessary to apply it practically. "The use that I make to myself of this is (that) I see the love of God that he gives me but one small, light lash, for I might have lost a far deal more, even to my undoing . . . , but I do see a great providence of God in the preservation of the little that I have, his name be praised."[40] Similarly, Wallington's account of the plots of the wicked against the godly, beginning with Cain's plot against Abel and concluding with one discovered on December 19, 1642, by which the malignant citizens of London were to seize the Tower, open the prisons, and make themselves masters of the City, is followed by a section entitled "Use of the Plots," which begins by asserting that

> here you may see of all this that hath been said how the poor Church of God is like a woman with child near her travail, which would fain bring forth and cannot. . . . And also you see many an excellent blessing and mercy in the very birth, for this honorable Parliament (as the Mother) to bring forth, and cannot. . . . Stand still and behold the salvation of the Lord, which he will show to his poor despised children, for the Lord will do all himself and that for our good. . . . And if reformation should

have come as easily as it did seem at first, we should not have so esteemed of it.[41]

Wallington's life and his reflections on his times were of no interest to himself, nor, he was convinced, to his posterity except to the degree that they displayed God's providence at work in the world. It was this dimension that gave otherwise trivial events their importance and made them worth preserving to the end of time.

The desire to preserve a record of God's providential acts will account for the existence and survival of such written records, but it is surely not an adequate explanation for their incredible quantity. Wallington may have labored under a compulsion, but he had not the excuse of the professional—the cleric or university fellow—for whom the written word was the normal mode of expression and communication. Wallington lived in the midst of a substantial household that included maid servants, apprentices, and journeymen in addition to his immediate family. He was also a busy shopkeeper, producing wooden wares that he sold along with other goods regularly purchased wholesale from chapmen, and he was, besides, a Puritan whose formal religious duties—family and private prayer, in addition to attendance at church and at weekday lectures—absorbed considerable time and energy. Yet at times the need for the discipline of writing seemed to override other considerations both of personal convenience and of family obligation.

On Easter Monday in 1643 he tells us that he intended to awake at one o'clock in the morning in order to find the time to write. Not surprisingly, he found himself instead loath to arise at such an hour, but he cured that wayward impulse by recalling "how my sweet Savior did arise early for my redemption, and shall I not arise early to write of his mercies?" Some hours later in the full light of day his wife, daughter, and sisters tried to persuade him to desert his study and accompany them on a springtime expedition across the river to the fields of Peckham on the Surrey side; but, although he confessed that he did "much delight to take my pleasure in walking in the fresh air with my dear ones," considerations of "the sadness of the times" and of his own resolution led him to determine to "deny myself of my outward comforts" and to remain at home to write. Evidently fearing that he sounded too censorious and pharisaical, he hastily added that he had "not once thought the worse of them nor the better of myself because they did not as I do."[42] Generous thoughts toward his wife and family he could allow himself, but such thoughts in no way weakened his resolve to remain at home at his desk. His sense that writing was a religious duty led him to forgo even those legitimate recreations a proper Puritan might permit himself.

Whence came the urgency to write and to write so much? On May 11, 1643, a day of thanksgiving, Wallington heard Hugh Peter preach on verses 23 and 24 of Psalm 136, "Who remembered us in our low estate, for his mercy endureth for ever, and hath redeemed us from our enemies," in the course of which Peter urged his auditors to "be not unwise, but keep your day book; write down your sins on one side, and on the other side God's little mercies, aye, write down the fall of the cross and that your Baal's priests are thrust out and faithful ministers put in their room. Tell the Lord we live by mercy." As Wallington observed, "this matter . . . did like me well, because by God's mercy I practice it already." And that is the point. Although he went on to note that he intended "to do it in a more exact manner," he recorded Hugh Peter's suggestion in the midst of a three-page summary of the sermon that occurs on the ninety-seventh through ninety-ninth folios of a notebook he had been keeping since January 1641.[43] At the same time he was collecting material for his voluminous notebooks of political news, his growing collection of letters, and his record of God's judgments on sabbath-breakers and drunkards. He hardly needed Hugh Peter's reminder to send him to his desk.

Undoubtedly familial example had something to do with Nehemiah's compulsive journal-keeping. At least in his later years Wallington's father, John, Sr., evidently kept a journal similar to Nehemiah's "A Record of the Mercies of God," for in a letter that John wrote to his nephew, the minister John Allen, in 1635, he asks that Allen send him an account of "some remarkable things in your country, for I do love to keep a monument of God's wonderful works of mercy and judgment."[44] A few years later Nehemiah provides what is perhaps another clue in a couple of letters he wrote to Henry Roborough, the curate of St. Leonard's Eastcheap, in the winter of 1640–41. The existence of these letters is in itself a curiosity, for Wallington, a neighbor and regular churchgoer, hardly had to write in order to communicate with his parson, and he evidently perceived the oddity of his proceedings, for he observed parenthetically at the beginning of the first letter that "forasmuch as I cannot speak my mind to you, I make bold to write." Since he then proceeded to bare his soul, his resort to writing is perhaps understandable, although he obviously expected that Roborough would not reply by the same means, for he concludes by suggesting that Roborough take his "own convenient time to send for me and examine me about these things." Less than a fortnight later he wrote again, confessing at the outset in the way of an excuse that he was "an ill-writer but a worse speaker," and going on to note that he had "intended to come to you every day this week (to speak my mind to you), and I think Satan hindered me, and this morning at three o'clock I had some thoughts in my mind of you, intending to come to you, but for fear I should be prevented as I have been, I made bold to write."[45] Wallington and Roborough did not differ greatly in age, and at this time they had known each other for twenty years. Roborough had been aware all along of Wallington's spiritual worries. Is it possible that Wallington was less inhibited by Satan's intervention than by his own diffidence in speaking, by his "want of wisdom" in his words? Years later, in August 1654, in the midst of negotiations over the taking of a new apprentice, Wallington carefully rehearsed his lines, but "though I had purposed what to say . . . , yet when he did come, I did forget and could not tell what to say but few words to little purpose, as if I did not care." Such incoherence by a master turner of more than 30 years' standing when confronted by an adolescent negotiating to become his servant filled Wallington with shame "that others should see how weak and simple I am in my dealings." But worse than the shame was his bafflement, for it "did so vex and terrify my mind that I know not what to do."[46] He was manifestly not an "ill-writer," but he may well have been "a worse speaker," unable normally to give verbal expression to the burden of his thoughts, shamed by his incapacity in comparison with his more socially adept and more articulate father and older brother, and hence given to retreating gratefully to the privacy of his study where, master of the written word, he could unburden himself in safety.

Whatever the compulsions that drove Wallington to write so much, he has left us nothing like a genuine autobiography. He tells us little about his childhood, and virtually nothing about his schooling or his training in the craft of wood turning. We do not know how he met his wife, Grace Rampaigne, or how their marriage was arranged. It is not possible now to discover where they lived, or where their house was in relation to his father's and brother's house, if indeed John, Sr., lived with John, Jr., in his later years. For all that

Wallington tells us so much about his spiritual life, he is largely silent about his public life in his guild, parish, and ward. He tells us far more about the politics of England than he does about the politics of his neighborhood. If, then, there is any justification for attempting a portrait of this most peculiar Puritan, it must lie in the intrinsic interest of the fragments of his life that can still be reconstructed. His life is important, then, not because he was a typical London Puritan artisan—the very fact that he wrote so much renders him inevitably exceptional at least in that respect—but rather because what we know about early seventeenth-century artisans, Puritan or otherwise, is largely statistical in nature, and Wallington's papers offer a unique opportunity to gain some insight into the thought and attitudes of one such artisan toward himself and his world, his family and friends, toward the process of getting and spending, and toward the revolution in England that he thought was the great manifestation of God's will toward his children in his time.

[M]y father did say to me, he did give me my name Nehemiah because
I should imitate the example of Nehemiah. Now his example is a
motive to me to do what is pleasing to God as in Nehemiah the first,
how did he enquire after the distressed Church of God, and when he
had heard of their miseries, Oh, how did he weep, fast, and pray to God
for them. And in the second chapter . . . how Nehemiah is content
to let go his own honor and pleasure and takes great pains with
enduring scoffs and mocks and all for the good of the Church. . . .
And in Chapter XIII there I see Nehemiah setting upon a reformation,
and his zeal for the cause of God and against the profanation of the
Lord's Day. But I needed to have gone no further than Jesus Christ,
for he is the best example that can be.

2. *To Begin a New Life*

Nehemiah Wallington was the tenth child and the fourth son of
John Wallington, Citizen and Turner, and his wife, Elizabeth Hall,
daughter of Anthony Hall, Citizen and Skinner, and his wife Jane.[1]
Retrospectively, Nehemiah saw his own birth in rather ominous, if
anticlimactic terms: "I, Nehemiah Wallington, had Christian parents, a holy father and a gracious mother. Yet they could not derive
grace in my soul, for May the 12, 1598, at five o'clock in the morning
was I born in sin and came forth polluted into this wicked world."[2]
Five days later he was baptized.[3] Important as these occasions
doubtless were to the Wallingtons, for Nehemiah they ushered in
what he later saw as the first stage in his life, when he "was in a most
vile and sinful condition."[4] When he came eventually to write his
"Record of the Mercies of God," he chose understandably to begin
not with these events but instead with an event 23 years later, dated
circumstantially "the last week of December on Tuesday morning
1621," when, "as I lay in my bed, I did propose on New Year's Day to
begin a new life."[5]

By that time, despite his comparative youth, Nehemiah was an
independent householder, living at the corner of Philpot Lane and
Little Eastcheap in the parish of St. Andrew's Hubbard, immediately
to the east of St. Leonard's.[6] He was already a master turner, free of
the Company by patrimony, and had on his father's advice hired his
first journeyman, Edward Cale; nine months earlier he had bound
his first apprentice, James Weld.[7] He was also a husband of some six-

month's standing, having married Grace Rampaigne on Sunday, June 18.[8] In short, late December 1621 found Wallington very much in the midst of things as a young husband, householder, and shop-keeper, a distinctly odd time from which to date a new life.

In truth, what Wallington subsequently describes is not a new life at all, but rather "eleven great and wonderful Deliverances" that God in his great mercy had given him in 1618 and 1619 from "eleven sore temptations of Satan."[9] A new life was in fact profoundly to be wished for, but, as Wallington was to discover, never to be completely realized. What seems to have prompted his decision to begin a new life with the new year was his recognition that he had just survived a major crisis with body and soul miraculously intact, for he had experienced the death of the soul that comes of despairing of God's love; he had sinned against the spirit and had been saved despite his sins.

For a generation or two in the late-sixteenth and early-seventeenth centuries, what we would probably define as late-adolescent identity crises were reasonably commonplace, particularly in the lives and biographies of the clerical saints. Conversions, which brought these crises to a happy conclusion, usually followed what was subsequently seen as several years of college life characterized by insufficient academic zeal and a longing for whatever fleshpots the university towns provided. Conversion itself was usually attributed to the action of obviously unmerited grace conveyed by the Word spoken by one of the great charismatic preachers of the university, after which the reborn soul characteristically dedicated his life to the professional ministry and associated himself with the community of the Puritan saints.[10] The years away from home at college normally provided the setting for this rite of passage, which transformed the doubting schoolboy into the dedicated professional preacher. For the future lay saint, apprenticeship seems sometimes to have provided the ambit for this bridging experience of growing maturity that came between the dependency of the family hearth and the adult life of the independent householder.[11] But Wallington was never apprenticed; instead, he experienced the most acute stages of his crisis in the bosom of his family, and although independence came early, the inner struggle continued for decades during which he had to remind himself constantly of the reality of God's unconditional love and the permanency of God's promises to his saints.

Nevertheless, the crisis that preceded this lifelong struggle was both acute and real enough. Wallington diagnosed himself in the psychiatric jargon of his time as "troubled in my mind and melancholy"; his condition might be characterized more simply as suicidal despair.[12] As he later noted, he had "many sorrows" and was "weak"; he had also been born into a godly family and learned early to practice private prayer, although as he said, "whether for fashion sake or custom sake I know not." He had as a consequence learned to pray effectively, and he had prayed conscientiously, he thought, that he might have a sight of his sins, not realizing how "bitter the sight" of his sins would be, "and the Lord did hear my prayers . . . and gave me a sight of my sins."[13] Knowledge of one's fallen nature was supposed to lead to a recognition of one's complete dependence on the unmerited grace of God whose salvation came in spite of man's rebellion, but as the physicians of the soul well knew, a sight of one's sins might instead lead to spiritual despair, to a conviction that one was irredeemably damned. Wallington realized that his despair was itself a satanic temptation, but he also reasoned that the longer he lived, the more he would sin and the greater his eventual and well-deserved punishment would be. Hence, logic suggested that he might abbreviate his punishment by ending his life, the sooner the better, and Wallington's account of his new life in fact begins with a description of a series of attempts to put a period to that life before it had fairly begun.[14]

Except for the depth of Wallington's despair and the extremity of his reaction to the loss of hope, he seems in this, as in so much else, a conventional Puritan of the second generation, the generation born into godly households and early aware of a responsibility to the godly community. Like Wallington, John Winthrop, the future governor of Massachusetts, claimed in later life that "in my youth I was very lewdly disposed, inclining unto and attempting (so far as my years enabled me) all kind of wickedness, except swearing and scorning of religion, which I had no temptation unto in regard of my education."[15] Such statements are doubtless testimony less to the particular wickedness of youthful Puritans than to the experienced reality of the doctrine of original sin. Further, that Wallington the artisan and Winthrop the university-educated gentleman speak about their spiritual experience in very much the same terms should occasion no surprise, for they read the same books, heard similar sermons, and shared, as a consequence, a common rhetoric of spiritual discourse.[16]

Their doctrine, to the degree articulated, was conventionally Protestant and, at least for the generation that reached maturity in King James's reign, largely beyond dispute. As a result, the theological fine points that preoccupied the Calvinist scholastics rarely figure in their writings, and what one finds instead are the fundamental doctrines that define the great drama of fallen man and God's redeeming love. Salvation was by faith alone. As Lady Brilliana Harley observed in one of her letters to her son Edward: "Luther had great fears till he had thoroughly learned the doctrine of justification by Christ alone, and so it will be with all of us: no peace shall we have in our own righteousness." Or as Wallington expressed it less abstractly: "I may look to my graces as evidence of my part in Christ and salvation but not as causes; I may make use of duties as means to bring me to Christ and salvation but not to be saved by them."[17] For the faith that saves was a gift given only to the elect, "a peculiar gift [given] only to his dear ones," a mercy extended to a few born as all men were in sin "before the foundation of the world."[18] Equally a part of the divine plan was the redemption of the fallen world, or at least of the elect saints, by the atonement of Jesus Christ, although the lay Puritan tendency seems to have been to express these doctrinal truths less in formal creedal terms than as gratitude for God's love manifest in redemption and Christ's love in taking on the burden of sinful humanity. "Here is God's love that I am out of Hell, not roaring with the damned, that I am freed from . . . tormenting diseases, that I have bread to eat . . . , but herein is God's love in that he has given me his only son (1 John 4:9); this is love indeed."[19]

The doctrines of justification by faith alone and of predestination to election were not, if these few lay Puritan writings are typical of their generation, a matter of controversy or even of great concern.[20] The Puritan clergy faced a challenge in the writings and preachings of the English Arminians; the laity faced a more immediate and personal challenge, which seems to have dominated their religious consciousness. On the one hand, there was the law, God's Commandments, which demanded from mankind—certainly from "the child of God" or "the servant of the Lord"—an obedience and conformity of act and intention that experience seemed to demonstrate was impossible, particularly to the sensitive and scrupulous. As Wallington recorded "It is not an easy thing to be a Christian; it is not reading of Scripture, or boasting of faith or Christ, though these be good; they cannot prove one to be an absolute Christian; there must be a conformity of life." Hence, the saint must learn to live with moral failure but could never be content with or resigned to such a condition. On the other hand, the saint was saved not by meritorious works, even where they proved possible, but by faith, and faith was a gift, a grace. As Wallington wrote, "Oh, that Christ would kindle this fire of love in my heart to him, for I cannot love him except he love me first and so enable me to love him."[21]

The difficulty was not in the doctrine, which was simple enough, but in living out its implications. And the difficulty was compounded by the fact that justification was supposed to lead to sanctification, a process that, if never complete in this life, was nevertheless supposed to be demonstrable: "as this love of the Lord is his peculiar gift, only to his dear ones, let it be your chief care to get assurance of that love of God in Christ; and since he has loved you, show your love to him by hating that which he hates, which is sin."[22] But if hating sin and reformation of life were not quite the same, how was one to know that one's hatred of sin was sincere, and that one was not simply a hypocrite?

The charge of hypocrisy was not one made only by an unsympathetic Ben Jonson on the London stage. Rather, the fear of hypocrisy and the uncertainty of being assured of a truly justifying faith were embedded in the Puritan soul. How could one tell whether a zealous pursuit of the godly life was not simply subjecting oneself to the "bondage of the law," showing oneself to be as "simple and ignorant as a beast" in supposing that one "could keep the law of God?"[23] In his young manhood John Winthrop believed he found in himself all the marks of a true saint:

> Now I came to some peace and comfort in God and in his ways, my chief delight was therein, I loved a Christian, and the very ground he went upon. I honored a faithful minister in my heart and could have kissed his feet. Now I grew full of zeal . . . and very liberal in good work. I had an insatiable thirst after the word of God and could not miss a good sermon, though many miles off, especially of such as did search deep into the conscience. I had also a great striving in my heart to draw others to God. It pitied my heart to see men so little to regard their souls, and to despise that happiness which I knew to be better than all the world besides.[24]

However, good lawyer that he was, Winthrop found that some temptations "set me to look to my evidence more narrowly," and what he discovered was "that a reprobate might (in appearance) at-tain to as much as I had done." How "to get assurance" was the preoccupation of a generation and the thread that runs through much of the autobiographical musings of the godly. The problem was not doctrinal but experiential. As Winthrop ruefully confessed:

> I had known long before the doctrine of free justification by Christ and had often urged it upon my own soul and others, yet I could not close with Christ to my satisfaction. I have many times striven to lay hold upon Christ in some promise and have brought forth all the arguments that I had for my part in it. But instead of finding it to be mine, I have lost sometimes the faith of the very general truth of the promise.[25]

And yet as Wallington insisted, in words that echoed Winthrop's on the utter necessity of such a faith to the godly life, "if I by faith did but close in with Jesus Christ and suck virtue from him, I might be a conqueror over them [sins], and His promise is that sin shall not have domination over me."[26] Like Wallington, Winthrop confessed to having been "long under great bondage to the law"; like Wallington, he eventually gained a conviction of his own election ("now was the time that the Lord would reveal Christ unto me whom I had long desired"); and again like Wallington, his late assurance of adoption was not accompanied by an end of weakness and backsliding.[27] Dead-heartedness and presumption went before a fall, and a fall inevitably brought on punishment. The task of the godly at that point, as Lady Brilliana Harley reminded her son, was to "look up to your God; consider why He corrects; it is to better us, that we may see the error of our ways and find how bitter sin is, that has brought such bitter things upon us, . . . for the Lord delights to show mercy."[28]

This promise of an ultimately merciful God was crucial, for the examined life was not an easy one. In fact, one suspects that it was the introspection demanded by the examined life that made the struggle for assurance, rather than the debates over controverted doctrine, the central concern of a generation of the godly. Be that as it may, many were puzzled by the Puritan insistence that predestination was a "comfortable" doctrine; yet for the troubled saint, the assurance that his ultimate fate had been established by a divine decree, and thus could not be changed by human failure, was all the hope he had. Winthrop confessed that he continued to experience "conflict between the flesh and the spirit, and sometimes with Satan himself," but could reassure himself that his "faith had not failed utterly" and that he had never been "quite forsaken of the Lord."

Wallington admitted that he continued to feel an "old inclination to old sins," but comforted himself with the thought that "this is the condition of all people of God . . . partly through Satan's temptations, and partly from original sin still remaining in the best, like an hereditary disease not totally cured till death." Wallington was even convinced that God willed it so, "to teach us in what great need we stand of the righteousness of Christ."[29]

Not all of the life of the saint was filled by a constant round of examination, judgment, and exculpation. There were moments when the troubled saint spoke another language, when, as Winthrop put it, "the Lord breathed upon my soul," leaving Winthrop "so ravished with His love, as I desired nothing nor feared anything, but was filled with joy unspeakable." In a similar vein Wallington recorded that on one March morning in 1643 "the Lord (like a tender Father or Mother) comes softly on me, withdraws the curtain, looks on me; when I least think on Him, He wakes me and takes me to Himself in such heavenly meditations that I did see things unutterable, which broke my rocky heart that mine eyes gushed out tears to think that ever such a holy, all glorious God should any way regard such an unholy, polluted creature."[30]

However, for the Puritans of Wallington's generation such moments of religious rapture seem rare indeed. Rather than mystical contemplation, a militant watchfulness seems to characterize the lay saint. As Lady Brilliana Harley urged, "keep always a watch over your precious soul; tie yourself to daily self-examination"; elsewhere she admonished her son to "let it be your resolution and practice in your life rather to die than sin against your gracious and holy God . . . ; watch therefore against the enemy."[31] The attention of the saint was never entirely introspective; rather, life was a constant round of action, examination, and judgment, followed by a return to the fray. Godly behavior, "a gospel conversation," was a chief way of glorifying God. "Believers," noted Wallington, "are the great witnesses that God hath in the world to witness for him against the corruptions of the world."[32] Such a stance led the saints to seek succor among the "professors" of a gospel conversation, as it drove them into battle against their worldly neighbors. The godly preacher might preach to the whole parish, but by Wallington's and Winthrop's generation, those who sought "to walk close with God" found themselves separating, if not separated, from the indifferent in their societies and neighborhood. Wallington, always socially ill at ease, found comfort in that withdrawal; Winthrop, forced by his position as a magistrate to consort with his social equals at the Suffolk sessions, found the experience intensely embarrassing in his early years. "Oh Lord," he wrote, "keep me that I be not discouraged." He needed help, for, as he admitted, "all experience tells me that in this way [i.e. the Puritan way of life] is the least company, and that those which do walk openly in this way shall be despised, pointed at, hated of the world, made a by word, reviled, slandered, rebuked, made a gazing stock, called Puritans. . . . " The saints, even among the gentry, needed to be assured that by placing themselves among the despised Puritans they were nevertheless on "a right course, even the narrow way that leads to heaven."[33] Winthrop seems typical in seeing the way narrow and foolish in the eyes of the world; Wallington seems typical in seeing such a life as anything but triumphant—if a pilgrim's progress, nevertheless a progress "of ebbings and flowings, risings and fallings, springs and autumns, gloomy and sunshine days of this my poor pilgrimage of my life."[34] In the course of that troubled journey Wallington recapitulated the pattern of redemption, for the first part of his life he saw as lived in "a most vile and sinful condition," the second as "strivings and strugglings against my corruptions"—his years of bondage to the law—until finally toward the end of his long life "the Lord hath filled my soul with joy and comfort and put in my mouth new songs of praises."[35] If such joy was only briefly experienced, a saint could ask for no more, short of the heavenly Jerusalem. However, in his twentieth year, that journey had scarcely begun.

Wallington begins his story not with his first attempt at suicide but rather with an attempt in his twentieth year to run away from his troubles. Calculating that it was better to flee temptation than to continue where he had "provocations to evil" (he was convinced that he was subject to an uncontrollable lust for one of his father's maidservants), he fled his father's house one late Saturday afternoon, crossed Moorfields to the north, and passed through a town— whether Hackney or Islington he does not say—to the woods beyond. There "hearing the wind blow the trees . . . , my conscience told me the wicked flieth when none pursueth (but the righteous are as bold as a lion), and the wicked are afraid of the shaking of a leaf." A woodcutter found him standing lost, perplexed, and in tears, suspected that he was a runaway servant, and urged him "to go home again," and "the Lord in his goodness caused me to run as fast home again as ever I run from home, the Lord's name be praised."[36]

There followed ten episodes, all matter-of-factly recounted, in which Nehemiah attempted to find a more immediate and final solution to his difficulties. That May, in 1618, Wallington overheard a neighbor describe a drink made of honey and sack as "rank poison" that "made him so sick . . . he thought he should not recover." Nehemiah tried the same concoction but found to his dismay that he "was not sick one jot, the Lord's name be praised." The following winter he was tempted to leap from the garret window, "but God of his great love and mercy caused me presently to go down the stairs as fast as I could." Later in the garret again he was tempted to hang himself from an alder pole stuck among the roof beams, but was deterred by the thought of what a blow such an obvious suicide would be "to my old father, my brothers and sisters, and the rest of my Christian friends."[37] That consideration was, in fact, to complicate all of Wallington's subsequent attempts at suicide. Had he hated his father and rejected the godly community, had he been able to view his suicide as an act of revenge upon an unloving parent and a hateful faith, he might have succeeded in carrying out one of his many contemplated attempts at self-destruction. Instead he found the need to protect family and friends a frustrating complication. Thus he abandoned the thought of cutting his own throat, for he realized "what a grief" such an obvious suicide would be. He feared the news of it would kill his father and lead "the wicked to speak ill of our profession, for thus they would say: 'look on these Puritans; see Master Wallington's son hath killed himself,' and so I would bring a slander upon our religion."[38]

Although the determination to protect his family and the godly community led him to abandon any thought of cutting his own throat, it did not lead him to abandon all efforts to end his burdensome life. He briefly contemplated death by drowning but realized that a fatal plunge into the Thames would not necessarily look accidental. Poison seemed the best answer, for he calculated that it would "make me sick and so die confessing my sins, and nobody would know how I came to be so"—a reflection revealing of the frequency of undiagnosed sickness in the London of his time. Ratsbane, a common enough poison, seemed the obvious solution; Wallington describes how he went to a grocer in Leadenhall Street where he was not known, and how he thought to allay any suspicion by asking "how I should use it to kill the rats." At home again he swallowed what must have seemed enough to kill a horse and went to bed "thinking never to awake again in this life," only to vomit up the poison later, "so that it did me no hurt, the Lord's name be praised."[39] Troubled in mind he may have been, but he must also have possessed an iron constitution.

How he thought his repeated attempts to do himself in would go unnoticed is never very clear. In all probability his very preoccupation with his own troubled feelings left him little energy with which to observe the impression he made on others. In any event it does seem apparent that his father's large household was well aware that his behavior bore watching, and, without ever confronting him with their knowledge of his intentions, they nevertheless intervened effectively on several occasions. On one such Nehemiah was so troubled by a quarrel at supper that he abruptly left the family table and ran upstairs to the "folks chamber," the family sleeping quarters, "making account to leap out of the gutter into Pudding Lane," but as he was opening the gutter door his brother John and Nathaniel Goody, his father's apprentice, "came up to me and persuaded me to come down and be quiet, and I yielded unto them."[40] At the time he contemplated poisoning himself his behavior evidently became noticeably erratic. When his father's maid Lidia found him alone in the shop after working hours and asked him what he was doing there, he replied with the startling words: " 'Who are thou, a Devil?' (for I did think the devil would come in the likeness of some maid or some beautiful woman, I being so full of lust), and many more such words I uttered unto her, but she ventured upon me, although she was afraid, and persuaded me to go up to bed." When he arrived in the sleeping chamber, he discovered Nathaniel Goody's sword and took it to bed, apparently to ward off evil spirits. His sister Dorcas and the maid Lidia arrived soon after, saw the sword tied to his bed, and, evidently fearing that he "should awaken and do them some hurt," carried it away while he slept.[41]

If Wallington's fumbling attempts at suicide should be seen essentially as inarticulate appeals for help by a young artisan conscious of his inner turmoil, if not necessarily aware of all its causes and implications, that objective had been reached by the spring of 1619. Although his overwhelming self-absorption seems to have left him largely incurious about the thoughts and feelings even of those closest to him, his account does make the sympathetic, if baffled, concern of his family quite evident. The reality of love and forgiveness is perhaps always hard to accept for those who believe themselves undeserving and who find it impossible as a consequence to live with their human imperfections. In any event, by the Sunday before Easter Nehemiah found himself unable even to will his own destruction. While the family on returning from church went into the hall to dinner, Nehemiah sat alone in the parlor unable to eat and crying over his dangerous state, for as he told his father, he was now convinced that "the Devil will not let me alone." Before he had seen the tempting Lidia as the devil in a fair form; now he seemed convinced that anyone who proffered help or support was the devil in disguise. As he told his father, " 'The Devil can come in any likeness; he can come in the likeness of my shoes,' and then I flung away my shoes. Then I said, 'the Devil can come in the likeness of an angel of light or in the likeness of Master Roborough.' With that Master Roborough [who had been at dinner with the family] opened the parlor door. Then I run to the other end of the parlor, and Master Roborough came to me and held my arms, for I began to be unruly, and I told him he was a devil." Nehemiah was urged to accompany Roborough to his home, where he was persuaded to read 2 Corinthians 5 while Roborough rehearsed his sermon, but when Roborough returned to St. Leonard's for the afternoon catechetical lecture, Wallington ran home again and went to bed, convinced, as he told his "loving and tender father," that "God had forsaken me, and that I should never be saved."[42] His father remained with him all that afternoon, reading to him and praying, and although Nehemiah had later bouts of melancholy, including one in which he thought he talked to the devil in the shape of a crow for the space of an hour, by early summer the worst of the crisis was over.[43]

Wallington marked the end of the acute state of his depression with the laconic comment that "so I was troubled till May [1619]; then the Lord of his unspeakable goodness gave me some comfort and caused me to draw out some articles for the reforming of my life, which afterward followeth."[44] In fact he did not copy out the articles until many pages later in the notebook, but what he does write subsequently makes clear two things. First, the new life he proposed to begin so confidently on New Year's Day in 1622 had actually begun in the spring of 1619 in the weeks that followed his terrifying breakdown on the sabbath before Easter. Second, it seems evident that despite his imperfect understanding of the nature of the changes that had taken place, even Wallington recognized that periods of melancholic despair were to remain a recurring problem. In May 1623, almost a year and a half after he dates the beginning of his new life, he notes that he "began to give over holy duties" such as private reading and family prayer. Whether as a consequence or as a cause of this failure of his regime of religious discipline—he evidently was not certain—he once again began to doubt whether God's mercies "were more in number" than his sins. Life again seemed without hope, and while traveling over the marshes on his way to Walton fair, he briefly contemplated drowning himself in the Thames. Wallington was in his forties before these periods of despair vanished altogether.

What is also evident is that he had only a partial grasp of the nature of the crucial changes that had occurred in his life. He realized, certainly, that his "articles for the reforming of my life" by giving his life a disciplined structure contributed greatly "to the peace of a good conscience."[45] He also realized that it was the better part of wisdom "to harken and obey the good counsel of my loving father, mother, my brothers and sisters, and other of my good and Christian friends." There was to be no more talk that those who sought to do him good were devils in disguise.[46] And his growing trust in the love and good will of family and friends was accompanied by a growing recognition that he would have to trust God's promises, that faith in fact was just such a trust. As he confessed, he could not "believe and rest on the promises of God in the word," although he had "tested of God's love like infidelious Israel." Admittedly, God had "done miracles for me, yet how am I ready to distrust and limit his power and goodness with 'ifs' and 'can the Lord do this or that'?"[47] The compilation of his notebook "The Mercies of God" was testimony to his recognition that he needed constant reminders of God's love. What he does not seem to have comprehended (or at least to have acknowledged in writing) is the importance of his marriage or of his becoming an independent householder to his growing confidence in himself and his destiny. In fact, to become a master turner after serving his father only "two years together," and to become an independent householder without serving as a journeyman bespeak a father more concerned with his son's sanity and confident independence than with the usual niceties of customary practice.[48] Marriage when scarcely past the age of 23 also suggests a father bent on obtaining for his son a loving "yokefellow" to help him, if not on the way to heaven, at least out of his preoccupation with lust.[49]

Nehemiah, obsessed by his sins, never seems to have fully realized how crucial the security of a loving family was to his sanity nor how much that security and that sanity had seemed jeopardized during his childhood. Instead, it was sin and in particular the male adolescent's sin of lust "which hath been in me ever since I was but eight years old" that seemed to be at the heart of the matter.[50] By the time he had begun to write "The Mercies of God" in 1619, he was prepared to bless God that "I had rather that my nose were held over some filthy jakes than yield unto my delightfullest sin." Nevertheless, he knew he had "a filthy, odious, and polluted heart" and also that "no unclean thing" could enter into heaven.[51] Hence he knew he was tempted by the act he had come to hate as a sin, and God's greatness was manifest not in freeing him from temptation but in enabling him to resist it when it inevitably came.

As in all stories of failed seduction, there is an air of farce about Wallington's accounts. On one occasion the young woman whom he attempted to seduce with "jesting and dalliance" at first resisted his advances, but when she later "came unto my house when I was alone and went into my bed . . . , God kept me, and his strength was seen in my weakness."[52] On another occasion he approached the object of his "exceeding burning desire" with words that had nothing of jesting and dalliance in them. Instead, "I did read much of the fearful sin of adultery, and I would often be speaking unto her of that grievous sin of whoredom, and when the conscience is awakened, Oh, how it will stare in one's face, and what a hideous doleful a cry it will be, when two souls cry together for vengeance."[53] What the object of this strange seduction thought of such peculiar speeches Wallington does not say. What he does make clear is that he acted out of fear, for he found "a sty of filthiness within me which did boil and bubble up," and only the mercy of God and the most heroic of human measures prevented his giving way to these compulsions. Because Jesus said "(Matthew 5:29) that whosoever looketh on a woman to lust after her hath committed adultery with her already in his heart," Wallington "made a covenant with my eyes that I would not look upon a maid." However, his imagination and appetite were a greater threat, and these he attempted to tame by collecting scriptural passages that condemned "adultery, fornication, uncleanness, wantonness" and the seductions of "strong women," by working hard at his calling, by fasting and arising "betimes in the morning," and by "abstaining from divers meats as eggs and oysters and wine and many other things which I loved very well." Recognizing that solitude gave free rein to the imagination, "I set up shop only thinking it would help me." Even "the honorable state of marriage . . . did not overcome this sin." In desperation "I thought to have done something to my body, but I durst not for fear of offending God." Ultimately it was not fear but the gift of faith that "did allay and quench this fire."[54]

When Wallington late in life again briefly sketched the events of his childhood and young manhood, a rather different picture emerged. Although the lack of faith that held him "under the bondage of the law" still seemed the central fact of those years, the sin of lust no longer cast such a shadow.[55] Instead, after noting the sinful condition into which he was born, the next fact about his childhood that he mentions was the death of his mother in 1603, when he was five and "a very froward and disobedient crying child."[56] There is no comment on her death—the fact is simply recorded—but Nehemiah had at some point in the early 1630's written a five-page "faithful memorial" of her life that he had inserted into "The Mercies of God." There he presents her as a model Puritan matron, "loving and obedient to her parents, loving and kind to her husband, very tenderhearted to her children, much affecting the sincere preachers of God's word, loving all that were godly."[57] However, it is clear that what he remembers is not so much the paragon as the sickly woman, grieving for her "dearly loved" father who had died the year before Nehemiah was born, for she became a semi-invalid following the birth of her last child, Sarah, on November 2, 1602. First she was "benumbed of all her limbs"; then, after midsummer, "she cast much blood for many weeks"; and finally after Bartholomewtide she began her final painful decline

> that made her cry many times, "No more, Lord, no more; no more, Lord, no more! Lord, is my strength the strength of stones, or is my flesh of brass that thou layest on such a load upon me? Lord, remember I am but earth, and that thou wilt bring me to the dust of death." Her pain was so great that she would . . . say: "Lord, what have I done, what is my sin . . . that thou dealest thus with me? . . ." She would often say unto her children: "Take heed of sin, take heed of offending God, take

heed of falling into His hands; if He begin, He will not by and by make an end. Take example of me; see how long His hand hath been upon me!"[58]

Nehemiah's mother died in November, a year after the birth of her last child. What Nehemiah made of her long illness, her agonizing death, or of her loss, he does not say.

John Wallington, Sr., promptly married a widow, Joan Hinde, who brought with her (among her other children) a young son, Philip, who became Nehemiah's constant companion. They were "brothers in evil," as he later put it, stealing carrots together from the carts in Leadenhall Street on the way to the school Nehemiah was sent to when he was seven. Although it is hard to believe that it was only their life of crime together that impressed itself upon his memory, the only other incident that Nehemiah recounts from those years was the occasion two years later, at the age of nine, when he and Philip stole a shilling from the parlor table. The two then ran off to an alehouse in Finsbury Fields beyond Moorgate, spent the shilling on cakes and ale, and soon found themselves so drunk that "when I did come forth into the air, my head was light, and I fell over the rails into the fields, and I could not rise. And a company of people compassed me around, spending their verdict on me, asking where I dwelt . . . [but] I spake not to them but hid my face in the earth."[59] Two years later, in 1609, the Wallington household was struck with an undiagnosed sickness, "my poor brother Philip dying first."[60] In little more than a month two of John Wallington's apprentices (one a stepson also) and his stepdaughter Anne had died, and Nehemiah was sent off to his grandmother Hall's house in St. Botolph's–without–Bishopsgate until the sickness was past.[61] Again, Nehemiah says nothing about his feelings in the face of so much death. What he does recall is going into his grandmother's garden and praying for the first time in private: "I did then promise the Lord that if he sent me to my father's house again, Oh, then I would have a care over my ways and do better than I had done."[62]

He survived this traumatic loss and separation also and returned to his father's house "in safety," but found himself, not surprisingly, still given to "disobedience . . . and quarreling and other sins." Those years between Philip's death and his own period of suicidal depression were given over—at least in memory—to halfhearted reform, to what Wallington called "a civil life, being somewhat conformable to holy duties." Despite gifts of improving books and the solicitude of his father and older brother John, Nehemiah found no real peace, his peevish quarrelsomeness constantly "breaking forth," to be followed apparently by new and equally short-lived attempts at reform.[63] Late in his second decade, restless in the face of "fearful temptations and despairing thoughts," Nehemiah ran away from home, not merely to the woods beyond Islington and Hackney, but 60 miles to Colchester and "from thence back again to Engerston [Ingatestone] where I tarried a fortnight to learn to work," an attempt at independence that ended when an invitation to drink healths led to a bout of drunken sickness. "Then I went into a room as dark as hell, and kneeling down I cried and prayed and then laid me down on the bed, being very sick, and I prayed and wept sore, for I was sensible of my sin, being as sick in my conscience as I was in my stomach."[64] It is hard to believe that Nehemiah's father had no inkling of the wrenching effect the death first of his mother and then of his "brother" Philip had had on Nehemiah, just as it is hard to believe that that patriarch was oblivious to his son's many thoughts of suicide. Rather, it looks as though John Wallington sought to give his wayward son as soon as possible the only foundation of loving security that insecure age knew—an independent household and a loving wife.

Nehemiah did, however, have some inkling of the peculiar importance of his relationship with his father, who was reputedly born in 1552 and would therefore have been 46 when Nehemiah was born and in his mid-sixties at the time of his young son's crisis—a formidable, still vigorous ancient. If Nehemiah did not openly acknowledge the full extent of his father's interventions, he nevertheless was well aware of his critical need for his father's acceptance and love. After describing the ten occasions on which he was tempted to do away with himself, Wallington had apparently intended to transcribe his articles of reformation. Instead, he launched into a long and peculiar account of how, in January 1622, his conscience so troubled him that "I thought that the tiles would fall down from the house and knock out my brains, and I thought as Cain did that everyone that meeteth me would kill me." The crime, however, was not Cain's and did not in fact involve his brother at all. Rather, what Nehemiah goes on to describe are three occasions when he stole petty sums from his father: the first, when he was about nine or ten and, accompanied by his stepbrother Philip, had stolen a shilling; the second, when he was about twelve and had kept the change when his father had sent him out for a pot of beer, money which he then spent on apples and penny loaves of gingerbread bought surreptitiously in Gracechurch Street just a block north of Eastcheap; and the third, at an unspecified date, when he had taken nine pence from the shop cash box, "thinking to keep it," but instead found that it was "as fire in my pockets" and so returned it the next day. Now a dozen or so years later, finding that prayer brought little comfort and no lessening of guilt for these childhood crimes, he took twenty shillings from his box and went off to make a fourfold restitution, "as God's law requireth." "Then my Father took it and told me he was loth to take it but only to ease my mind, and my Father did speak very comfortable unto me, and he told me he had forgiven me. Then was I very glad, and, Oh, the lightness of heart, Oh, the peace of conscience and the joy of the spirit I had then."[65] Intellectually, Nehemiah was certainly able to distinguish between God and his father, but emotionally it is not entirely clear that he did so. Certainly without his father's forgiveness he found no peace.

Years later, in a curious letter to his old friend Henry Roborough, the curate of St. Leonard's Eastcheap, Nehemiah recalled that that minister had "been acquainted with my heavy troubles of mind and many grievous temptations of Satan about twenty years ago." Wallington then remarked significantly that he had "so continued in that sad condition till the death of my loving Father, which is near two and a half years ago, and then parting with an earthly Father . . . found a heavenly Father."[66] He amplifed the point in a letter he wrote two years later to his old friend James Cole, by then in Connecticut. After noting again that he had lost an earthly father but gained a heavenly one, he added quite explicitly that "I did find after my Father's death more joy and comfort in my poor soul from God than ever I did before."[67] Certainly Wallington never could have admitted to wishing his father's death, but he may well have found it easier to live with the knowledge of God's perfections than those of his formidable—if tender and loving—father. Be that as it may, he did regard his spiritual progress as terribly slow and the years after his father's death as a second beginning. In 1642 he wrote that he was "ashamed to see how many young ones outrun me in the way to heaven, aye, those that are . . . but one year old outgo me in many parts that am above twenty years old, I mean by the new birth."[68]

The inner springs of Wallington's prolonged spiritual uncertainties are now beyond recovery, if indeed they were ever very clear.

One consequence of all his spiritual turmoil seems to have been a real sympathy for others troubled as he had been and to some extent continued to be, for as late as a decade after his crisis he was prepared to admit that the fears his family and friends continued to have for him were justified: "because I have many sorrows and am weak, and sometimes I am out of the way, you are fearful of me, and I cannot much blame you for it, for sometimes I am fearful of myself."[69] Wallington collected stories of suicides, not apparently out of morbid curiosity or a sense of superiority, but because he knew their terrible examples were a warning and a lesson particularly for himself. Suicide was a temptation to which the godly, he knew, were particularly prone. In 1633 he recorded the story of an Essex farmer of good estate, "a grave, ancient professor indued with many good gifts that many sought to him for comfort in their troubles, and one morning he arose and spoke to his wife to give him the key of the chamber and cut his throat, and none can find out the cause wherefore unto this day." If such could happen to the "wise and learned," surely all need watch themselves. Further, we rarely know the cause and the temptations and should, therefore, "take heed of judging, as the Apostle Paul saith." In particular, it was the "melancholic and solitarious" who were most exposed to the temptation of suicide—who knew that better than Wallington himself?—and who were therefore most in need of a watchful self-discipline.[70]

The problem, he knew, was not intellectual but practical. In theory the Puritan's "comfortable" doctrine of election should have been sufficient, for although he knew himself to be "a poor weak wretch, ready to be blown away by every blast," he also knew that he was "secure," for "whom He loveth, He loveth unto the end."[71] Unfortunately, the introspective in particular were given to doubt, not least because any rigorous self-examination produced ample evidence of sin even among those whom God loved. Hence, discipline was not so much the road to righteousness as a means to avoid the passive and morbid preoccupation with inevitable failure that was the lot even of the saint. God's love in redemption demanded no less than a loving obedience, even though that obedience remained imperfect. That is what the new life meant—not a life of easy fulfillment, at least for Wallington, but one of endless struggle.

Shortly after his twenty-first birthday on May 25, 1619, Wallington began that struggle by drawing up his first set of 30 articles "for the reformation of my life in all things that are disagreeable to the holy law of God whereunto I bind myself unto the Lord my God and to the peace of a good conscience," an oath he later expanded in 1622 to include the proviso: "and also to perform those things which a loving and kind husband ought to do to his wife." Additional articles were promulgated on New Year's Days and on birthdays, so that by January 1, 1631, Wallington's articles numbered 77 all told.[72] These resolutions were not intended merely to express good intentions for future behavior; they were rather orders and decrees Wallington enforced on himself by fines ranging from a farthing to two pence (to be paid into the poor box on his desk after each infraction) and apportioned according to a mad calculus by which Nehemiah determined, for example, that sleeping on a Sunday was a mere one-farthing infraction, whereas failure to love God above all creatures and things was a one-penny crime, and committing an offense that brought dishonor to God "whereby God's name is evil spoken of" demanded the supreme sanction of a two-pence fine. The articles were to be read once a week (article 70), but in fact their enforcement required constant introspection of the most vigilant kind. To enforce article 13, which required Wallington to arise before six on a Sabbath morning, must have been simplicity itself, but to require that he not stifle the impulse to pray when moved to it by the Holy Spirit—or in fact any good impulse—on pain of a two-pence fine suggests an ability not only to monitor one's conscious thoughts but even to catch the first stirrings of a vagrant impulse.

Nevertheless, if Wallington's articles are Puritan scrupulosity blown up to heroic proportions, they have a certain logic to them. The articles do not at all run the gamut of ethical behavior; the "holy law of God" (at least to Nehemiah in 1619) by no means encompassed all Ten Commandments, and in fact scarcely included the first five. The first six articles concern prayer and require that Wallington join his family twice daily in worship, pray for God's children in trouble, and turn to God in his own troubles. Articles nine, ten, eleven, and 22 have to do with the second and third commandments, with loving and fearing God above all, with committing no action that would bring dishonor to God, and with refraining from taking God's name in vain "rashly, idly, or carelessly, when God is not glorified nor man edified." Articles thirteen to sixteen are concerned with keeping the Sabbath, and articles seventeen to 21 with church attendance in general. Articles 23 to 29 deal with regular Bible reading and the regular reading "in some other good book." God is to be entreated to bless his Word to his faithful reader, who in turn is to meditate on the Word every day and to make "some use of it or else to pay to the poor a farthing." Articles seven, eight, and twelve enjoin Wallington to be patient under affliction, to keep careful watch over thoughts, words, and deeds, and to cleanse his heart "from the very first motions of all sinful thoughts." In effect 29 of the articles are concerned one way or another with duties toward God and with the self-discipline necessary to be a proper child of God. Only article 30 looks to the Second Table duties, those owed to one's neighbor rather than to God, and requires that Wallington obey his father and mother and "be dutiful to all my betters" (the requirements of the Fifth Commandment).

The balance of the next 26 articles, drawn up when he became an independent householder and a husband, was necessarily very different and outward-looking. The first five concerned the proper relationship between husband and wife—by no means an easy one, since the articles required that he be "loving and kind" toward his wife, and at the same time that he accept loving correction from her for his sins as well as that he lovingly point out her faults to her, while carrying himself as "head and governor." However, his new duties did not remove his old, and he enjoined himself to maintain "loving and kind relations" with his brothers and sisters, to accept their reproofs for his sins when he had done amiss and to avoid quarreling with them (articles 36 to 40). The next seven articles address themselves to his relations with others: he is not to look at a woman with lust in his heart—clearly no longer the major problem and preoccupation it had been before he married—nor is he to speak "light, filthy, frothy, or unsavory words," nor to bear malice toward any or wish hurt to any. Articles 48 to 51 focus on the proper pursuit of his particular calling and require not only his diligent exercise of it but also his care in not concealing faults in his wares or engaging in deceit in trading. Finally, he was to avoid grieving at the prosperity of his neighbors, a fault to which his lack of economic success made him especially prone. The last two articles of his second set sought to curb the peevish ingratitude that, along with envy and discontent, he saw as all too characteristic of his attitude toward life: the antidote was to "be thankful to God for the least of his blessings."

In his middle twenties Wallington became increasingly conscious that he had a role to play as a godly householder. He was now the "head and governor of a family" that he must "teach and instruct."

As a godly paterfamilias, he could no longer engage in frivolous conversation or mock and jest. A certain solemnity was required that avoided the extremes of too much familiarity or too much rigor (articles 57 to 60). He had assumed an exemplary role, but one in which role and reality should be one. Hence he must not only "lead such a life" that others, seeing his "holy life and conversation, may be won thereby," but he must also "declare and speak of the mercies and goodness of God unto others and what He hath done for my poor soul" (articles 65 and 66). Wallington was not only to "obey God in every thing as He hath commanded," but also "to avoid all appearance of evil" (articles 68 to 72).

It was this emphasis on roles and appearances, on a self-conscious seriousness and rectitude, that so readily led to the charge of hypocrisy, yet there was no easy way to avoid it. Nehemiah had known for years that he had been born into a special community of God's children; consciousness of that membership had shaped the way he had responded to despair in his early twenties; and now, as an independent householder, consciousness of his responsibility to the community of the godly necessarily shaped his public life. Being among the elect was not the issue: Wallington was not to be certain of his election for years to come. However, his decision to draw up these articles, in fact to begin a new life, was a decision to obey God's commandments "so far as He will strengthen me," and that commitment involved both a life of private virtue and the acceptance of a public role as a member of a chosen people, of a new Israel in an increasingly corrupt and wicked world. When Parliament was dismissed in 1629 "and no good thing is done," but the "abominable sin of Idolatry hath toleration," Wallington again promised "by the assistance of the Lord to be more watchful over my ways, and diligent in good things, and to double my service unto thee." Such political catastrophes were not simply the inevitable consequence of previous political blunders. By Parliament's failure God was seeking to teach a lesson, and Wallington took the point as he demonstrated by quoting Isaiah 26:9, "Seeing thy judgments are in the earth, the inhabitants of the world shall learn righteousness."[73]

Wallington made the last of his New Year's resolutions on the first of the year in 1631. By the middle of that decade he had "given over these my articles" in despair at having gone so far "in debt to the poor that I am never able to pay," and doubly overcome by the realization that in so doing he had come "to break promise with the eternal God." Looking back in later years at the beginnings of his new life and "at the first working of grace in my heart," Wallington came to see that his articles had been a mistake, not because he had sought, by their means, an impossible perfection in this fallen world, not, certainly, because he had thought "to merit heaven" by their fulfillment, but because he had thought that he could by himself "run in all haste apace, even a gallop to Heaven." The proper response to the gift of grace was indeed obedience to God's commandments—in that much Wallington had clearly embarked upon the right course—and, as he confessed, "Oh, how faine would I be holy!" But, as he was to discover over and over again, the desire to live a life of holy obedience and the capacity to live according to God's holy will were two quite different things. The gap between desire and accomplishment could be narrowed by a great struggle but never closed in life. There was consolation in remembering that Christ was a loving savior and that God's "mercy is above his justice"; but rather than storming heaven at a gallop, Wallington found himself "like unto Pharaoh's chariots when the wheels were struck off," making his way "to heaven slowly with much ado."[74]

The long list of articles and the New Year's resolutions were only the first of a series of measures Wallington took in response to the recurring need to begin again, "to strive to renew my life in new obedience." In 1629 he sought to reinforce the discipline his articles imposed by keeping in addition a written record of his sins, hoping by that means so "to break" his "proud heart" that he would come in humility to recognize his utter need for a savior and his complete dependence on Jesus Christ.[75] In the late 1630's he sought in frequent attendance at the Sacrament of the Lord's Supper, "as often as occasion is offered," a more positive aid to a disciplined life, and by so doing to take advantage of "God's promise . . . that He will not send the hungry away empty."[76]

Wallington's resort to the Sacrament was a major departure from a religious practice otherwise dominated by sermons and prayer, by words and the Word. Yet he found it impossible to approach even that ritual act with a simple faith in its inherent efficacy. In 1639, after a year or two of the practice, he found himself "troubled in mind" that he had so little benefit from his frequent attendance, and, typically, he turned to the recently published treatises of two Puritan divines for aid and instruction.[77] He then filled a quarto with what he had learned about the nature and substance of a sacrament, about the necessity, reasons, and uses of it, and about how to receive it worthily; by 1641 he had started a second volume in which he recorded his prayers and meditations preparatory to his monthly taking of the Sacrament and the "fruit and benefit" he received from each communion, a book that he significantly entitled "The Growth of a Christian." Preparation for the Sacrament, in fact, became simply another occasion for self-examination—a time to ask "full pardon for my sins," and a time to give thanks for all God's mercies "particular and general to the whole land."[78]

Yet for all Wallington's tendency to intellectualize his faith, to turn even ritual into an occasion for words of examination and praise, he nevertheless realized that the Sacraments were part of the "mystery" of religion, "outward things" dedicated to "holy and spiritual ends." The point was not "to taste a piece of bread or to drink a draught of wine," but to come into the presence of a living God. If he were to give an account, he wrote, of what he was about as a communicant, he would say:

> Lord, I am going to that ordinance wherein I expect to have communion with thyself and the communication of thy chief mercies to my soul in Jesus Christ. Yea, I am going to set the seal of the covenant, on my part to renew my covenant with thee. I am going to have communion with the saints, to have the bond of communion with all thy people to be confirmed to me that there might be a stronger bond of union and love between me and the saints than ever.[79]

The uses and benefits of the Sacrament always remained a major preoccupation at least in his spiritual diaries, but Wallington did recognize that he found in the Sacrament two experiences largely missing otherwise in his religious life. As he noted at one point, "it is a mighty thing to have Christ and such spiritual things made real and not to be a fancy." It was the eye of faith that discerned the Christ beneath the bread, but that spiritual seeing was real; in a life in which religion in a formal sense meant largely talking to God in prayer and listening to his Word in sermons, the action of faith in the Sacrament brought about a genuine communion beyond words and made "Christ and the soul as one."[80] At the same time the Sacrament supplied another ingredient otherwise largely absent in Wallington's Puritanism, a confirmation of the community of the saints. A covenanted church was perhaps a more obvious solution to the saint's isolation, but although Wallington made use of personal covenants and readily joined in taking the national covenant in 1643, he never abandoned his parish church.[81] Hence it was in the monthly sacrament, rather than in the visible reality of the covenanted church, that Wallington found the promise of the true communion of the saints and the one occasion when he could break out of his rather lonely confrontation with the demands of the Word for the promise of the warm fellowship of the children of God.

The Sacrament of the Lord's Supper played a significant part in Wallington's spiritual pilgrimage during the last twenty years of his life, but year in and year out he, like all Puritans, depended on preaching and prayer for spiritual sustenance and guidance in leading a godly life. Wallington's views about the efficacy of the preached word were entirely conventional. He took notes on many of the sermons he heard, rehearsed them, and read over his jottings; he also bought printed sermons when he could. However, the function of the sermon was not simply expository, prophetic, or hortatory, for otherwise reading them would have been sufficient. Sermons were significant to Wallington not merely as a customary mechanism for communicating the Word, but much more importantly as the central act of worship: "the hearing of God's Word it is part of God's worship; it is a tendering of the creature's homage to God, a testimony of the respect that creature did owe to God." Sermons were the "great ordinance for converting and edifying of souls in the way to eternal life," but it was the preached word alone that had that special efficacy. For the Word to be profitable, it must be believed and applied, but belief depends on faith, and "faith comes by hearing."[82] Sermons, not sacraments, were the ordinary vehicle of grace.

Like most Puritans, Wallington was an inveterate hearer of the preached Word. He had been "brought up in the ways of God from a child," he wrote, and had learned to go to church "not only on the Sabbath day but also the weekdays to the lectures." He had in fact on one heroic occasion heard "nineteen sermons in one week."[83] Such opportunities for hearing the Word were, he claimed, of relatively recent origin. In 1654, when he noted that the morning exercise of preaching, established first at St. Mary's at Hill, had been moved to the neighboring parish of St. Andrew's Hubbard, it was possible to hear 30 sermons a month without leaving that parish. When his father first came up to London in 1572 and was apprenticed in St. Andrew's, the parson was a nonresident pluralist, and the senior Wallington never heard a sermon preached there in his eight years of residence.[84] By 1642, 70 years later, the problem facing Nehemiah Wallington was not the paucity of preaching but the temptations posed by the very number of preachers crowding the City as the First Civil War approached and, a few months later, as the Westminster Assembly gathered. While listening to Joseph Caryl preach on Monday, September 5, 1642, Wallington wondered whether he "might not as well benefit by hearing of Mr. Roborough as by hearing of some others, he being a minister of God and teaching the truth as well as others." Wallington feared that the fault was in himself, that he might "have a nice squeamish stomach and must have fine faces or else it will not down." If so, he feared that God "in judgment" might give him "an itch in the ear that [he] know not who to hear nor how to relish wholesome doctrine."[85] Nevertheless, as fast days and days of thanksgiving were added to the regular Sabbath sermons and lecture days, there was no escaping a variety of preaching, and in April of 1643 Wallington noted that he had heard Hugh Peter, William Rayner, Simeon Ash, Nathaniel Holmes, John Wells, Henry Burton, a Mr. Jordan, and a Mr. Knowles (probably Henry Jurden and Hansard Knollys), as well as his own parson Henry Roborough.[86] Fast days in particular were spectacular affairs, involving three or more ministers and lasting from eight in the morning to seven on a dark winter's evening. On one occasion Simeon Ash, having spent most of his allotted two hours in prayer, "said he would tell us what he might have said or stood upon, his text is 2 Chron. 12:7."[87]

Nevertheless, for all his apparent enthusiasm for the preached word, Wallington recognized that at times his spirits flagged. At the tail end of 1642, on December 21, he noted that he had gone "to the Fast again, but with much pulling back, considering the hindrance in my shop, the pinching of my body with hunger and cold." But more than these outward discomforts, what worried him was that he could not find his "heart humbled" and therefore had "but little benefit and profit to my poor soul."[88] The fault, he realized, was not in the preacher but in himself. Later the following spring he lamented at a fast that "although Mr. Roborough did pray so heavenly and preach so profitably, yet my heart would not yield . . . ," for "yet did I remain dead and drowsy, the day being very irksome and duties very tedious unto me, like unto one that never knew or heard of God."[89] Only a special spiritual athleticism or the unusual tensions of the early 1640's could have made endurable the day-long fasts with their endless prayers and preaching in any case. What filled Wallington with fear that he would be pursued by all the curses that destroy those who fail to keep God's ordinances (Deut. 28:45–48) was his awareness that "many times" he wished that even the Sabbath would be gone: "and I have thought long till the sermon was done, and looking at the hourglass wishing it were run out, I have suffered mine eye to gaze about in thine house and my mind to wander on vain thoughts that will not profit, and I have many times slept at church, hearing of God's Word."[90] From an early age he had wrestled with that temptation and had tried "when dullness begins to come upon me" to rally himself by pinching himself or by biting his tongue or sticking himself with a pin. Later he adopted the practice of taking to church peppercorns or ginger or cloves which he would bite when he found himself nodding, "so . . . by the goodness of God I got some victory over this sin."[91] Nevertheless, to the end of his life this lonely, God-struck artisan, limited in his public life by his education and vocation to the fashioning of wooden bowls and stools rather than of words or the Word, wondered "why I should so reverence God's ministers that my heart springs when I am with them, and yet so little love or mind in hearing of the Word."[92] That he might have missed his true calling was a thought that never seems to have entered his mind.

Wallington knew, as did all Puritans, that "the right manner of sanctifying the name of God [was] in hearing his Word," but however necessary the discipline of sermons and sacraments, both sometimes failed as a form of effective worship and as a means to a lively faith. On such occasions Wallington invariably blamed himself, for the sermon or the Sacrament was merely a vehicle by which the faithful renewed their sense of God's presence and of the reality of His will and commandments. The proper response was "an earnest desire to walk in all the ways of God."[93] If that response was lacking, the fault surely was neither in God nor in the means of grace, but in sinful and wayward man. Day in and day out, when all else failed Wallington turned to that other standard discipline— prayer—as an antidote to tediousness in hearing sermons or dullness in his duties. Prayer was an active discipline, and particularly in family prayer Wallington found that role of preacher and teacher, exhorter and prophet, that his vocation and station in life denied him in public. King David "saith . . . seven times in a day will I praise thee," and that good Puritan Robert Bolton was reported to pray "six times daily, twice with his wife, twice with his family, and twice alone by himself."[94] These were precedents Wallington sought to follow.

Even late in life he was wont to rise early before dawn to pray. On July 9, 1654, by "God's mercy at almost four o'clock I did arise and in my closet . . . I did praise the Lord for his many mercies to myself and in remembering us in sending rain."[95] Not every morning began as cheerfully, but private prayer was always its ordering principle. Four days later on July 13

> about two o'clock I did awake and I could not but think what a base, filthy, vile heart I have, my conscience hagging me for my sins of omission yesterday. . . . And now these sins . . . seem to me as black as hell. . . . Then I lay examining my life by the law of God and did see my lost condition, but then I did think of that in Romans 7, what Paul said I applied unto myself, as also I did think of God's free grace and love in Jesus Christ and how Jesus Christ is in heaven pleading for me. So a while after three o'clock I did rise and in my closet there did pour out my complaint to God, how my own troubles seemed more to me than the sorrows of his Church, or the weighty things of the kingdom, Oh wretch that I am.[96]

It was in fact his very failure to pray as he had intended on the previous day that occasioned these fretful reflections. Prayer in his closet was then followed by "meditations and conference" with his wife, "reading and praying" with his family, and so to the day's work.[97] If the following day was the Sabbath, he began "near six o'clock [in the evening] . . . with some joy to think of that day," and shut up his shop by seven so that his family and servants could begin their preparations, too. On the following morning, after private prayer, he gathered his family at six o'clock and launched into what amounted to a service of family worship: "one did read Leviticus 26, of which I did speak what God put into my mind; then I went to catechizing, and then to read out of *The Garden of Spiritual Flowers*, very useful to our souls, and some others read out of the Psalms. And so to prayer with my family wherein I did find some comfort."[98] Only then was the Wallington family ready to go forth to join "the public congregation" at St. Leonard's. At the end of a long Sunday the process was reversed, repetitions of the sermons before the family followed by family prayer, and finally, "when we were all parting to our beds, some words of exhortation I spake to my family not to forget those instructions which God had made known to us but to remember them all week long."[99]

Prayer was "a mighty great ordinance, a greater than any other, because . . . it sanctifies all things." By prayer man acknowledged his creaturehood; by prayer he glorified God and sanctified "the very Word to my use." Prayer was the Christian's first duty: by prayer one glorified God for mercies received, for sins pardoned, for assurance of God's love, and for the knowledge of his will.[100] Prayer not only was fundamental to a right relationship of man to God but was an active principle in the created world. "Prayer hath a casting voice in all the great affairs of the kingdom," for prayer was, under God, the ordering principle in history. "The great things of the world . . . are according to the prayers of the Saints: they bring down blessings upon the godly; they pour forth judgments upon the wicked."[101]

Necessarily, then, Wallington experienced prayer not as a spontaneous act but rather as a heavy responsibility. Prayer was always preceded by self-examination and by meditation upon the immediate object and end of the prayer to be prayed. Family prayer involved an even greater responsibility, for Wallington saw himself as Ezekiel's watchman, set by God to safeguard those in his care, "and if any perish for want of my care, their blood God will require of me." Hence, before family prayers "I sent up some desires to God that He would teach me that I may teach them, and not only with words but with holiness of life."[102] Good actions, that which Wallington called "a Gospel conversation," should follow, for action should follow knowledge and the stirring up of the affections, and the "holy and gracious lives of the saints" serve both to honor God and "to further the great designs God hath in the world."[103] Prayer was active both in itself and in its consequences, and Wallington's last "duty" of the day was normally a final act of examination to assess the results of prayer and to discover by so doing the direction of God's will. Happy the day in which he could write at its conclusion that "upon examination I find a return of prayer in that God did follow me from duty to duty (without weariness and sleepiness, though I awakened at three in the morning till nine at night) with some comfort."[104]

In the course of a long life Wallington resorted repeatedly to the disciplinary techniques of the Puritan's examined life—resolutions and covenants, sermons, sacraments, and prayer—and much of his writing recorded the empirical results, the daily assessment of their efficacy. Wallington eventually came to see that he had made some progress in his struggle. He knew he had survived both a youth spent in a "most vile and sinful condition" and a crisis in his early twenties when he first became spiritually self-conscious and "the sight of my sinfulness [was] most sad and dismal with heavy temptations."[105] Yet for the next 30 years life seemed a constant and inconclusive struggle. In the 1630's resolutions were abandoned in favor of the discipline of the Sacrament of the Lord's Supper, but in spite of that discipline in early 1641 Wallington confessed that he "did feel . . . corruption stirring to impatience and untoward filthy thoughts boiling within" him. Two years later, in late 1643, "further examination" revealed "so much unthankfulness and backwardness to good, with formal performances of duties," that he found he desired death and yet was fearful of it.[106] In fact Wallington found himself in a paradoxical position. When he looked at his life, he saw quite correctly that he was "no swearer, no drunkard, and no unclean person in gross act or open wicked liver," but how in all that outward show of godliness did he differ from "the proud pharisee?" The only honest answer was not at all, for the outward acts of the godly and of the hypocrite might well be identical and indistinguishable. As Wallington begged the reader on one occasion (and surely when he did so, he wrote from his own experience):

> Oh, consider, all you that are civil honest, you that pay every man his own, you that hear the Word of God gladly, so did Herod; you that teach others, so did Judas; you that offer sacrifice, so did Cain. And oh, consider this, you that are kind to God's children and ministers—and I pray you do not mistake me, for I do not speak against these things . . . —and not in love to God and aiming at God's glory, Oh, then, woe, woe be unto you, when God shall awake your conscience, for, Oh, then it will terrify you to the quick.[107]

That was the problem, dilemma, and paradox. The right action must be matched by the appropriate motive, but the very process of discovering or uncovering motive by self-examination inevitably produced an unwanted self-regard, a focus on oneself that seemed to vitiate the very love of God the good act should witness to. "As St. Paul saith, I was unblamable in my conversation to the world, . . . yet when the Lord opened the eye of mine understanding and awakened my conscience, Oh, then what a sty of filthiness and a sink of uncleanness was in me."[108] As Wallington admitted, "I looked too much on myself and not upon Christ," the consequence of which was that he found himself still in bondage to the law. [109]

The examined life itself offered no obvious answer to this conundrum. Wallington knew all the Puritan gambits for assuaging the tortured conscience. If self-examination showed evidence only of one's sinful nature, nevertheless God assuredly "looks not so much [at] what we are but what we would be, neither doth he measure us so much by our actions as by our affections."[110] But where were one's affections anchored, if one nevertheless sinned against one's better judgment? If introspection showed that one possessed but an imperfect faith, nevertheless "hath a man no faith, because he hath not the faith of Abraham? Hath a man no love nor zeal to God and his glory, because he hath not the love of Moses and the zeal of Elias? . . . God will not reject the least degree of grace, Christ will not quench the smoldering flax nor break the bruised reed."[111] But were not sins the very evidence, not of faith, but of doubt? In late 1643 Wallington wrote despairingly that he was prepared to praise God even "for a dream of faith, even for a desire for a desire and some hope in my Savior Jesus Christ that he will strengthen my palsied . . . hand of faith."[112]

In the final analysis it was not introspection but reflection upon the nature of Christ that seems finally to have produced a conviction that he was numbered among the elect. Is Christ "very merciful? Then he will spare me and take pity on me." To know God's will and commandment was to face judgment and to be judged wanting, but "to know God in the face of Jesus Christ is sweet and comfortable."[113] A sense that he was among the elect did not come suddenly, but it did come. Wallington, unlike many of the saints, could never date the time of his conversion, but at some point in his early fifties he ceased, as he put it, to be in bondage to the Law, and "the Lord Christ appeared unto my soul in strength and comfort and filled me with much joy."[114] Nothing had apparently changed. As Wallington wrote in late August 1650 to his old friend James Cole in Hartford, Connecticut, he had been "struggling with the world near these thirty years, and yet the world still frowns on me as at the first."[115] Further, he was still as troubled by doubts and temptations as before, although he now accepted that anxious state as inevitable and even comforting: "that man that never had doubtings may fear he never had faith, seeing faith is mingled with infidelity and not perfect in the best."[116] What had changed was neither his outward condition nor his inner state; rather, there was an awareness of what "the Lord Christ hath done for me and what He is unto me," for the Spirit of God had "whispered in my soul saying 'son, thy sins are forgiven thee.' "[117] Or at least so Wallington translated the experience of "the abundance of inward joy which I find in my soul many times." Nevertheless, if the actions of grace were obscure, the results were manifest. Whereas before, introspection frequently offered only new evidence of his infidelity and backsliding, now "upon examination of my heart I did find I am a child of God and not a hypocrite, for I have the grace of true repentance which is (an hatred and) a turning from all sin and a turning unto God which no hypocrite can do."[118] Not every morning brought so happy a discovery, but the sense of sin remaining could now be successfully rationalized as that necessary remnant needed to prevent "trust in our own righteousness."[119] As Nehemiah wrote to James Cole, he had found "more of God and heavenly joy" in his old age than he had ever experienced before and now found in these last years that his "heart is bent for God's glory and longs to be at home."[120]

For he shall judge the world in righteousness and shall judge the
people with equity.
—Psalm 98, as quoted by Wallington

The world is like an ill fool in a play; the Christian is a ludicrous
spectator . . . , which thinks those jests too gross to be laughed at and
therefore entertains that with scorn which others with applause,
yet in truth we sin if we rejoice not.
—Joseph Hall

3. The Theater of the World

Despite the constant call to the examined life, introspection did
not leave Wallington oblivious to the world around him, as though
locked inside his trembling mind in morbid self-regard. The beginning and the end of each day were devoted to God and the inner
life—to examination, soul-searching, reading, and prayer—but during the long hours between, the presence of the outer world was
inescapable. As a householder and an artisan, Wallington had duties
toward family and kin, servants, neighbors, and customers. As a
child of God, Wallington also had duties toward the community of
the godly and to the church, its sermons and sacraments, its prayers
and days of humiliation and thanksgiving. These social responsibilities took Wallington out of his closet and down to his parlor, his
shop, and the streets of London beyond; however, his attitude toward the world around him was not formed merely by the sum of
his duties in it.

The world as created was necessarily God's world, and, as such,
demanded the careful scrutiny of man, God's last creation and the
only creature short of the angelic intelligences capable of compre-
hending to some degree the divine order, or at least the divine intention, inherent in that handiwork. For the God Wallington knew was
not a divine clockmaker who, having wound the instrument and set
it running, took no further interest in its performance. Wallington's
God continued to act on and through his creation to carry out his
intentions, but what remained problematic was how much of God's

purpose was within man's comprehension. Wallington did not expect God to speak to him from a burning bush: the days when man walked and talked with God directly were, like the age of true miracles, firmly in the distant Biblical past. When Wallington thought about this question in abstract epistemological terms, he, like Thomas Beard, whose *The Theatre of Gods Iudgements* so obviously influenced him, tended to give a good Calvinist answer. As Beard notes at the outset of his "Epistle Dedicatory," "It is a principle in Natural Philosophy . . . that the works of God are wonderful, and his judgments past finding out: and not without great reason, for if we turn over every leaf of God's creatures . . . , we shall find that every leaf . . . not only demonstrates a Divine power . . . , but also our own weakness, which is not able to comprehend the least part thereof."[1] Creation manifests God's power, but the meaning of particular events and their role in the divine plan is part of what for Calvin was the "hidden counsel of God."[2] In the face of this "hidden counsel" Wallington advises that man not "vainly judge," but rather "magnify his works . . . that God may have the glory . . . albeit we do not conceive always the right cause and reason of them."[3]

Up to a point Wallington's thoughts and perceptions moved comfortably within the confines of these Calvinist limitations. If God's secret will remained hidden from man, even fallen man possessed in Scripture the essentials of God's plan for man's redemption. Furthermore, the same source made obvious God's continued sovereignty over his creation, no matter how corrupted, decayed, and debased that creation had become by man's disobedience "now in the last days."[4] Hence, there could be no reason to doubt that the world was ruled by a divine Providence, mysterious though its workings might be to man at any given moment. As Wallington noted in his preface to his "Memorial of God's Judgments," begun in 1632, "Gentle reader, I thought good to take notice of the hand of God now amongst us."[5] The point was not that God's actions were necessary to teach ignorant and erring man lessons not available in Scripture. Wallington's second collection of stories of providential actions was entitled "Ensamples of God's Wrath upon those that have broken his Commandments."[6] God's essential will for man was known in his commandments; what the providential event taught men—a lesson evidently learned only from constant, dramatic, and sometimes brutal repetition—was that God was a living God, that His will endured, and that He would not be mocked. God intervened in the world, then, not to teach an abstract lesson or to increase man's understanding of the moral universe as such, but rather to drive sin-prone man to obedience. As Thomas Beard enjoined the reader at the conclusion of his lengthy catalogue of God's judgments: "Forsake, therefore, if you tender the good, honor, and repose of yourselves and yours, the evil and corrupt fashions of the world, and submit yourselves in obedience under the scepter of God's Law and Gospel, fearing the just retribution of vengeance upon all them that do the contrary, for it is a horrible thing to fall into the hands of the Lord."[7] For Wallington there was a peculiar horror in these providential acts of divine retribution, a pointedness that drove the moral lesson home with dramatic effect, for he chiefly took notice of the vengeance visited on those sinners "in the very act of their sins, having neither time, power, nor heart to repent."[8]

Everyone knew that God had commanded Moses to tell the Israelites to "remember the Sabbath to keep it holy." Even the most innocent-seeming and trivial breach of that absolute command could bring instant punishment. On a Sabbath early in June 1632, two young men in Whitechapel went down to the Thames side and boarded a ship, "and one said to the other, 'I will get on the top of the mast first,' and so he did; then the other said, 'I will be down first,' and so he was, for in making haste he fell down and burst in pieces and so died, never stirring more, for his skull broke. . . ."[9] Wallington had heard the story from the mouth of the survivor, and so was prepared to vouch for its authenticity, but he records so many Sabbath-breakers overtaken by sudden deaths that he had no reason to question the connection between the breach of the commandment and the dire consequences. There was in fact an evident statistical correlation: "there was an honest minister did say (dwelling by the waterside) that he had observed for some years that there fell out more casualties upon the water on the Sabbath day than on all the week besides."[10] However important such stories were in proving God's continual watchfulness over the ways of man, and His determination to have the Divine Will respected (at least by those who observed God's propensity for punishments at once swift, condign, and usually fatal), such judgments did no more than confirm the permanent validity of those demands on sinful man first given to Moses in the wilderness of Sinai.

Where Wallington, like Thomas Beard before him, parted company with Calvinist orthodoxy was in seeing in God's judgments and mercies, signs and portents, a kind of continuous revelation of God's will and not simply a continuous confirmation of commands once given and recorded for all time in Scripture. History teemed with meaning, and the meanest event was freighted with significance. And although God's will and meaning were hidden in the event itself, they were not hidden from the discerning observer. As Thomas Beard noted,

> History . . . teacheth and instructeth all those that apply their minds unto it, to govern and carry themselves virtuously and honestly in this life . . . : for these the high and wonderful works of God do most clearly . . . present themselves as his justice and providence, whereby albeit he guideth and directeth especially his own, . . . yet he ceaseth not for all that to stretch the arm of his power over all . . . ; for he hath a sovereign empire and predominance over all the world.[11]

One reason the godly were under a continuous obligation to examine their lives was precisely that only such constant examination could keep each individual cognizant of God's current will and purpose. The problem, as Wallington saw it, was not in the obscurity of God's message but in the obliviousness of man. We either ignore those afflictions visited on us in our daily lives, or, "if we do take notice, we look no further than the secondary means, as thus when we are sick [we assume unthinkingly that] it was such an air that made me sick," not bothering to ask who should afflict us or why: "they do not say, it was for such a sin, and I will reform it."[12] Historical events were a kind of continuous sermon from which the godly should gather both the right doctrine and the right use. After recording the burning of London Bridge on the night of February 11, 1633/34, Wallington prayed that "the good Lord our God teach us, so that we may not be vain beholders or hearers of this wonderful and fearful, yet just work of the Lord, but that we make such use of this and all other His judgments as He requireth in His word we should do. . . ."[13]

Obviously such a view could freight history with a fateful portentousness. Though Wallington could see an element of mercy in the fire on London Bridge—for "there was but little wind, for had the wind been as high as it was a week before, I think it would have endangered most of the City, for in Thames Street there is much pitch, tar, rosin, and oil in their houses"—he also thought there was much to be learned from that frightful event.[14] The first lesson that such a fearful judgment taught was that God would "have glory and praise for his own works": whether merciful or catastrophic, all must be acknowledged as the work of one divine master.[15] But the second lesson was that the fire was a dreadful judgment on London's sins,

> which now are grown to their height: as idolatry, superstition, woeful profaning of the names, titles, attributes, creatures, and of God himself, with the perfect language of hellish swearers in every child's mouth, whoredoms, adulteries, fornication, murders, oppressions, drunkenness, cozening, lying, the contempt of the Gospel with slandering, mocking, flouting, chibing [sic], silencing and stopping the mouths of God's prophets and servants, and other gross secret sins.[16]

Given such an endless catalogue of sins—and Wallington added as a kind of afterthought an account that he had just heard of a group of married men in Southwark who had "lived in the sin of buggery and were sworn brothers to it" some seven years, committing this sin on Sabbath mornings at "sermon time"—the wonder was that the punishment of London had not been more severe, for such judgments as the fire could be seen as no more than "fatherly corrections."[17] Remembering how he had "looked down Fish Street hill" from his bedroom window and had seen the fire "vaunting itself over the tops of houses like a captain flourishing and displaying his banner," Wallington recalled Jeremiah's prophecy to a sinful Jerusalem: "But if you will not hear me to sanctify the Sabbath day, then will I kindle a fire in the gates thereof, and it shall devour the palaces of Jerusalem, and it shall not be quenched."[18] By and large, history was the scene of judgments that were at once punishments for public and private sins and warnings to reform or "to flee the wrath to come."[19]

Nevertheless, Wallington found in his providential view of history a surprising element of hope. He knew it was vain to expect that at some point mercies might outweigh terrifying judgments, given man's sinful nature. Rather, he found a source of comfort in the fact that God was not bound by the necessities of secondary causation, by the ordinary workings of cause and effect, for "the Lord often by strange and unheard of means brought mighty things to pass." Hence, creatures and created things do not "work always according to their own nature, which they received of God at their first creation, but sometimes by the mere will and pleasure of their creator in such that, whensoever it pleaseth him, the creature[s] work both above and contrary to their natures."[20] The day God commanded the sun to stand still so that Joshua and the Israelites could slay the Amorites (Joshua 20:12) served Wallington as an example of such a divine act, and God's unchanging omnipotence meant that such interventions in the ordinary course of events could occur at any time. Wallington did not have in mind the obvious fact that many, although sinners, escaped "God's just severe judgments upon them." That was due merely "to God's free love and grace that will show mercy to whom he will show mercy."[21] Rather, what Wallington had in mind was God's ability to bring about mighty ends even though the means seemed weak or inadequate to the purpose. In particular he had in mind God's promises to the godly, the fulfillment of which could only be doubted at the price of infidelity. It was evident that on the whole the godly did not prosper in the world, yet it was a mistake to assume that, because "outward means faileth them," so "God also then had forsaken them."[22]

This assumption about the workings of Providence not only comforted Wallington in his relative poverty but comforted the godly during the political and ecclesiastical discouragements of the 1620's and 1630's. During those years England had ample warnings "that the sword is coming"—strange portents like "a fearful thunder with storm and lightning in 1626," and the sighting of a meteor in Berkshire in 1628.[23] Yet however helpless the godly minority might feel in the face of social and political forces seemingly beyond their control, to despair of God's mercies and deliverances was clearly not the answer. As the type of the godly community, Israel, with its history of repeated defeats and exiles, nevertheless had as well its history of miraculous deliverances, and Wallington saw "comfort and courage" as available to "all those that have learned . . . to cast themselves on His providences and to wait for His blessing . . . in such manner and by such means as best pleases His majesty." It was a view of history peculiarly suited to the first generation to make a revolution. However discouraging events appeared—and England from the late 1620's was certainly inhospitable to the godly—Wallington was sure of an ultimate triumph of some kind, "for it shall certainly go well with you; you have that great God on your side."[24]

Yet such an assurance of ultimate triumph even in the face of apparent defeat was difficult to maintain, given a doctrine of Providence that seemed to put God on the side of those whom life rewarded with success, for those who failed or were crushed by God's

accidents were surely the victims of divine judgment and well-deserved punishment. The problem was a real one for Wallington, and
he returned to it on a number of occasions, seeking an explanation
that not only squared with the divine economy as he understood it,
but that also provided the necessary psychological satisfaction. In a
sense, the personal equation was the easier to solve. The accidents,
disappointments, and tragedies with which his life abounded were
no more than to be expected, for, after all, even the godly sinned.
What distinguished the godly was not human perfection but divine
election. When Wallington looked at his own life, it was evident that
he had transgressed against every one of the commandments, "having broken the same ten thousand times."[25] Further, the godly
sinned self-consciously, for they not only knew God's will in Scripture but had an empirical, "experimental" knowledge of His Providence in the world and knew, therefore, quite precisely what were
the wages of sin. As Wallington exclaimed at one point, "Oh my
God, I have lived in contempt of thy Providence."[26] A certain amount
of personal tragedy, then, was the inevitable lot of sinful man; it was
the task of the godly to understand the cause and to reform their
ways. That they were not overwhelmed by well-deserved judgments
was in itself a sign of divine mercy.

The collective fate of the godly presented a different problem. As
Wallington admitted, "the matter standing thus between God and
his people, his people may seem to have cause to say with Gideon, if
the Lord be with us, how hath this befallen us, and where are all the
wonders which our forefathers told us, saying the Lord led us out of
Egypt, but now hath the Lord forsaken us and given us into the
hands of the Midianites."[27] One answer to such a complaint was to
recognize its inevitability and to glory in the role of persecuted
saints, "for I can see, most gracious God, that none can live godly in
this world, but they must suffer persecutions."[28] From the beginning
of time, from Cain's plot against Abel, "the wicked always hate the
godly and plot against them." Hence, "you may see now how Antichrist, even these bloody-hearted papists, doth plot against the
poor Church of God, as in '88 and that hellish Gunpowder Plot. And
how have they laid snares for the poor children of God, as with the
reading that sinful book of liberty [the Book of Sports], so with the
cursed Book of Canons [of 1640] with that execrable oath. . . . But
He that sits in heaven laughs them to scorn and hath brought all their
devices to naught."[29]

What comfort Wallington could derive from this line of argumentation depended upon how much conviction he and the godly had that their cause was God's, for otherwise there was little personal comfort to be had from knowing that one's persecutions fit into that larger war between Christ and Antichrist which would end only at the end of time. Short of the millennium, the saints must suffer persecution and the spoiling of their goods "with joy," certain that they "have in heaven a better and more enduring substance."[30] And when they find themselves in the hands of the Midianites, they might consider what "divers and weighty reasons" God has for visiting them with such providential judgments: first, that "all God's children know that sin is the mother of all their woe"; second, "that his people may thereby be brought to a diligent examination of themselves"; third, that thereby they may "prove their faith" and "exercise their patience"; and fourth, that God may better avenge himself on his enemies. This latter was doubtless the most psychologically satisfying. When "the people of God fall into any difficulty, their enemies out of spiteful mind begin to think that they are wholly gone." Their enemies then begin to triumph over them, "to mock them and to prognosticate their utter ruin: they begin to shake their head at them, to put out the tongue and to cry out, Aha! Aha!" But all this is but a snare and a delusion, for "the Lord raiseth up himself and turneth all the boasting of the adversaries . . . into a lie, and turneth also his people's case so . . . that their woe is turned to joy, and their grief confounded, God glorified, and his people comforted"—a satisfying denouement, even if the time of this ultimate triumph was less predictable than the evil day of the Midianites.[31]

In the meantime it was obvious that both saints and sinners lived out their lives in an extraordinarily dangerous, not to say hostile, environment. Catastrophe experienced was a judgment or punishment, catastrophe escaped a mercy or deliverance; one called for prayers of humiliation, the other for those of thanksgiving; but in any event Wallington's accounts of the workings of Providence are full of tales of sudden death and destruction. And the very arbitrariness of the violence and destructiveness of the times, and the general helplessness of man in the face of flood and fire, accident and disease, seemed to drive Wallington to find some meaning, justice, and comfort in what was otherwise a not very hospitable world.

Of those great natural catastrophes that periodically overwhelm the country dweller—storms and floods, winds and droughts—Wallington as a city artisan had only a distant awareness. In the summer of 1643 he noted a terrible tempest of thunder and lightning near Norwich, not because it flattened the ripening grain, but because an "abundance of rooks and daws sitting upon the trees were stricken dead, insomuch that one hundred and eleven of their carcasses were found the next morning by the farmer's servants." What made this "accident the more observable is that not any profitable creature about the farmer's house was so much as touched," but the storm fell instead "only on those ravenous and sharking creatures that are hurtful to man." What this prodigy might mean was, as Wallington confessed, as "yet unknown to man," but he concluded the account rather smugly that by "inference we may conjecture that it may mean God's judgments upon the plundering and pillaging cavalier rebels, who, like rooks and daws, live now ravenously by the sweat of honest men's brows."[32]

On one occasion in the summer of 1654 he was made starkly aware of the seriousness of a drought, for the conduit that ran down Gracechurch Street and brought water to St. Leonard's Eastcheap and the surrounding parishes ceased to run by late June, "which common people have much felt." On June 24, Midsummer Day, Wallington noted that the water-bearers, who used to dress up the end of the conduit "with flowers, bows, and garlands," this year hung it about

> with mourning cloth, with two long pieces hanging down at each end with a piece of paper written thus: the cause of this our mourning is our exceeding want of water which formerly we have enjoyed. And there were two water-bearers, a man and a woman clothed in black, which they called my lord and lady, and they went round about the conduit with many other water-bearers after them with the tankards under their arms with the mouths of their tankards downwards in a doleful manner, saying at every corner of the conduit: "It is not for bread nor for beer we mourn, but we mourn for water."

Wallington recognized the seriousness of the mock funeral, for many of the poor water carriers were "like to be undone for want of work." For Wallington, although he suffered little more than inconvenience, it was obvious nevertheless that the drought was a judgment of God from which "the inhabitants of the world should learn righteousness."[33] On July 9 Wallington rose at four o'clock to praise God for his many mercies, in particular "for remembering us in sending rain"; but although that summer storm broke the drought, it was not until October 10 that water once more ran in the conduit down Gracechurch Street, "a great cause to be thankful."[34]

In the course of his account of the drought Wallington noted that the price of a tankard of water had risen from a farthing to twopence, but what really frightened him was the "danger the City is in, if now there should be fire on it."[35] Fire was the great scourge of urban life and figures largely in Wallington's accounts of providential judgments. In a city not yet rebuilt in brick and stone, fire came like that other great visitation, disease, and before it man seemed virtually helpless. Most London parishes had their ladders and hooks to pull down burning roofs, their brooms to sweep water from the broken conduits along the gutters, their leather buckets and their woefully inadequate pumping engines. In the face of a fire like that on London Bridge in February 1634, Wallington's reaction to which we have already described, Londoners had little recourse but to flee. Even the most trivial of accidents with candles and open fires could have the most dreadful consequences. A careless maid, lighting a candle at dusk on a February evening in 1634, burned down the better part of a house in Honey Lane before the fire was brought under control, a fitting judgment, for the family had been "gadding forth," as Wallington put it, on a Sabbath.[36] In August 1644 in the parish of St. Andrew's, Hertford, a goodwife and her mother sanctified the Sabbath by tarrying at home to do the family wash, and while they were hanging out the clothes to dry, "their only child fell into the fire and was so burnt that it died presently."[37]

Such horrific consequences were doubtless the wages of sin, but Wallington well knew that all households were constantly exposed to accidents with candles and open fires. At about one o'clock at night in October 1628, a candle left alight above the sleeping Wallingtons burned through its wire candlestick and fell, setting Nehemiah's hair on fire: "I feeling . . . it smart, I started up and put it out, and I did consider the great goodness of my God which never slumbers nor sleeps in preserving me and mine so wonderfully from fire."[38] The following year in July, Wallington's servant took a candle to bed in the garret where he and the apprentice slept above Wallington's bedroom—a piece of carelessness against which Wallington after his own recent experience had warned him. Again the candle burned through its wire holder, this time setting the bedding on fire. Nearly smothered by the smoking straw, the servant woke to see the straw glowing like "two pences of gold on the ground; then he awoke his fellow and both of them stand up and pissed out the fire as well as they could."[39] Once again Wallington could only acknowledge God's goodness and mercy, for the garret contained baskets of wood chips and piles of light lumber as well as the two beds, and had the fire spread to those flammable materials, it would have been unquenchable. Yet such accidents were clearly commonplace. Late in November of 1630, Wallington records that his daughter Sarah, playing before the fire with a small pair of bellows, tripped and would have fallen into the fire "had not the Lord kept her, for as she was falling my wife gave a sudden start and shoved her at one side." That one survived at all in the midst of such homely perils was evidence of "God's great mercy," for shortly afterward Wallington noted that he had heard of "a child in Bearbinder Lane that did fall into the fire and was burnt to death."[40]

Sometimes a moral was obvious in Wallington's accounts of these conflagrations, but sometimes Wallington, clearly appalled by what he had learned, could only record the facts of the fire as he heard them and note that by God's mercy he had once again escaped. In the spring of 1639 a drunken carman's servant, returning home late at night to a stable in Pickle Herring in Southwark, had set a candle down carelessly in the hay and straw and started a fire which burned seven horses and more than 50 houses besides. "Oh, this filthy swinish sin of drunkenness which was a cause of this fearful fire!"[41] When during the Royalist occupation of Oxford in 1644 a fire "consumed in all about three hundred and thirty houses" on a Sabbath afternoon, it was easy to see that its cause lay in a troop of soldiers who had met that morning at "a fiddler's profane taphouse near the Red Lion," where "with their wenches, music, drink, and tobacco," they had spent the morning in drinking healths, one to the king, the next "to the confusion of them at Westminster and to the destruction of the city of London." In the light of such blasphemies, "drunkenness, music, scurrilous songs, cursing and swearing and profaning God's holy day," it was a wonder that the whole wicked city was not engulfed in one universal judgment.[42] However, the story of a domestic tragedy in nearby Cheapside in 1633, in which a child of three, left alone by a maid for a moment while she went to fetch an apron, wandered too near an open fire and set its clothes alight, burning it fatally, was recorded without comment.[43]

Late in life Wallington recorded two spectacular fires that he witnessed, seeing them less as judgments than as demonstrations of the "high hand of God," and since he survived them, as undeserved mercies. On July 20, 1654, the *Mary*, a ship laden with a cargo mostly of cloth and about to set sail for Barbados, caught fire in the Thames, slipped its mooring near Pickle Herring on the Southwark side, and drifted upriver toward London Bridge, where the retreating tide left the burning ship aground "by the Providence of God . . . on a shelf within a stone's cast of the bridge on the Southwark side." There within half an hour the fire reached seven barrels of gunpowder, blowing the ship out of the water and breaking slates and windows for hundreds of yards along the south side of the river, "divers hurt and maimed and some strangely preserved." A Mr. Duncan, "dwelling on the other side of the bridge, coming to help his neighbor, . . . a mercer, to remove his goods for fear of fire, going up into the leads to see how the fire was was suddenly struck dead with a piece of timber from the ship." Altogether thirteen were blown up or killed, including one in St. Magnus's parish just to the south of Little Eastcheap. The next day a second ship, the *Amity*, lying at Cox Key, was blown up by the carelessness of a gunner, killing among others the shipmaster's boy whose mother had come upriver from Ratcliffe beyond Shadwell to visit him: "the master, then standing on the key, called him to come to his mother, he then being in the cabin; when he saw his mother, he went into the cabin again to fetch some oranges and lemons that he had in his chest for her, but before he came out the ship blew up" and his body was never found. "God's exceeding great mercy I am not one of them," Wallington concluded, "for I am sometimes afraid of sudden death, not only because things are out of order, but I would not die in the act of any sin nor in discontented condition."[44]

Sudden death seemed to Wallington an all too common occurrence, frequently as a consequence of an all too sudden vengeance of a God who would not be mocked with impunity. In 1634 Wallington noted the report of a man at Chipping Norton who, on being reproved for playing ball on a Sabbath, replied that "he would play as long as he could see: a man coming by with a charged piece, he desired that he might shoot it off; the man gave him leave, and he shot out both his own eyes." A Danbury drover, warned not to drive his cattle on a Sabbath, similarly challenged God by replying, "Let me see who dare stay me." The drover had scarcely got out of town before he fell off his horse and died soon after. "So you may see that the great Lord of the Sabbath stayed him with his vengeance."[45] One of Wallington's own apprentices, despite frequent warnings of the grim fate of Sabbath breakers, was persuaded by another to go out to the fields on a Sunday to wrestle. There the apprentice, "holding the other up in his arms a long time and after striving together, the other fell upon him and bruised his stomach," so that "a short time after he died of it."[46] Some who mocked God in particularly heinous ways met appropriately spectacular deaths. In 1639 in Salisbury

> a jolly fellow brewed strong ale to maintain sport on the Lord's Day, and in the month of May would have a maypole set up on the Lord's Day, and on the night before he and his jovial crew went in despite of the Puritans to cut the tree, and on the Lord's Day in the morning he driving his three horses down the hill a little beyond Salisbury . . . the tree not being tied fast . . . turned round by reason of one wheel going higher than another . . . [and] so fell over [that it] beat out the fellow's brains upon the ground.[47]

By contrast, the sudden deaths met by drunkards, although suitably edifying, were relatively humdrum. A man drinking at Aldersgate slipped while going downstairs and cracked his skull, dying "about an hour after . . . ; I was at his burial myself," Wallington notes.[48] A Mr. Shaw at the Blue Anchor in Pudding Lane just down the street from Wallington's house came home drunk one night and was locked up by his wife, who would not let him accompany her when she went out again. When she returned, she found him dead at the bottom of the stairs from a broken neck.[49] On the other hand, drunkards occasionally managed to combine that relatively minor sin with other more spectacular offenses and thereby met equally memorable ends. Four from a village in Derbyshire met at an alehouse to drink a barrel of ale, and being "inflamed with liquors . . . would needs do something to be talked on." Finding the church door open, "they drove a cow into the church, and that which is appointed for churching a woman they read it for the cow and led her about the font," for which they were "strangely and fearfully punished: for he that played the priest was presently dumb . . . ; another of them was stricken with blindness; the third with madness; and the fourth broke his neck by falling from a rock the same week"—a properly satisfying outcome for such "a wicked and horrible" act.[50]

Sudden death seemed in a way a "natural" consequence of such sins as Sabbath-breaking and drunkenness. But at times Wallington seemed impressed less by the workings of divine Providence than by the sheer dangers to which one was constantly exposed. Late in January in 1633 a "company of boys" went to the ducking pond in Clerkenwell to slide on the ice; the ice broke and six drowned. All that Wallington could think to say of this untoward event was that "they were hopeful youths, and the parents of them were of good estate."[51] In Cheapside at the site of the old cross, there was a place eight or ten steps deep where "a laboring man went down to mend some pipes to convey the water, but the damp [gas] came and killed him, so that he was taken up dead."[52] In Bishopsgate Street a master carpenter, laying boards two stories up, slipped and fell, breaking his skull. Five days later, again in Bishopsgate Street, a scaffold broke on which a bricklayer was at work, pitching him down upon a wall so that he broke his back.[53] While Wallington was at the Romford Fair, a horse kicked a man with its hind leg and killed him. The very streets were a constant source of fatal accidents. In Thames Street a cart slipped, crushing a man against the wall of St. Botolph's Church. A Highgate woman riding a mare to Islington was knocked from its back by a stallion harnessed to a cart behind. The mare bolted, the stallion followed, and the cart wheel ran over the woman's head so that "her brains did fall on her neck cloth."[54] When walking along Kent Street, Wallington saw a page jostle a maid, who slipped, falling beneath the wheels of a passing coach.[55] Coming home along Thames Street on a November evening at twilight and intending to turn up Bread Street hill, Wallington was passed by a cart burdened with a high load of faggots that overturned at the corner: "had I gone a little faster, I could not conceive but I should have been killed. . . . So all the way . . . home I lifted up my heart, praising God for my deliverance."[56]

At times even Wallington's house seemed bent on his destruction. On June 5, 1626, just a week after Wallington and his father had signed the lease to his house in Little Eastcheap (Nehemiah's first house and shop had been in the neighboring parish of St. Andrew's Hubbard), he set about its repair.[57] While a carpenter worked on the roof beams and gutter above the garret, Nehemiah set to work with a pickax removing crumbling bricks from the chimney breast in the front room of the second story, preparatory to the arrival of the bricklayer. As he stooped by the fireplace to pry up a brick, "a great deal of dust fell down into my neck, as if God should say unto me, Nehemiah, I will give you warning, but I called unto the carpenter and asked him why he flung dust in my neck, but he gave me no answer. Then as I was going out of the room to call him again, a piece of ceiling fell down and hit me on the head." The entire chimney then collapsed, taking the gable end of the house with it and tumbling the brick and rafters into the street. Nehemiah's wife, Grace, hearing the frightful noise, "came running out of the chamber, looking very pale and saying, 'Oh, husband, where are you?' She then being with child miscarried with that sudden fear." The apprentice, James Weld, had escaped injury in the shelter of the staircase. The carpenter, who had swung himself up onto the gutter, called down through the clouds of dust "to ask how I did, thinking I had been killed or hurt." Wallington's father, who had been in the shop on the ground floor, rushed across the street as soon as the timber ceased falling and also called up to ask "how I did." Nehemiah, who could "scarce answer," he was "in such a maze," was eventually able to call down that he "was reasonable well," although he could not help "weeping tears" at being "delivered from such a danger." Despite all the destruction to the front of the house, no one was hurt: "Thus God preserved us all, but especially me, his poor servant." Nehemiah went on to add that the repairs for which he had laid out five pounds now cost "near to five and thirty, but blessed and praised be the Lord it was no worse with us."[58]

No other household accident was nearly so spectacular, but the shop in particular remained a place of danger. On a Saturday late in November 1630, when all but the infant Samuel were in the shop— Wallington and his father, Grace and little Sarah, and the two apprentices, Obediah Seeley and Theophilus Ward—Theophilus, who was showing chairs in the back room, dislodged a heavy one with his "bustling" about, apparently one at the top of a stack, which crashed down into the shop through the doorway and demolished a powdering tub that Wallington was in the process of selling to another customer. "It was God's great mercy . . . that it hit none of us, for if it had, it would have maimed us, if not killed us." Not long afterward a heavy iron cleaver fell down the stairwell from the garret, landing in the shop close to where Grace and their daughter Sarah were sitting in the upper end of the shop, "but did not hit them, the Lord's name be praised."[59] Two years later, while "my sweet child Sarah was playing in the shop, and as I was shewing of bed staves" to a customer, a huge ash log, propped against the wall, was dislodged and fell toward Sarah, and "had I not by God's providence caught hold of it (I think verily), it would have knocked her down and killed her . . . , for it was as much as ever I could do to stay it, it was so heavy."[60] Such stories appear interspersed among other accounts of God's manifold mercies to him and his family, and the accidents described were clearly no different from many others except that the Wallington household had survived them unscathed.

For it is clear that Wallington knew that the godly were not immune from judgment. In fact, although it was evident that by no means all suicides were members of the godly community, Nehemiah was not alone in having had such self-destructive tendencies. In April of 1632 Wallington heard about a neighboring minister at St. Mary le Bow who, "being much troubled in mind about his insufficiency in the ministry," asked his father to carry a petition for the prayers of the godly to nearby St. Antholin's, a church long famous for its Puritanism and its early morning lectures. But before the father had returned from that pious errand, the young minister had hanged himself.[61] Sometimes the suicides of the godly were doubly troubling because they seemed to have no cause,[62] but at other times the cause was frighteningly obvious. One June morning in 1635 a Mr. Monk in a neighboring parish arose before five o'clock and cut his throat. "Then he run forth in his shirt very bloody, flourishing his sword in his hand and leaped into the Thames (at Botolph's Wharf) and hit himself on a boat." Someone threw a rope around him, but he slipped from it and dove to the bottom. Then the watermen dragged him up with their boat hooks, and, as he was brought home, "he did roar most hideously, crying that he was damned, and he had prayed often, and God would not hear him. . . . He lay crying very strangely and hideously till the next Wednesday, and then he died."[63] Wallington tried to draw some lessons from these sad events. The self-destruction of the apparently godly showed the need "to take heed of judging, as the Apostle Paul saith"; what was also needful, especially in the godly, was constant watchfulness and especially the avoidance of melancholy and solitariness, "for Satan works much upon such."[64]

If orthodox Puritans seemed particularly prone to religious melancholy and suicide, the more radical Baptists seemed to Wallington given to acts of mad folly. In 1645 a Baptist in Whitecross Street was heard to say, evidently in an antinomian frenzy, that he would work upon the following Sabbath. Shortly thereafter, he was running downstairs after his wife with a broomstick in jest, when "the broomstick end hit against the wall, and the sharp end run into his belly and so [he] died presently, only saying this word: 'I have killed myself!' So he lived not to profane the Sabbath.'"[65] In 1646 in Dover, Kent, a woman who was "a most obstinate Anabaptist" cut off the head of her child, "and having severed the head . . . , did present the dismal spectacle to her husband and bid him baptize him then if he would."[66]

Although Wallington was generally confident that God withheld his judgments from the godly only to give them time to perfect their repentance,[67] Providence on the whole seemed to demonstrate that God was on the side of the godly and against the churchmanship and politics of their Arminian and Royalist opponents. After John Cotton had left his living in Boston, Lincolnshire, the bishop had urged the parish to install an organ in the church; and although the parish objected to the expense, the bishop prevailed by paying for it himself. "But [the organ] being newly up . . . a violent storm came in at one window and blew [it] to another window and brake both organ and window down"—a story for which Wallington named two credible sources, a Parliamentary captain and a minister lodging with Mr. Skelton, apothecary, in the Old Bailey.[68] Wallington had also heard about a minister at Hitchin, Hertfordshire, who urged the churchwardens to set up an altar in the approved Laudian fashion. One of the churchwardens warned the minister bluntly that some would then worship it in the Catholic fashion. This the minister denied, promising to preach against any such idolatry. However, when the altar "was finished very bravely, the minister came toward it and bowed three times, and the last time he bowed so low that he could not rise up again, but was crooked, and as he was going to the Bath for help, he died by the way."[69] Idolatry, like Sabbath-breaking, was so directly provocative to the divine majesty and so contrary to God's express commandments concerning his proper worship that Wallington was never surprised when such acts were followed by the most condign of punishments.

Providence showed itself equally a partisan of the godly, punishing those who would persecute or denigrate the saints in a most exemplary and edifying fashion. In 1625, when the "wicked cruel bishops" caused Edward Elton's book on the Commandments to be burned in Cheapside, and a partisan of the bishops had come to triumph at the fire, "that great and mighty God that hath the command of the wind and fire . . . did command his wind to blow one of those sheets of paper out of the fire again and to lap about this man's face (as he stood to see them burn), and it did so burn his face very much that he was in miserable pain."[70] In 1633 it was "credibly" reported that John Taylor of Postingford, Suffolk, accused his minister, Mr. Abbott, to the High Commission, although he would not have it known that he was the instigator. Abbott, learning of it and "meeting him by the way, told him of it," but Taylor denied the accusation and "wished that he might never go home, if he did so; and, as he was entering his own ground, he fell off his horse dead, never speaking more."[71] Wallington recounted a third such incident that took place early in February in 1640 in Mr. Munday's house in Little Britain just east of St. Bartholomew's Hospital. Two men were conversing, the first remarking on the pitiful sight of Burton, Bastwick, and Prynne in the stocks, shorn of their ears for publishing anti-Arminian tracts. " 'Push,' quoth the other, swearing a bloody oath, 'it were no matter if they had been hanged, base schismatical jacks to trouble the whole kingdom with their base opinions.' " After uttering this fierce and passionate condemnation, he fell to "bloody and fearful curses," whereupon he suddenly began to sweat and faint, "and taking out of his pocket a handkerchief to wipe his face and head, his ears fell a bleeding," which, needless to say, "wrought a strong amazement to all that stood by."[72] During the years of Laud's ascendancy, such stories must have provided what measure of comfort was available to the embattled godly.

These stories, however, were merely signs and portents of more dramatic providences to come. Once the conflict was joined, God's partisanship became open. Wallington reports that he "heard credibly" in 1639 of a soldier at Newcastle with the army King Charles had assembled to meet the rebellious Scots, who announced publicly that "he would not return till this hand (of his) had plucked out the heart's blood of a Scot." His arm was suddenly struck lame and painful, and when the surgeon to whom he went the next day asked how it came to be so, "he said he knew not, except God were angry with him for saying he would not return till his hand had plucked out the heart's blood of a Scot."[73] God, in fact, had a penchant for turning the oaths of the king's partisans against them in dramatic displays of the divine power. On May 22, 1642, during a sermon by Mr. Wells at St. Katherine's Creechurch in Leadenhall Street, the preacher urged his auditors "not to sleep but to stir themselves up." On hearing this Mrs. Clark, Wallington's informant, jogged the knee of a slumbering Mrs. Atkinson in a gentle manner so as to awake her. Nothing grateful, Mrs. Atkinson, "being a deboist [debauched] woman," called Mrs. Clark an "envious housewife and drunken sow, and saying, Oh, you bold drunken slut, do you kick me?" Mrs. Clark suffered this tirade in silence, but on returning home told her husband and declared herself unwilling to continue to share a pew with Mrs. Atkinson. Mr. Clark then informed Mr. Wells and the churchwardens, who sent for Mr. Atkinson to come to the vestry, and when he came and was informed of the complaint, he charged that Clark lied and that Mrs. Clark had kicked his wife, an exchange of charges that led to an increasingly acrimonious scene which ended with Atkinson calling Clark a "blockhead and a Roundhead" and other "reproachful words." Atkinson then hurried home and returned shortly with his wife, "who came thither in a great heat and full of bitterness" and swore to the vestry that if Mrs. Clark had not kicked her, "she wished she might never go home else alive and that she might never speak more." Having pronounced in this way her own sentence, "as she was going out into the churchyard, she sank down dead and [was] never heard to speak more except . . . just as she was dying," when she cursed Mrs. Clark, "saying, 'a pox take you: you are one of the holy sisters,' and suddenly her tongue (as was observed) turned black." What is particularly interesting about this account of what is essentially a quarrel between neighbors is that for Wallington the salient point was the political and religious bias displayed—the reference to "holy sisters" and "Roundhead"— for he titled this section of the book "Judgments of God upon those that mock in calling of Roundheads," and he followed the Atkinson-Clark story with one of a woman "who was a scorner and a derider of such as do truly fear God, commonly calling of them Round-heads," and who subsequently gave birth to a child having no head but instead "having upon each shoulder an ear and eyes in his breast."[74]

Words had an almost magical quality for Wallington, and those who cursed or reviled the Parliamentary cause regularly perished in the act. A cavalier, meeting "some honest people that stood in his way" in a Buckinghamshire lane, took offense at them and called them Roundheads, "and before he was out of their sight, his horse did stumble, and he fell and broke his neck." Even more provoca-tively, during the siege of Reading in January 1642/43, a Royalist cannoneer recited "their common, hideous, hellish verse: 'God damn me, God ram me nine mile in hell, if ever a Roundhead in England do dwell.'" When he next fired his cannon, it exploded, killing him and many others.[75] Given the "blasphemous" and "devilish healths" that were common in the king's armies, Wallington could only "admire . . . the patience of God" who forebore to destroy them all. The following oaths were reported in 1642 and were, Wallington thought, sufficient to "make our hearts to ache and our joints to tremble": "We drink a health to King Charles in whom we live, move, and have our being; we drink a health to the confusion of the Gospel of Jesus Christ; we drink a health to the confusion of Pym's God; we will drink and be drunk, and whore, and be damned and will not be beholding to God to save us; we had rather be in hell with our courages than in heaven with the Roundheads." The blaspheming of the Royalist soldiers was so notorious that Wallington was quite prepared to believe the story of the troop of Cavaliers who, coming to plunder a town, swore that they would kill all the Roundheads they found there. When "some of that rascally crew" asked how they would know a Roundhead, since many wore their hair long, the answer was given that each suspect was to "wish God to damn them," and all who would not were to be robbed and slain as Roundheads. "These abominable things make me tremble in writing of them."[76]

These terrible oaths and healths were to Wallington's mind the ultimate sin of the Cavaliers—worse even than their making war on Parliament, which made them rebels in his eyes—for by these abominations they denied the true God and whored after a false. Nevertheless, the very act of joining the king committed the Cavaliers to the devil's party, with results that were as terrible as they were predictable. At the engagement near Brentford on November 12, 1642, it was reported that the king's soldiers shot off their ordnance "many times . . . , yet God would not suffer them to go off against us." It reminded Wallington of "Pharaoh's enchanters who, when the dust was turned to lice, said, 'This is the finger of God,'" and it led the Cavaliers to say, "if the devil would help us as the Roundheads' God doth help them, they would not so much fear the Roundheads." For Wallington this was proof of the words in Deuteronomy 32:31 "that their God is not as our God. . . . For they provoked him with strange gods that provoked him to anger with abominations."[77] But the devil did not help the Cavaliers, for he was as subject to God's will as man was. Rather, the devil came as a judgment on those very Cavaliers who invoked his name. Wallington heard that on December 21, 1643, the devil came in the guise of a man toward three Cavaliers guarding the bridge end and outer works at Bridgwater, Somerset. One of the sentinels bid him stand and, when he came on, fired his musket at him, but it was the sentinel who "suddenly fell down dead." "Then the devil went on and tore the bridge and iron chains to pieces and threw down their works," and the two remaining sentinels fled terrified to "relate what befell them."[78]

Perhaps the most frightening judgment was visited on a troop of Lord Goring's command in garrison at Salisbury in March 1645. Some of these soldiers were drinking healths at the Catherine Wheel, and "after they had drunk the king's health, the queen's, Rober's [Prince Rupert's], and some others, one of them began a health to the devil." Another refused on the grounds that "he did not know whether there were a devil, and if he could see the devil, he would pledge his health. Whereupon there was immediately a great stink in the room and a smell of brimstone withal, and immediately an ugly creature that frighted them all appeared amongst them and took the man and carried him out of the window, nothing of him remaining but some blood spilt about the window."[79] To Wallington the Cavaliers had become "worse than devils," for "the devils believe there is a God and tremble at his judgments, but these men do neither."[80]

Wallington had grown up in a world full of danger and had become accustomed to sudden death by fire and drowning, by accidental falls, and by the ubiquitous horses, carts, and coaches that made the narrow London streets so perilous. Although many of these fatalities seemed arbitrary, Wallington was certain that he lived in a moral universe that made sense of all such violent dangers, for they were judgments and punishments, or, if one survived them, mercies and deliverances that offered empirical evidence of God's will and empirical proof that God would not be mocked. One could even find a certain satisfaction in contemplating all these cases of sudden death, for if one lesson to be learned was "to take heed of judging of any," others were to "praise God for making others examples to you," and "to admonish [us and] to stir us up to prepare for" death, an exercise that should enable sinful man to get his priorities aright.[81] The point of these displays of divine Providence, like Job's tribulations, was to teach man the nature of the universe and of the God who ruled it, even that ultimate lesson that God and man were radically different and that God's ways were in some final sense un-searchable and unknowable.[82]

But increasingly during the years of Laudian ascendancy, and most obviously during the 1640's, the familiar, if dangerous, world became the scene of a Manichaean conflict between the forces of God and the devil; and if the English revolution failed in the final analysis, as Wallington was sure that it had by the 1650's, it was not because God had ceased to provide exemplary lessons adequate to the education of the new Israel. On May 2, 1655, Wallington recorded the reasons why "the Lord of late hath been pleading with this city by fire and rebuking of it with flames of fire," reasons ranging from the "many strange false forms of worship that are tolerated in the midst of us, the many pretenses of worshiping of God in such ways as never entered into His heart to enjoin"—doubtless a reference to the emergence of the Quakers along with the "Anabaptists," as Wallington continued to term them—to "the hardening of their hearts and shutting up of their bowels toward poor creatures that are in misery."[83] The volume of judgments ends not with some signs of public repentance but with accounts of "some sad-sorrows that have befallen the people of God."[84]

There were still lessons to be learned, but there was no evidence that God's English Israel was prepared to learn them.[85] Wallington survived the Laudian persecution of the saints, even his own frightening trial before the High Commission, convinced that God would ultimately vindicate His saints. His providential beliefs equipped him to survive repeated defeats by the various enemies of the godly who could be so readily identified with the Antichrist. But the defeats of the 1650's resulted from the quarrels and loss of nerve of the godly themselves. Disillusionment followed, for Providence offered no hope for an Israel that had betrayed its own high calling.

God hath given you husband, children, family, and other blessings,
but you enjoy none of them without a cross. . . . But this grief God
recompenseth with great benefit, for our savior Christ is our good
warrant, that this is the lot of God's saints, to enjoy his blessings with
afflictions. So that the more you be sorrowful, the more you be sure
that the loving God hath given you your portion.

—Edward Dering

4. Family and Friends

Nehemiah Wallington began his first extant notebook on "The Mercies of God" by invoking the "many mercies and favors and many great deliverances from dangers of our bodies I and mine have received from God."[1] Although his ultimate concern was with the discipline necessary to "holiness of life and conversation," with his religious duties, and with what comfort they brought to his troubled soul, nevertheless fear of the dangers of physical harm, particularly to family and friends, was never far from his thoughts. Half a lifetime after recording that initial prayer of gratitude for deliverance from danger, he noted late in December of 1654 that he had "spent most of the day in reading and prayer with my family in which I did find some comfort. And though now two are sick again in my family, which brought me some fears, yet quickly my fears were gone in thoughts of God."[2] In his long life Wallington found neither a means to escape from the ever-present dangers of the world nor a cure for his constant anxiety about them. He recognized that God's "rod of afflictions" was constantly exercised against him in an effort "to wean" him "from the world"; nevertheless, he also recognized how incompletely God had succeeded despite that constant chastisement, for "his afflictions and love" inevitably "ran out too much" on his "wife and children, even more than upon God."[3] To love God's creatures unreservedly was to court sorrow, for God reclaimed them by accidental death and disease with dismaying regularity; yet for all his censorious priggishness and for all the egoism of his consuming concern for the safety of his own soul, Nehemiah was a man of warm affections, worrying over his family into what should have been serene old age and clinging to old friends, though separated from them by the broad Atlantic.

Except for a fragment about his mother, who died when he was five, Wallington never deliberately set out to write a memoir of any member of his family. Yet the hints and comments he left behind do reveal a good deal, if only inadvertently. What they make clear, first of all, is one unusual aspect of Wallington's situation. Whereas most members of the artisan class left hearth and home to seek an apprenticeship, Nehemiah remained at home in the bosom of his family until just before his marriage. Furthermore, whereas few young artisans were London born—Nehemiah's father had apparently not been, nor was his son-in-law, John Houghton—Nehemiah was born and died in the tiny parish of St. Leonard's Eastcheap.[4] Precise figures exist to show how unusual Wallington was in this respect. Between 1610 and 1620, the decade in which Nehemiah would have been apprenticed—he was admitted free of the Company of Turners by patrimony on May 18, 1620—the Company bound 265 apprentices.[5] Only 8.3 percent were London born (12 percent if Middlesex is included), and as many young apprentices were from Somerset as from Surrey (14 each), as many from Lincolnshire as from Kent (10 each). More came from Wales, Scotland, and Ireland (15) than from any single English county with the exception of London itself.[6] The consequences of such long-range movement by the young are difficult to calculate with any precision, but it is obvious that, unlike most of his fellow turners, Wallington had not been separated from his immediate kin at adolescence.

What the senior John Wallington's attitude toward his own family may have been cannot now be known. He may have shed all connections happily on reaching London, or it may simply be that John's parents were long dead by the time Nehemiah was born 26 years later.[7] Whatever the case, paternal grandparents or other paternal kin do not appear in Nehemiah's various autobiographical references, except possibly a "cousin" John Wallington to whom Nehemiah addressed a letter in 1648 entitled (in Nehemiah's letter book) "reproof for gross sins, advising him to repent," in which Nehemiah rebuked this purported cousin for numerous failings, in particular that "filthy, odious, loathesome, swinish, beastly sin of drunkenness," which had made cousin John "odious to God" and had also led him to profane "the Lord's day" and to "steal and rob your poor father."[8] If this cousin's actions were as represented and if they were typical of the paternal kin, it is conceivable that Nehemiah's father's Puritanism, which was evidently acquired after he came to London, may have estranged him from his family. On the other hand, it is dangerous to argue from silence, and the one letter to cousin John may just as easily suggest that John Wallington, Sr., had a brother with whom sufficiently close relations were maintained for Nehemiah to be aware of his cousin's moral failings.

Be that as it may, John Wallington, Sr., seems to have found domesticity to his liking and to have viewed his own role in his growing family as that of the benign patriarch. Within nine months of his marriage to Elizabeth Hall,[9] a godly young woman of twenty and the daughter of a London skinner, the first Wallington child, a daughter christened Anne, was born. In the course of the next twenty years John and Elizabeth had another eleven children, another Anne, an Elizabeth, two Johns, two Sarahs, a Mary, Martha, Samuel, Nehemiah, and Dorcas.[10] Less than a year after Elizabeth Wallington's death on November 20, 1603, John remarried, this time to a widow, Joan Hinde, whose young son Philip was Nehemiah's childhood companion until Philip's tragic death in the sickness of 1609.[11] Like Elizabeth Wallington before her, Joan died in her fortieth year, ten months after her marriage, leaving behind no children by John Wallington but, in addition to Philip, an older daughter by her first marriage, who became "sister Hinde" married to a "brother Cross" of Chelmsford whose son was in the Parliamentary army in the winter of 1642.[12] John then married again for a third time to a slightly younger widow, Alice Harrison, two of whose children, Richard, age seventeen, and Anne, age ten, died in the Wallington household in that terrible early autumn sickness in 1609, just weeks after little Philip Hinde.[13] Alice and John had one child together, Nehemiah's half sister Patience. Alice lived on till the summer of 1634, dying just four years before her husband; although Nehemiah mentions Patience on a number of occasions, he never writes of his stepmother Alice.[14]

The size of the Wallington family—twelve children by the first wife, a thirteenth by the third, plus at least four stepchildren—was clearly exceptionally large, although not unequaled. We are fortunate that a parish clerk at St. Leonard's was particularly conscientious in recording the names of fathers at christenings during the ten years from 1602 through 1611. This allows us to identify 70 fathers, including John Wallington, and by tracing their names forward and backward in the register to reconstruct their families—at least to the extent that their children were christened in the parish of St. Leonard's Eastcheap.[15] Three hundred and ten children were brought by those 70 fathers to be baptized, an average of 4.43 children per family. Fifteen fathers brought only one child to the font (21.4 percent), but seven fathers (10 percent), among them John Wallington, brought ten or more children to be baptized—a small but significant minority, for these seven sired 79 offspring, 25 percent of the total.

The repetition of given names among the Wallington children—two Annes, two Johns, and two Sarahs—suggests that the Wallingtons, despite their fecundity, were no more immune to the high mortality of the period than other Londoners. Several of the children certainly died in infancy, and we know that the first Anne died within the month and the first Sarah within eighteen months of birth. Others doubtless did so as well, but their burials are not recorded in the parish register. Six survived to marry: Elizabeth, the eldest surviving child, who at 21 married a local turner, Richard Bradshaw, in 1607; Mary, who at 23 married another local turner, Thomas Fawken (also spelled Facon), in 1614; Nehemiah, who at 23 married Grace Rampaigne in 1621; Dorcas, who at 26 married Richard Kiffet; John, Nehemiah's older brother, who married Mary Valentine, certainly by 1627 when their first child was christened (John, Jr., was 32 in 1627); Sarah, born in 1602, married at an unknown date (Nehemiah mentions that he visited her in Lewisham, across the river in Kent, in 1625); and Patience, the half sister, who was married about 1632 to Henry Church, haberdasher.[16] However, only four of his thirteen children were still alive when John Wallington, Sr., made his will in 1635: two daughters, Mary Fawken and Dorcas Kiffet, and the sons John and Nehemiah.[17] Elizabeth Bradshaw, whose youngest child was born in the spring of 1620 and who would have been 50 in 1635, apparently predeceased her father, as did Patience Church, the youngest of children to live long enough to marry, presumably in Patience's case in childbirth. Henry Church, the latter's husband, was one of the overseers of John, Sr.'s, will.

The second generation apparently fared no better. Elizabeth and Richard Bradshaw christened nine children. One was stillborn, one died within the month, a third at thirteen months, a fourth at age three, and a fifth at age eight. The other four may have lived to maturity; at least their burials are not recorded in the parish register. Mary and Thomas Fawken appear to have had two daughters, one of whom survived to adolescence. Dorcas and Richard Kiffet had at least one son, John, who lived to be apprenticed to his uncle John Wallington, Jr., in 1654. This same John and his wife Mary had five children: one stillborn, two who died under the age of two, a fourth who died under the age of ten, and the fifth, John's namesake, who died in his fourteenth year. Nehemiah and Grace also had five children, four of whom died before their third birthday. Only one, Sarah, survived to marry John Houghton, another turner, on July 20, 1647. John Wallington, Sr., lived to be 86, John, Jr., lived to be 64, and Nehemiah 60. Their longevity was much less typical than the high mortality among their children.

In St. Leonard's Eastcheap, the parish clerk recorded 190 burials in his register between 1602 and 1611 and noted the age at death for 171 (90 percent). Of those whose age at death is known, 20 percent died under the age of one, 42 percent by age 10, and almost two-thirds (64 percent) before reaching their majority (age 21). Only 8 percent lived past the age of 50, and a mere 3 percent past 60, the longevity reached by the surviving Wallington men. During the decade in question the plague struck London with unusual virulence in 1603: 70 burials were recorded for that year alone in St. Leonard's, more than a third of the burials recorded for the whole 1602–11 period, and a figure that surpassed the last demographic catastrophe in 1563, when 67 burials were recorded, and the next to come in 1625, when 58 burials were noted. If 1603 is eliminated, it is possible to develop a demographic profile of the parish that is not skewed by the extraordinary mortality produced by the plague, a disease that seems to have had its most devastating effect on the large population of apprentices and servants.[18] With the plague year eliminated, 30 percent of the known total died under the age of one, 44 percent died by age 10, but only 59 percent died before reaching the age of 21. Fourteen percent lived to be 50 or older, and 7 percent 60 or older.[19] In fact, the St. Leonard's data suggest that there were two periods of high risk: the first year of life, when approximately 30 percent of the recorded deaths were noted, and the period from age 16 to 25, when another 24 percent of the recorded deaths occurred in normal years (26 percent if 1603 is included). The latter age group includes a large population of immigrant apprentices and servants, plus young wives—two groups particularly at risk.[20]

What made Nehemiah Wallington's situation unusual was that, as a native Londoner, he could not have escaped knowledge of the appallingly high levels of mortality among the young. Yet at the same time, because he remained at home until he married and then moved briefly only to the next parish, he necessarily grew up among the survivors. His older siblings, Samuel and Martha, born during the three years preceding his birth, may well have died before he arrived, but during his early years his sisters Elizabeth (born in 1585) and Mary (born in 1590) and his older brother John (born in 1594) would have been very much in evidence, as would have been his younger sisters, the babies Dorcas and Sarah. The death of his own mother in 1603 obviously affected him deeply, as did the death of his stepbrother Philip in 1609. Undoubtedly these two traumas overshadowed the death of his first stepmother, Joan Hinde, in 1605, and of his second stepmother's children, Richard and Anne Harrison, in the weeks after Philip's death in the autumn of 1609. Nevertheless, by that date his eldest sister Elizabeth had married Richard Bradshaw and had given birth in the spring of 1609 to twins, one of whom lived, a son John.[21] By the time Nehemiah was twenty years of age, seven Bradshaw nieces and nephews had been born in St. Leonard's parish, three of whom may still have been alive, and sister Mary had married Thomas Fawken and was pregnant with her daughter Mary. In other words, in 1618—Nehemiah's twentieth year and the year of the onset of his crisis, with its attempted and contemplated suicides—Nehemiah was not a lonely apprentice far from his family and isolated in a strange city. Rather, he lived in the midst of a large family: his father and second stepmother were very much in evidence, as were a brother and four sisters, a half sister, two brothers-in-law, and three nephews and nieces (two more, Mary Fawken and Hannah Bradshaw, were born in July). He was surrounded, in other words, by more than a dozen close kin all living a stone's throw away from one another in one tiny parish. A decade later, in 1628, Nehemiah's father and stepmother Alice were still alive, as were at least three of his siblings (Mary Fawken, John, Jr., and Dorcas Kiffet), and at least one nephew, John Bradshaw (he had been on the expedition to relieve La Rochelle). Patience was still at home unmarried. Brother John's first daughter died in July 1628, but by then Mary was pregnant with their second child, a son to be named John. And Nehemiah and Grace had a son, Nehemiah, who died in November 1628, and an infant, Sarah, born in December 1627. By Nehemiah's thirtieth year, then, he had at least ten remaining kin in the parish. And these are minimal figures. Nehemiah's sister Sarah across the river at Lewisham may still have been alive, but Nehemiah last mentions visiting her in 1625. More of the Bradshaws may have been alive, but no new Bradshaw children are recorded as baptized after 1620, and Nehemiah mentions only the Bradshaw son John.[22] There must have been Wallington kin, siblings and relatives of John, Sr. (as mentioned earlier, Nehemiah wrote to a cousin, John Wallington, in 1648), and there may have been cousins on the Hall side of the family (John Wallington, Sr., signed an indenture with his brother-in-law, Anthony Hall, of Tottenham, Middlesex, in 1597).[23] There was the Allen family, whom Nehemiah mentions several times, a family related to the Harrisons, and through them to the Wallingtons by way of Alice Harrison, John Wallington, Sr.'s, third wife. There was Nehemiah's stepsister, the daughter of Joan Hinde, who was married to "brother" Cross and living in Chelmsford; and there were the Churches, to whom the Wallingtons became connected through the marriage of Patience and Henry Church.[24] Finally, Nehemiah had Rampaigne relatives, the two brothers of his wife Grace: the elder, Zachariah, was married and living in Ireland, and the younger, Livewell, approximately Nehemiah's age, was a minister first at Burton, Lincolnshire, and later at Broxholme.[25]

The real question concerning all these relationships with parents, siblings, children, and more distant kin is not of their very existence—for, given the high fertility of the period, large families and extensive blood and marriage connections were inevitable—but rather of their quality, the reality and depth of the feelings involved. By and large, historians have advanced three generalizations characterizing these relationships in broad terms. First, parental relations have largely been seen as cold, patriarchal, and authoritarian. Second, relations with children have been characterized as distant and low in affection, in part as a psychological protection against the loss inevitable when mortality among children was so high, in part as a consequence of the callousness developed in response to such appalling losses. Finally, it has been suggested that kin relations, so rich in complexity and importance for the vast cousinhoods of the aristocracy, had little meaning for those of lesser social status, who frequently left family and neighborhood at adolescence, and for whom neighbors might be of much greater importance than distant kin.[26]

The question of Nehemiah's own relations with his parents is complicated by the fact that his mother died when he was five, and his father, who was eleven years older than his mother, must indeed have been a patriarchal figure even when Nehemiah first knew him—46 at Nehemiah's birth, soon to be in the livery and one of the first wardens of the Turners' Company when it received its royal charter in 1604, a prospering and respected member of the community from Nehemiah's earliest memories.[27] Nehemiah's most vivid recollection of his mother was evidently of her final illness, which he described with a concreteness of detail that suggests that its full horror was etched indelibly in his memory. The birth of her twelfth and last child, Sarah, at five on a Sabbath morning late in November of 1602 left Elizabeth Wallington an invalid. Nehemiah explains and justifies that last painful year as a time when "the Lord chastened" her, giving her "a sharp and bitter portion," so as "to make her willingly to come to him." But what Nehemiah remembered were the cries wrenched from her bed of pain: "No more, Lord, no more; no more, Lord, no more! Lord, is my strength the strength of stones, or is my flesh of brass that thou layest on such a load upon me? Lord, remember I am but earth, and that thou wilt bring me to the dust of death." However, aside from these prolonged agonies, Nehemiah remembered his mother largely in conventional terms as a proper Puritan matron—"a godly, religious, and virtuous woman," who was "full of pity," "loving and obedient to her parents, loving and kind to her husband, very tender-hearted to her children, much affecting the sincere preachers of God's word, loving all that were godly, much misliking the wicked and profane." She had committed to memory "the stories of the martyrs," presumably from Foxe's book, and knew as well some secular history from "the English chronicles," but whether she could read herself is not clear. She was an excellent seamstress, being noted for her drawn work and the fineness of her embroidery. Nehemiah in fact recollected her largely in terms of a series of conventions and noted that she was a very "pattern of sobriety."[28] Doubtless such impersonal terms were easier to put down on paper than a five-year-old's memories of a dying mother.

Nehemiah's relations with his magisterial father are by comparison rich, complex, and of long duration, for Nehemiah was 40 when his father died full of years in August of 1638. Wallington seems to have confused his father with God, which is understandable enough, given his age and benign authority in household and community. For the son, a great burden of guilt seems to have been removed when his father died: as he told his old friend James Cole, "I lost an earthly Father and found a heavenly Father, that is, I did find after my Father's death more joy and comfort in my poor soul from God than ever I did before."[29] Such a confusion would not be surprising, for Nehemiah frequently thought of God in the image of a father: "For the Lord is as a Father that hangs betwixt anger and pity, resolved on neither, but incline[d] to that that the carriage of his children may call for, by sticking further if they stoop not, and desisting from stripes, if they do."[30] However, the picture of John Wallington, Sr., that emerges in Nehemiah's pages is not of a man poised between pity and righteous anger, as ready to break the stubborn as to comfort the humble; rather, we see a man who, for all his success as a man of affairs and for all the many responsibilities a large family and his position in the Turners' Company brought, nevertheless had the ingenuity and took the time to shepherd his son, young enough to be a grandchild, through an exasperating period of several years when suicidal depression and spiritual self-doubt rendered him incapable of helping himself. Nehemiah was not unmindful of this, and his confusion of God and his father came about, it seems, precisely because in his saner and more sanguine moments he realized that he served "not a straight-handed God, neither a hard Master, but a loving and kind Father which will not let a cup of cold water go unrewarded."[31]

After receiving news of the death of Nehemiah's and Grace's first child, a disturbing letter in which Nehemiah had apparently written also of Grace's sickness, Livewell Rampaigne, Grace's brother, wrote Nehemiah a letter of consolation and comfort—for the daughter already dead and for the wife whose fate was, to Livewell, then unknown. In the course of it Livewell refers to Nehemiah as "an indulgent father and a loving husband."[32] It is just such an image that the senior Wallington had always displayed to Nehemiah; at least there is no hint either direct or indirect of the minatory and authoritarian domestic tyrant so dear to the theoretical writings of the period. Nehemiah conscientiously catalogued God's various chastisements and consoled himself with the knowledge that such "afflictions are common to all God's children."[33] However, he provides no evidence that his earthly father dealt with him in any such fashion. Instead, he pictures a worried parent all too aware of Nehemiah's precarious mental health, indulging his son's melancholy and erratic behavior, inquiring solicitously "how he did" when Nehemiah was too depressed to join the rest of the family in the hall for a Sabbath dinner.[34] Later on the same occasion, when the family had returned to church for evening prayer, Nehemiah had gone to bed, claiming illness, "but I was not so sick in the body, as I was in my mind." It was at this melancholy moment "that my loving and tender father came up to me in the chamber and sat down by the bedside and did read unto me and prayed unto God for me, and he did think I would have died that afternoon."[35] At least he had the kindness to take his son seriously and to apply the only remedies that "troubled in mind" but godly young man could believe in.

Moreover, his father remained actively involved in Nehemiah's life long after such interference must have been customary, indulging him when possible but providing safeguards as he did so. Nehemiah asked for his independence, and his father, then master of the Turners' Company, arranged for his becoming free of the company by patrimony, which was the proper step procedurally, but then arranged for him to have his own shop without serving two years as journeyman, which was irregular to say the least.[36] Although the senior Wallington set Nehemiah up in a shop a few yards away from the parental home on the corner of Philpot Lane in the parish of St. Andrew's Hubbard, "my tender father caused me to come home and sup and lie at his house every night." When Nehemiah indicated that such a measure clearly defeated his desire to be alone, "my father then caused me to hire a journeyman, one Edward Cole, to lie in the house with me." One suspects his father's anxious hand in Nehemiah's marriage to Grace Rampaigne shortly afterward, but Nehemiah simply records with absolute complacency the words from Genesis, "The Lord God said, It is not good that the man should be himself alone. I will make him an helpmeet for him."[37] Nehemiah may, of course, have been confusing his earthly with his heavenly father once again.

The constant involvement of John Wallington, Sr., in the life of his son may have been unusual only in the sense that few fathers lived long enough to continue such an active interest. In any event Nehemiah never seemed to regard such paternal activity as untoward or unwanted. There is some evidence that Nehemiah was not the only member of the family so helped. In 1622 Thomas Slutter, Turner, willed the Turners' Company 30 pounds to be loaned to young freemen of the company free of interest for three years. Although there were six suitors, the first two turners to receive the loan were Thomas Fawken, the senior Wallington's son-in-law, and Nathaniel Goody, his former apprentice.[38] Fawken must have been a frequent source of worry to his father-in-law in these years, for he was constantly breaking company ordinances and evidently continued in financial difficulties despite the loan.[39] When in 1626 John Wallington, Sr., "was a suitor for his son Nehemiah that he might have 15 pounds of the 30 pounds which Thomas Slutter gave to the company to be lent unto two young men . . . for three years gratis," the embarrassing fact came to light that Thomas Fawken had been unable to repay his loan.[40] The following year he appeared before the company warden and assistants and refused to pay his quarterly dues on the ground that the company had unfairly distrained 20 pounds of his goods at the Smithfield Fair to pay for various fines and arrearages he had incurred. Fawken had then lost his temper, and, as the clerk noted with some consternation, "behaved himself this day like a man distracted of his wits, railing against the Company and beating the table with his fists, and being requested to be quiet, he said he would not, neither would he endure me to read what was written in this book . . . and his father-in-law, Mr. Wallington, sitting at the table could not persuade him to be quiet." As the clerk noted, "these 20 years I never saw the like abuse offered the board."[41] Two years later John Wallington quietly repaid the 15 pounds lent to Thomas Fawken, and in 1632, on one of the last occasions that the elder Wallington, now 80, attended the board, he paid the arrearages owed by another poor member of the company. "God stir up more men's hearts to be so charitably minded as Mr. Wallington is," the clerk added.[42]

In the meantime the elder Mr. Wallington had co-signed with Nehemiah the lease to his house in St. Leonard's in 1626. In 1630, when Nehemiah's former journeyman was exposed as having cheated Nehemiah of several score pounds in the course of his two years of service, it was the elder Wallington and the elder Cole, the father of Nehemiah's friend James Cole, who mediated the controversy.[43] The year before, the elder Wallington had taken on one of Nehemiah's servants, Theophilus Ward, as apprentice, and as late as 1630 the elder Wallington sometimes worked in Nehemiah's shop. In fact, it is obvious that the elder Wallington took Ward on as an apprentice because Nehemiah could not without violating guild rules; however, Theophilus continued to work for Nehemiah, who referred to him as "my servant."[44] The following June, despite his having been an independent householder and shopkeeper for ten years, Nehemiah found himself unable to meet the small debts owed to the chapmen who supplied his shop with additional wares. "As the sun doth break forth on a cloudy day, so did the Lord in the midst of my cares send in customers that I took some store of money, and my father helping me with thirty shillings, I had enough to pay my chapman."[45] Ten days later he and his father jointly bought a consignment of shovel trees and trenchers, and a year later Nehemiah noted that his father arranged a small family loan, this from the haberdasher son-in-law, Henry Church, when Nehemiah once again found himself temporarily short of cash.[46]

The elder Wallington may well have been exceptionally kind and understanding as well as exceptionally long-lived. He noted in his will that although he had been "a trader in the world many years," nevertheless he had "never troubled any man in suit of law," nor had anyone ever sued him.[47] Yet even his son and namesake, as prosperous and successful as his father and always a competent man of affairs, never seems to have regarded his father's treatment of Nehemiah as so indulgent as to be eccentric. On the contrary, young John seems to have shared his father's sense of familial responsibility and solidarity and to have had a special regard for Nehemiah's weaknesses and failings. When Nehemiah found himself named along with Burton, Bastwick, and Prynne in a Star Chamber bill in 1638, he was much troubled particularly by the Star Chamber oath, which he feared would force him either to forswear himself or to implicate his friends. In two different accounts he left of that frightening event he mentions the support he received from his brother, although his brother, who was also named in the bill, obviously had worries of his own: "I was much troubled in my mind about the oath and my brother John spake very comfortable to me and was (as he hath been always) a loving brother to me in this my sorrow"; "and my tender brother did say to my father, his [trouble] was not so much for himself as for his poor brother Nehemiah."[48]

Part of what was distinctive about the Wallingtons was a sense of family which, if not as broad as that of the gentry and aristocracy, nevertheless extended beyond the nuclear grouping of parents and children. Shortly after Nehemiah married, feeling the weight of "the charge of so many souls," he bought a copy of William Gouge's *Of Domestical Duties*, which was first published in 1622, "so everyone of us may learn and know our duties and honor God every one in his place where God has set them." A few years later, with the same intention in mind, he drew up a list of "31 articles for my family for the reforming of our lives," to which the adult members of the family "set our hands." Besides the signatures of Nehemiah and Grace, the document contained that of the apprentice, James Weld, and the three servants—Obediah Seeley, Theophilus Ward, and Susan Pate.[49] Such a document suggests that Nehemiah tended to see "family" as simply another term for "household," but his usage on other occasions makes clear that, though he did tend to include his household in his family, the latter included much more. The Wallingtons remained "in this doleful city" during the plague of 1625, and "hearing of bells tolling and ringing out continually could not but make us wonder at the hand of God to be so hot round about us." In the course of meditating on God's terrible visitation, Nehemiah asked himself with typical morbidity: "What if the sickness should come into this house, who would I be willing to spare? Then would I say, the maid. Who next? Myself. But what if God should strike thy wife, or thy father or thy brother John? How would I take it then?" Nehemiah goes on to express the hope that he would "take it patiently" and comforted himself with the thought of "the sorrows and troubles they were gone out of and the pleasure and joy that they were gone into."[50] In these musings Nehemiah writes of "Hearing how God swept away whole families, . . . taking away fifteen or sixteen out of some households," a statement that clearly confused biological families and economic households. But his final speculation goes beyond his household to include his brother and father. On another occasion he writes of "wife, children, parents, brothers, and sisters," which is functionally pretty much the family that Nehemiah recognized as such.[51]

Though such a conception of family did not specifically include the more distant kin of aunts and uncles and cousins, in fact Nehemiah assumed that family responsibility included such relations. Furthermore, "brother" and "sister" included for Wallington relations by marriage, for the distinction "in-law" was not one that Nehemiah made or apparently considered important. An incident that occurred in 1632 illustrates perfectly the functional definition of family as Nehemiah understood it. The year before, Nehemiah had signed a bond as surety for a debtor's appearance at the end of the loan period to pay the principal. Although the borrower had in the meantime died, the lender apparently decided to attempt to collect from Nehemiah, as though the latter had been surety for payment rather than merely for appearance. However, all this became clear only later. As Nehemiah describes it, he found himself on an April evening between 8 and 9, working in his shop, while his wife Grace was above, preparing supper "for her brother and sister which were come out of the country, thinking to be merry together" (presumably Livewell Rampaigne and his wife), when two serjeants and others appeared in the hall and announced they had come for the 80 pounds named in the bond, which they were prepared to take in goods at that very instant.

> My wife seeing a stranger coming . . . and saying he was come for four-score pounds worth of goods and hanging his cloak on the door, saying he would begin with the pewter, first it did fright her very much, looking very pale on the matter, and went down into the shop and wrung her hands, bursting out weeping, and then being with child did miscarry, and I run to Temple Bar to find my brother Cross to ask his counsel, but I could not find him, but before I came again my brother John and my brother Kiffet told them, if they would be contented till morning, they would be bound that nothing should be stirred. . . .

In the course of the next two weeks "brother" Cross managed to straighten out the tangled affair so that in the end the deceitful creditor was forced to pay two pounds for Nehemiah's costs, but in the meantime the full resources of the family were mobilized: not only brother John, to whom Nehemiah always turned in trouble, but also brother Kiffet, who was, as Dorcas Wallington's husband, actually Nehemiah's brother-in-law, and brother Cross, who, as "sister Hinde's" husband, was related only through marriage to a stepsister.[52]

However, such an affair does not tell the whole story, for family responsibility was not limited, as this incident seems to imply, by proximity. As has been mentioned, Nehemiah records visiting his youngest sister Sarah in Lewisham, on one occasion in the autumn of 1625 making a family expedition of it and taking his wife Grace, their children Elizabeth and John, their maid Ruth, and Nehemiah's half-sister Patience, on a trip by boat made memorable because the boatman nearly upset them all by rowing over a ship's cable and then going aground at low water several times. "But God of his goodness carried us safe thither at last, where we were all very merry together, and so we came all safe home again, the Lord's Name be praised for ever. Amen."[53] Even after Sarah's death brought an end to excursions to Lewisham, Wallington customarily took family outings to Peckham fields on the Surrey side, a neighborhood he must have come to know on his trips to visit his sister.[54]

In part because Nehemiah was literate and could correspond, even more distant relatives were not beyond the reach of his concern. He evidently felt particularly close to his ministerial brother-in-law, Livewell Rampaigne, with whom he shared religious zeal and humorless didacticism. Nehemiah preserved four of Livewell's letters, written between 1625 and 1632, evidently because of their exemplary instruction. Indeed, these letters are veritable compendia of Puritan moral instruction. For example, in response to a letter from Nehemiah that included accounts of the fall of La Rochelle and the death of yet another Wallington child, Livewell offers four uses to be made of public afflictions: first, that God's special favor to England in escaping La Rochelle's fate "is duly to be observed and with praise forever to be acknowledged"; second, that "God's dearest servants . . . are not privileged from bloody and fiery trials," from which the English should take warning; third, that the English should examine whether they had been remiss in the prayers for their co-religionists in trouble; and last, that from their fate the English should learn a grateful patience with their own troubles. Nevertheless, these letters also testify to a genuine affection between these two God-driven men.[55] As Wallington children died one after another, Nehemiah turned to his brother-in-law for solace and received both heartfelt sympathy and sensible advice. "When I consider," Livewell writes in early 1629, "God's rod is on you still in sickness of your child, in want, but above all in trouble of mind in a wounded spirit, Oh, Brother, my heart bleeds within me for you." But later in the same letter Livewell writes with a certain brisk sensibleness: "Comfort yourself with such meditations and do not cast down yourself with unprofitable sorrow, so offering advantage to the tempter."[56] It may well have been just this willingness to face unpleasant facts, this healthy regard for the harsh realities of life, that made him such a useful friend to Nehemiah, whose response to the very real horrors of his life tended to be a paralyzing depression and fearful incomprehension. At any rate Nehemiah carefully preserved Livewell's letter written late in 1625 in response to his grim news of the many deaths in the plague summer of that year and of the grave sickness of Grace, his wife and Livewell's sister. Livewell confessed when he wrote that he did not yet know "how it hath pleased God to dispose of my sister":

> If He have in his infinite goodness withdrawn His hand, restored her health to her, and her to us, we have just cause of joy and thanksgiving; if otherwise, as I much fear by your postscript, if He have taken her to Himself, we have just matter of humiliation and exercise for Christian patience and courage. And yet my confidence is that God has in the midst of judgment remembered mercy, that if she be dead, she is dead in the Lord and hath now the happy performances of all these gracious promises which are the comforts of our miserable lives.[57]

Altogether, in its combination of pious hope and commonsense acceptance, it was a surprisingly mature letter for a young brother of 24, still months away from his ordination, to have written to his brother-in-law. His concluding promise that, despite the feared death of his sister, "the bond betwixt you and I shall not on my part be broken" is evidence of the depth of the relationship between these two kindred spirits, despite the 130-odd miles that separated Burton near Lincoln from London.[58]

If the Sarah Rampaigne who came with her two children to live with the Wallingtons in 1635 was Livewell's widow, as is most probable, then the bond between these two "brothers" continued beyond the grave.[59] Sarah remained as a member of the household until her death nineteen years later. Although after her death Nehemiah confessed that it was his "sin" that he was "never content when my sister was living"—and it must have been a strain having an additional family of three crowding into the Wallington household, with its two bedchambers and garret—Wallington always referred to Sarah Rampaigne as "my sister" and recorded, for example, an occasion on January 12, 1642/43, when, rather than being accompanied by his wife, he and his "sister went to the public fast, and there was old tugging with our God for favor and mercy in helping us."[60] Sarah died at about five in the afternoon of July 12, 1654. Grace had come to Nehemiah earlier in the afternoon and had asked him "to buy a lobster for my sister, for she had a mind to one." But although he "fetched one suddenly, . . . my sister Sarah could not eat any of it, for presently after she died as she sat in a chair."[61] Despite the fact that there was no attempt to gather kin—there was scarcely time for that—it was evident that Sarah was dying, for Grace asked her "whether anything lay on her conscience." "No," Sarah had replied, "nothing doth lie on my conscience, but I desire a dram of mercy; it is a dram of mercy I would have."[62] Two days later, after the funeral, Nehemiah recorded that "this day my sorrow of my heart was made for the breach in my family in the loss of my sister Sarah."[63] However burdensome her presence may have been from time to time, Wallington had apparently never considered asking her to leave, for she was a member of the family and her passing left Nehemiah feeling "heavy and sad."

During the previous eight years the Wallington household had sheltered another Rampaigne, a nephew Charles, son of Grace's older brother Zachariah, who had perished at the hands of Brian Maguire's rebels in the winter of 1641. It is doubtful whether Nehemiah had ever met Zachariah, the eldest member of the Rampaigne family, who was evidently a wealthy planter with a considerable estate in county Fermanagh near Enniskillen. However, Nehemiah had somehow learned of the circumstances of his brutal murder on the road to the coast where he was cut down while his four children begged for his life: "Oh, do not kill my father, Oh, do not kill my father." Two of the children perished that first winter from starvation and exposure, but two survived, as did Zachariah's widow Dorothy, his second wife, who at some point in the next year or so acquired an Irish Catholic protector and lover.[64] The Wallingtons learned of all this in 1647 when Dorothy, who had come to England, apparently to liquidate what was left of the Rampaigne estate, had written letters to her Irish lover, letters that were intercepted and somehow reached the Wallingtons' hands. Nehemiah was horrified: "Oh, sister, my heart aches and trembles to consider of your sad and miserable condition . . . in regard of your poor soul." To "lie down with that Irish rebel" was bad enough, but having done so, to dissemble her pregnancy and to continue such "sin and wicked ways without repentance"—this was an abomination that would call down from God "just judgment" and from Nehemiah a veritable shower of apposite Biblical citations from Psalms and Proverbs, Hebrews and Ezekiel, Matthew and James.[65] While Nehemiah prayed that God would "bless and sanctify these wholesome instructions," Grace wrote a more practical letter to sister Dorothy, suggesting that her surviving child by Zachariah, a son Charles, be sent to stay with the Wallingtons, for Dorothy, like an "unnatural mother," had neglected his education. "Oh, let his soul be precious in your eyes, and have a care to put your child to some good trade that he is most capable of." Although Grace confessed that she had "one child of my own, besides my sister Rampaigne and her two children have none to go to for help but to us, and my husband hath poor kindred of his own, . . . yet because my affection is to the child, being the child of him who I so dearly loved," she urged Dorothy to send Charles to London and promised to persuade Nehemiah to take him on as an apprentice for only 20 pounds.[66] Whether because she wished to pursue her Irish liaison unencumbered or because Grace's proposition did indeed seem a "kind offer," Dorothy evidently acceded to her wishes, and Charles was raised till his majority as a member of the Wallington family. On July 18, 1655, having completed his apprenticeship, Charles was made free of the Company of Turners, just three years before Nehemiah's own death.[67]

These complex households that included not only the nuclear family and servants but also aged parents, widowed in-laws, and various nephews and nieces should not surprise us. The high mortality rate involved parents as well as children. Richard Kiffet, failed turner—he was listed as a girdler when his son was apprenticed—had been dead at least fourteen years when his son John was bound on May 30, 1654, to serve John Wallington seven years as apprentice. John Kiffet may well have been brought up in John Wallington's childless household, for his mother Dorcas had remarried on August 13, 1640.[68] John Wallington, Sr., seems to have been living with his elder son at least three years before his own death, for in his will he mentions a number of household articles (e.g., "an ancient drinking glass with three naked boys on it that was given to me of my wife's father on the first day of marriage, and a pair of bellows with St. John Baptist head on a platter graven, the which were Sir John Rainsford's in King Henry the Eighth's time") that he wished "should remain in the house of my son John"—suggesting by that phrase that he had moved his household goods into John's house, and himself as well, perhaps since the death of his third wife the year before.[69] In the absence of family, the old and orphaned would doubtless fall to the care of the parish overseers, but there is no evidence that Nehemiah, whose prosperity was certainly modest at best, ever expected the public authorities to bear the burden of supporting family members in need, any more than he would have expected his "brothers" to ignore his periodic pleas for help.

These family relations are visible, if only intermittently, because written evidence survives in a father's will or in letters to distant relatives. The relations that are the most opaque are those that were the most intimate—those between husband and wife and between parents and children. Nehemiah was married to Grace Rampaigne for 37 years, but he does not mention her that many times in the course of the surviving notebooks. He copied out four notebooks for her—Grace was apparently literate—a book of "choice Psalms" in 1639, a book titled "The Mighty Works of the Lord, which is a Prop to Faith" in 1646, and two books of sermons, one in 1636 and another in 1647, but he never tells us how he met her, wooed her, or wed her.[70] She helped out in the shop on at least one occasion, when her "care and diligence" prevented the loss of a customer, but there is no way of telling whether she customarily did so.[71] Occasionally in his various pious meditations he mentioned what a blessing it was to have a good wife, but these sentiments tended to be conventional. In the sixteenth of his catalogue of eighteen remedies for discontent he noted that "I did consider God's mercy in giving me a comfortable yokefellow to draw in one yoke to heavenward." Clearly, having a "comfortable yokefellow" was a great mercy, but it was not "that mercy above all mercies," which was the realization that "God having given me his only son Christ, how shall He with Him give me all things."[72] A wife was a blessing, but not to be compared to salvation; so the loss of a wife was a source of great grief but not equivalent to the grief caused by the knowledge of sin, for that was an offense against God: "great is the grief of an husband that loseth a kind and virtuous wife, and who can express the sorrow of a father or mother for the death of their dear and only child. But yet all the sorrow in the world is not like that sorrow and grief of heart for sin."[73] These are conventional pieties and, however orthodox, tell us nothing about the actual relations in the Wallington household.

The picture of Grace Wallington that emerges from Nehemiah's chance observations, as opposed to the stereotypical wife described in his formal meditations, is of a woman of powerful feelings who yet had a kind of commonsensical realism about the harsh facts of seventeenth-century life that her depression-prone husband never acquired. Nehemiah noted without comment two occasions (there obviously may have been more) when she miscarried—once in 1626 when the gable end of the house plunged into the street, and she feared that Nehemiah was crushed beneath the falling timber, and again in 1632 when the serjeants came to collect the bond of 80 pounds, and she thought the family faced imminent ruin.[74] Her young husband and the household they had made together were obviously the object of Grace Wallington's passionate concern; so was the fate of the Puritan movement that seemed embodied in the Parliamentary cause in the early 1640's. At the time of the fall of Bristol in 1643, when Parliamentary fortunes had reached their nadir, Nehemiah recorded with something of a tone of surprise that "surely I never did know my wife's heart to break so much for anything, as it did at this time in prayer."[75]

Yet for all her obvious capacity for deep feeling and passionate concern, it was Grace who had to provide an example of steadiness and to comfort her despairing husband as one child after another sickened and died during her decade of childbearing. In 1622 Nehemiah had made a New Year's resolution to carry himself "as a head and governor" toward his wife, and Livewell Rampaigne in his letter written to the Wallingtons in 1628 also assumed conventionally that Grace was "the weaker vessel" in need of Nehemiah's comfort as Nehemiah was of God's, but these were cultural conventions, not descriptions of social realities.[76] Wallington knew intellectually of the terrible vulnerability of infants and of women in childbearing years. The birth of their firstborn, their daughter Elizabeth, came after "great and sharp labor" which began on an autumn Saturday and continued until five o'clock the following afternoon, when "it pleased the Lord of his great mercy to give her safe deliverance of a daughter, but there was but small hope of the child's life." In a revealing afterthought Wallington confessed that "although (this mercy) childbearing is a common mercy of God, yet it is none the least, and therefore we ought to take notice of it, and to be thankful (unto God) not only for a month but forever to live thankfully."[77] When the plague struck again in 1625 with a ferocity unequaled since 1603, Nehemiah was particularly sensitive to the fact that infants and young mothers were exceptionally vulnerable: "we did hear that threescore children died out of one alley," and he later recorded that he "did hear of threescore women with child and in childbed that died in one week in Shoreditch parish and scarce two that was sick with child that escaped death."[78] Doubtless some became callous in the face of such a slaughter and found in indifference an antidote to the predictable loss. For Wallington, however, each new child was an endless source of anxiety, a being to be cherished and prayed over, and each death, however expected, was a crushing blow. Under Grace's patient ministrations he learned to go on with his life, but it is probably significant that his last bad bout with the temptation to suicide occurred in 1632, the year that Grace had her last miscarriage and their youngest son Samuel died.

The death of little Elizabeth in October of 1625, just short of her third birthday, almost overwhelmed Nehemiah. Her birth had been difficult, but she had lived, and Grace had been able to nurse her. Early in her second year, in February 1625, she had the measles but recovered. The whole family survived the plague that summer until October, when the bills of mortality had already recorded a decline in the death rate. Then, on a Saturday afternoon, Ruth, the servant maid,

> told my wife that she had a pricking in her neck, which words put us all in fear, and toward night she went to bed. And about eight o'clock at night [my] wife was in the kitchen washing of dishes, my daughter being merry went unto her mother and said unto her, "what do you here, my wife?" And at night when we were abed [Elizabeth shared her parents' bed], says she to me, father, I go abroad tomorrow and buy you a plum pie." These were the last words that I did hear my sweet child speak, for the pangs of death seized upon her on the Sabbath morning, and so she continued in great agonies (which were very grievous unto us, the beholders) till Tuesday morning, and then my sweet child died at four o'clock in the morning, being the eleventh day of October, and was buried that night.[79]

Nehemiah was beside himself with grief. As he confessed, he "forgot" himself so much that he broke all his "purposes, promises, and covenants" with God and refused all comfort from men. Finally Grace, who was already seven months pregnant with their second son, told Nehemiah: "Husband, I am persuaded you offend God in grieving for this child so much. Do but consider what a deal of grief and care we are rid of, and what a deal of trouble and sorrow she is gone out of, and what abundance of joy she is gone into. And do but consider, it is your daughter's wedding day and will you grieve to see your daughter go home to her husband Christ Jesus, where she shall never want, but have the fullness of joy forevermore?" Nehemiah was clearly nonplussed: "do you not grieve for this child?" And she answered, "No, truly, husband, if you will believe me, I do as freely give it again unto God, as I did receive it of him."[80] In these moments of high stress Nehemiah always found it difficult to summon the theologically appropriate feelings.

Having responded wrongly to the death of his first child, Nehemiah was not then surprised to feel a second "lash" from "the hand of God," for before the week was out Grace was sick, so sick "that my [step-]mother, the midwife, the doctor, and others of my friends that did see her . . . said she would not continue long with me, she then being with child and in two months of her reckoning." This time Nehemiah responded properly with prayer, "and the Lord did hear my prayers." Grace lived and in due time gave birth to a son, Nehemiah. After such high drama Nehemiah was amazed at the quick return to normality, and in a bemused afterthought writes that "after all this, what quarrelings, grievous reproaches, and slanders I and my wife had, the Lord knows that knoweth all best."[81]

Yet if Nehemiah never really learned the lesson of that first death, it is perhaps not to be wondered at, for Grace's patient acceptance is surely harder for us to comprehend than Nehemiah's nervous anxiety. The birth of their first son, John, was apparently unremarkable, but early in his second year, just after little Elizabeth's recovery from her bout with the measles, this "merry" child so "full of play" had the first of what seemed to be a series of epileptic seizures. At three in the morning they heard him groan, and when Grace put him to nurse, "he was all in a sweat." That morning when Grace placed him in his cradle to sleep, "he fell into a fit much like unto the falling sickness, for his eyes, mouth, and hands did work very much, and he did foam at the mouth, and at the going away of the fit, he did cast up the white of his eyes much like one that is dying, which was very woeful to the father and mother and the rest of the beholders." Dr. Sanders, when summoned, diagnosed "the convulsion" and prescribed a cordial, after which "by the blessing of God he had but three fits that night more." In all he had ten seizures that first day, ten the next, and he lay "skriking [*sic*] and very sick till the next Sabbath day when he broke forth in the measles."[82] John recovered, "thanks to our prayers and the prayers of his church for him," but a little more than a year later, just six months after Elizabeth's death, John became ill and would take no nourishment but some cold beer.

The night before he died he lay crying all that night: "Mame, Oh, John's hand, Oh, John's foot." For he was struck cold all one side of his body, and about three o'clock in the morning Mrs. Trotter that watch with him wakened my wife and I and told us he was departing now. And my wife started up and looked at him. He then being aware of his mother, he said, "Mame, John fall down, op-a-day; Mame, John fall down, op-a-day." And the next day he had two or three fits . . . and at eleven o'clock at night he said unto the maid Jane "some beer," and she gave him some beer. Then he said "op-a-day." These were the last words that my sweet son John spake, and so ended this miserable life on Tuesday the fifth day of April 1626.[83]

Four months earlier little Nehemiah had been born, arriving before even the midwife could be summoned. Grace had sore breasts—the inflammation did not abate for six weeks—and Nehemiah was put out to nurse.[84] Grace's pregnancy the following year terminated in a miscarriage in June 1626.[85] Within the year little Nehemiah, who was not yet three, sickened and died: "a bitter portion indeed it was to part from an only son." Once again it was Grace who had to comfort her grieving husband with a lesson in Christian resignation, the cogency of which he was forced to admit and which afterward he would record as a heavenly meditation. "Husband, say we should put our child forth to nurse, and when we see time fit to send for our child, and if the nurse should deny us our child, . . . we should then be very angry with her. Even so stands the case with us, for God gave us this child to nurse for him for a while, and now he requires it of us again. Therefore let us give it to him willingly." This time Nehemiah was able to reply with an equally pious observation: "God doth intend us more good than we are aware of, for where a man's treasure is, there is his heart: now our child is gone to heaven, our heart will be there."[86]

The notion that parents had but temporary custody of children given to them by a fatherly God, who would reclaim his own when the time was ripe, may have helped reconcile London parents to the fact that they were unlikely to succeed in raising more than a few of their offspring. However, it never allayed the anxiety caused by sick and failing children. The Wallingtons' last child, Samuel, was born a year and four months after little Nehemiah's death, after a lengthy and painful confinement, but he "did not thrive." Like John before him, Samuel began to have convulsions at about six months of age, and this time Dr. Sanders confessed himself unable to help. Nehemiah in desperation "could not tell what to do but to commend him unto God," but then the Wallingtons were told of a Mrs. Mason, presumably a cunning woman, who was fetched and who placed "plasters unto his head, stomach, and his feet; then he had seven or eight fits of the convulsion more by the Sabbath day at night." Although he recovered briefly, he continued to waste away, and three months later they were counseled to send him into the country, and they put him to nurse in Peckham. There he survived another ten months, but a week after Grace had last visited him word was brought that he was very sick. Nehemiah hurried off the next morning to learn the truth of the matter "and one met me by the way and told me my son was dead. Then I returned back again with the heavy news, and we went to the burial of our sweet son Samuel on the 13th day of October being Saturday, which was a very wet day, and we went a mile and a half from their house to his grave, and we were wet to the very skin, for it was a very wet and doleful day."[87]

At the end of ten years of childbearing, only little Sarah Wallington remained alive. She had had smallpox at the age of three and survived. As a toddler she had narrowly missed falling into the fire, as we saw in an earlier chapter. Reflecting on that accident and on the fact that Sarah had been "very merry all that day and prattling to me prettily," Nehemiah thought what a mercy it had been that God had preserved the child, for "whereas now I am delighting to see my child merry, I might have been heavy and weeping over it." The following summer, in August 1631, at about six in the evening, Sarah, who had been playing before the shop door with a neighbor's child, had wandered off unnoticed down Tower Street through Barking to Tower Hill. There as she was going along the road into East Smithfield she had fallen "and hit herself sore on the forehead." A woman passing by had comforted the child but, unable to discover where she lived, had begun to carry her into Wapping, supposing she had come from that riverside parish, when she was stopped by a passing servant who recognized the Wallington child and told the woman that she came from Eastcheap. In the meantime Nehemiah had discovered that Sarah was missing and had begun a frantic and futile search through the neighborhood, only learning of Sarah's rescue when he returned defeated some hours later. Although he was properly grateful for Sarah's return, he realized that once Sarah had wandered three parishes to the east, it was only the luck of the passing servant that prevented her from being lost to the Wallingtons forever, "for it might have been that we should have seen [Sarah] no more, . . . and then what strange, distractful thoughts should we have had, and how could we eat or have slept that night with thinking what is become of our poor child, thinking . . . maybe it is drowned at the waterside, or some other mischief had befallen it."[88] Two years later, in the summer of 1633, Sarah was again sick, this time with the measles, and early in her seventh year she was sick "with a casting and a scouring . . . we thought she would have died [of]." Nehemiah always acknowledged at each recovery that God should have praise and glory forever, but it is clear that it was the lot of a parent to be "full of grief" and "distractful thoughts."[89]

Nevertheless, Sarah lived, and in 1641, when she was fourteen, Nehemiah mentions that she had a desk of her own in his study— he evidently had taught her her letters. Yet despite this happy image, her growing maturity generated a new set of problems and anxieties.[90] The Wallingtons did not put Sarah out to service, but Nehemiah nonetheless copied the letter of a pious father to his daughter on her going into service to a "noble and virtuous gentlewoman whom God hath called you to wait upon," which doubtless expresses what Wallington would ideally have said on such an occasion. The father's "earnest prayer" is that God will make her "serviceable" by giving her "that humble, grave, and sober frame of heart as becomes the gospel of Christ Jesus," and that his daughter will "obey her commands readily, observe her instructions carefully, [and] bear her reproof patiently." Servants, like all children, were to carry themselves with humility and sobriety: "Let your words be few, your carriage humble and sober, grave, peaceable, your countenance be cheerful, your diligence evident to the whole family." In addition, the Puritan servant was "to let the fear of the great God be always before you: read the Holy Scripture often, pray unto your God frequently, fervently, and believingly, hear the word preached attentively." Finally, the dutiful child should not exalt itself above its station but should be "courteous, loving, and kind to all in the family."[91] Doubtless had Wallington had a son, he would have written a similar letter on apprenticing him to a godly master. Instead, at about the time of Sarah's eighteenth birthday, Nehemiah determined "to marry my daughter in the fear of God." With that responsibility off his hands and the lease of the house renewed, the house repaired, and all his "taxes and cessments [assessments]" paid, he hoped "then in my old days to sit down and rest from cares and troubles of the world and the rest of my time to employ in holy duties."[92]

In 1646 Nehemiah succeeded in renewing his lease—if not in paying all his parliamentary taxes in that time of dead trading—but it
took him another year to arrange for Sarah's marriage. He does not
mention the machinations preceding that event, but his letter book
contains an anonymous epistle dated 1632 and titled "A godly letter
sent to Master I. W. and his wife M. W. advising them how to have a
special care in the matching of their beloved daughter." The "I. W."
so addressed is undoubtedly John Wallington, but it is almost certainly Nehemiah's father rather than his brother. Patience, the elder John Wallington's youngest daughter, had married "brother
Church" sometime in 1631, but the daughter in question is apparently a stepdaughter, since the person to whom the letter is addressed is said to be "in place of a father." The identity of the daughter cannot now be determined, but it is likely that the letter was written by Nehemiah himself, who would not have been comfortable
addressing such a frank and critical letter to his patriarchal father in
his own person. For although the letter purports to be a piece of
"friendly counsel," "a word spoken in season," and "a watchword
to prevent evil," it suggests that the father is more bent on making a
good match than on securing the good of his daughter's soul. "As
you are parents, you are . . . to provide for their good. So nature
binds a man; the heathens do no less. But consider, as you are Christians, you must go further." The soul, after all, is "more worth than
a world," for "it is the price of the blood of Christ." Hence, "wherein
do you exceed heathens, if you provide only for the body . . . in
outward things of this world, whether it be a good situation of
dwelling, or riches, or a good trade." What is feared is that although
the body will be well cared for, "the soul [will] perish for want." The
daughter, "a tender branch that hath been hitherto watered and
pruned and preserved," is now to "be left to the wild beasts of the
forest . . . without defense, without support." What the writer is
particularly afraid of is not that the father has been moved by riches
or civility but that he has been swayed by the "shows and pretences"
of religion: "the more pretence, the more hypocrisy." The writer insists that "where grace is, it may discern grace in another," but none
is to be seen in the prospective husband. To marry a daughter to such
a man is to turn a precious soul over to "a blind guide."[93]

What the upshot was of this letter—if indeed it was ever sent—
we never learn, but even if it was not written by Nehemiah, it is
evident that he approved its sentiments, and this must have compli-

cated the arrangement of Sarah's marriage. Of that event Nehemiah records only that on "July 20, 1647, my daughter was married." Her husband was John Houghton, a fellow turner, the son of a Bedfordshire yeoman who had been apprenticed to a London turner for nine years late in 1637.[94] Houghton would barely have had time to complete his mandatory two years as a journeyman when he married into the Wallington family; he must have been an exemplary young man, but the marriage was scarcely prudent, and Nehemiah with his customary candor does not disguise that fact. He had not lost a daughter but gained the extra burden of a son-in-law, and had done so when he was still supporting his sister-in-law, Sarah Rampaigne, and when he was about to take responsibility for bringing up Zachariah Rampaigne's son Charles. As Nehemiah confessed, "now I did think to live at less care and a little more ease and rest in my old days, but I was mistaken, for here is not my rest, but cares and troubles did more and more increase, having a greater family and so great a charge of souls, when I cannot keep my own soul."[95] Although the Houghtons' residence under the Wallingtons' roof was short-lived, Nehemiah's anxiety about the fate of his daughter continued—and, as it turned out, rightly so.

In the short run John Houghton must have achieved a modest success, for in 1649 he was chosen to enter the livery of the Turners' Company.[96] The record is then silent until the autumn of 1650, when on September 18 Sarah Houghton gave birth to her first twin, a son John, and on October 9 the second, a daughter Sarah.[97] The twins were baptized at St. Leonard's, which suggests that the Houghtons were still resident with the Wallingtons or that Sarah had returned home for her confinement. Nehemiah notes the death of his grandchild Sarah in 1652, and at some point during these years the Houghtons moved upriver to Fulham, for it was from Fulham that a messenger came on an April morning two years later with the news of the death of the other twin John. Nehemiah never learned to accept the loss even of grandchildren with the proper degree of Christian resignation, and as he confesses, "I did find it very hard to praise God for taking from me as giving unto me." He prayed, as he knew he ought, that God's will would "be done in earth as it is in heaven," but he recognized that such a prayer, "coming not from my heart, conscience tells me I lie." In times of stress he never did find it easy to summon the appropriate responses of acceptance and gratitude, and he consoled himself, not for the first time, with the thought that a forgiving God would accept the thought for the deed. "My comfort is that God accepts my desires in his Christ."[98]

During the summer of 1654 new troubles came on thick and fast. Sarah was pregnant again, and on July 7 Nehemiah recorded that

> this evening being full of care and pity for my child Sarah, my bowels yearning within me for her, I then did think of the Lord in Psalm 103:13,
> > And look what pity parents dear,
> > Unto their children bear,
> > Like pity beareth God to such,
> > As worship him in fear.[99]

John Houghton's business was evidently failing, and, as Nehemiah noted three weeks later, what was hardest to bear was the knowledge "that we know not how to help each other." Sarah had come home late the night before from Fulham "both weary and lame, which made my heart to yearn and my bowels with compassion to turn within me." The unworldly Nehemiah, never very successful himself at business, was the last person to counsel his son-in-law, and he knew it and suffered for his impotence. A week later when he was preparing for the Sabbath and the Sacrament, Sarah, who was sick and had already sent for her mother, now sent for Nehemiah "to pack up their goods to come to be at our house." Although the move left Nehemiah "in much weariness of body and grief to my mind," he was able to acknowledge God's many mercies which "brought us all home safely." It is not surprising that he turned that evening to the Book of Job, "where I did see a righteous and just man full of trouble, and I did see that I ought to acknowledge that the Lord gives and the Lord takes away."[100] And God was by no means through with his servant Nehemiah, for the Houghtons' troubles were far from over.

Two days later, on August 8, John Houghton set out for Cornwall, apparently on business, and they "parted with tears," for Nehemiah told his "son" that "I did think I shall see him no more in this world, for the time of my change is at hand." Nehemiah had four years yet to live but had clearly come to feel that the world was too much with him. On the evening of October 14 he found "at examination . . . a return of my prayers . . . in preserving and sending my son in safety again," but whether the trip had been a success is never clear.[101] A little more than a fortnight later Nehemiah notes that "my dear daughter Houghton was delivered of a lusty boy before any outward help could come, for which my heart was much raised in praise of God," but the day after he was again castigating himself for his sin of unthankfulness, for "when divers did say to me, 'God give you joy in your grandchild,' my heart did not echo praise to God for it."[102] Within the week the elder Wallingtons were awakened at three in the morning by their son-in-law, who came with the news that Sarah was very sick—she said "she had a fire within her, which words was much trouble to my heart"—and Nehemiah went back to wondering whether he could, like Job, "receive evil from God as well as good." Sarah was too sick to attend the baptism of her child, also named John, and with no assurance of her immediate recovery the infant was sent "as far as Oatland" to nurse. Sarah was not well enough to accompany the Wallingtons to church until Christmas eve, some six weeks after the onset of her illness. It was evident that Nehemiah was to find no relief from his anxieties about children and grandchildren short of the grave. As had been the case so often in his three decades of marriage, he noted in one of his last entries that he turned in his perplexities to take counsel with Grace: "upon examination I find that I spent two hours in the morning in speech with my wife, some of the world, some of heaven, and how I may glorify God."[103]

By comparison with the emotionally freighted relationships within the family, friendships seemed a relatively uncomplicated blessing. Nehemiah does not tell us how he made his friends, but the record shows that he clung to them with a tenacity that suggests their importance to this lonely and socially awkward man. His best friend was undoubtedly James Cole of Whitechapel, a young trades-man of approximately Nehemiah's age, although Nehemiah refers to him on one occasion as an "ancient Christian"—that is, one long assured of his election.[104] It was to James Cole as well as to his father and another friend that Nehemiah turned to arbitrate the dispute between him and his journeyman Roberts in 1630; it was again Cole whom Nehemiah named as one of the overseers of his informal will, which he drew up in 1632.[105] Nehemiah twice wrote that their hearts were knit together "like David and Jonathan," a very precise comparison, for it suggested not only the closeness of their friendship but also its religious basis, for they were very much covenanted brothers in the faith. In one letter Nehemiah addresses James Cole in Davidic terms as "a valiant champion in the Lord's quarrel [who] hath stirred me up (with others) to stand in my place and rank where God hath set me."[106]

Friendships normally leave few traces except on the lives of the friends themselves. Yet something of the relationship between this particular David and Jonathan can be told because James Cole fled London in the early summer of 1634, seeking safety in one provincial Puritan community after another, and in the course of that flight sent letters to his family and friends that were passed along to Nehemiah and that he carefully copied into his letter book. As Cole explained in a letter to his wife's parents, "great debts and dangers . . . hath lain heavily upon me many years"; and although he did not fear imprisonment, had he stayed in London and gone to prison he should "have had little hope either to have relieved [his] family or to have paid [his] debts, which now there is some hope of both."[107] Nonetheless, Cole recognized the moral ambiguity of the step he had taken, and in a letter he addressed to his wife from Ipswich—in which he asked to be remembered to his "loving and well-wishing parents and kinsmen," his "familiar lover and unfeigned friend Nehemiah Wallington," and the rest of his "faithful friends"—he acknowledged that his "sins" had brought him to his present "doleful heaviness and sinking sorrows," that some would suffer in their estates by reason of his absence, and that he "cannot escape much reproach and great revilings" as a consequence. He beseeched his wife "to deal with [his] creditors in fair words and not in bad terms and pray them for to rest with patience on God for [his] raising, which casteth down and raiseth up again at His pleasure." In the meantime, until he could send for them, he begged his children and servants to accept his wife as their "governess" and asked his wife to "catechize my children and nurture them in the fear of the Lord." His distress at the position he had placed his family in is evident—"the thoughts of you and of my children doth pinch my heart"—and he concluded the letter by noting that he had become so "burdened with salt tears" that he could not continue.[108] In reality he had not anticipated the pressure his family and friends in London would bring to bear on him to force his return. The losses of his creditors and his distress at his being unable to "make them restitution" turned out to be secondary to the reproaches of the godly community. As Nehemiah's father wrote: "You know the chief care of a child of God is and must be still to glorify God in the place and calling wherein God hath set him. And his care must also be that he grieve not his fellow members, the Saints of God, and so carry himself that he does not open the mouths of the wicked to speak evil of the ways of God."[109] Cole's letters are full of explanation and exculpation, but in the final analysis he could only appeal to "God's providence which works all things for his own glory and our good."[110]

Cole's father accused him of abandoning his wife and children; his father-in-law reproached him "with running from my country"; and John Wallington, Sr., pointed out that his place was in "Whitechapel with your wife," and that he should "dwell with her as a man of knowledge and instruct her and your children and servants in the ways of God, and appoint their work which are now all of them in a mournful maze and know not what to do till you come that should direct them all."[111] James replied, but did not David flee to Gath? As for his father's "bitter letter," he was determined not to answer it at all. Nehemiah wrote that Cole's mother had taken his "going away to heart and is very sick," and that he feared "it will be her death." Nehemiah also pointed to the fearful effect of such an example: "If such a captain as you fly, what shall become of such a weak soldier as I am?" As his father was to do in a later letter, Nehemiah reminded Cole of the impact of his actions on the godly community in London: "And how have you given a stumbling block to the weak. Oh how have you grieved the hearts of your wife, your parents, and the rest of your loving friends. Oh how you have made the hearts of the righteous sad. . . . But above all, how have you given the Enemy cause to rejoice and triumph, and the name of God, your good God, to be dishonored by the wicked." And so Nehemiah urged him "in the name of God, return, return," and promised Cole that the news of his shame "is not yet much spread abroad." In fact, "it is no shame to come home again; it was a shame to go from home."[112]

Unlike the others, Nehemiah did not mail his letter, for, not knowing how to send it safely, he decided "to carry it to him" himself. On a Saturday morning he went downriver to Woolwich, where he took ship for Harwich on the Essex coast, disembarking there at midnight. He then took a small boat up the River Orwell to Ipswich, where he arrived "near two o'clock on the Lord's day in the morning, and then delivered my letter to my brother Mr. Cole and went into the fields and conferred together." At Nehemiah's urging, Cole agreed to seek the counsel of Mr. Samuel Ward, the famous Puritan preacher at Ipswich, and Ward's advice, like that of all the godly community, evidently was to return home.

> So betimes on Monday morning we set forth on foot from Ipswich toward London and scarce rested till I was there, my brother Cole parted from me at Elton and went to Barking till his wife came to him, but I went home and upon Tuesday morning at five o'clock I was in my chamber by my wife's bedside very weary. . . . Some say it is near threescore miles from Ipswich to London, too hard a journey to go on foot on a day and a night, but love endureth all things.[113]

Love endured, but friendship was not enough to hold James Cole in London. Shortly afterward, in August or September 1634, Cole was writing from Warwick to thank his neighbor Scott who had written a letter dictated by Cole's wife and had arranged for Cole's oldest son to join him. Once again Cole had sought shelter in a known godly community and wrote with evident amazement at what he found.

> With us where I do now sojourn there be two congregations that is in two great men's hands, where is neither crosses, nor surplices, nor kneeling at the Sacrament, nor the Book of Common Prayer, nor any other behavior but reading the Word, singing of Psalms, prayer before and after sermon with catechism, which I did think it had not been in any congregation in this kingdom, if I had not seen it and, through God's mercy, have been partakers with them in the use of God's ordinances.

This discovery prompted Cole to ask "how the gospel flourishes in London," for, as he noted at the end of the letter, he would be content "with poor means" so he might continue to "enjoy such Christian liberty."[114]

At the end of November Cole wrote to his wife that "my lord's desire is to employ me in New England," and when Nehemiah next wrote eight years later, having finally found "a fit opportunity to send to you," it was to James Cole of Hartford, Connecticut. Nehemiah wrote, reminding James that they had "been like David and Jonathan" and lamenting that they should never meet again in this life, although they should assuredly meet "in the world to come." He went on to tell Cole how he had been haled before the Court of Star Chamber, because he "had some books which were not to the lordly prelates' liking," but had escaped with no more than the loss of time and money; how his father had died and how he had found "after my Father's death more joy and comfort in my poor soul from God than ever I did before"; and how "as you know, the whole land was overrun with idolatry and popery and all manner of abominations." Nehemiah then went on to describe the politics of the past three years in terms of the framework of historical understanding he and James Cole shared—that of a cosmic battle that pitted "devilish plots" against "the mercies of the Lord." So the "most filthy, execrable Book of Canons [of 1640] with a most odious cursed oath which should be imposed on all our ministers" was part of the devilish plot, whereas the failure of the prelates' pursuivants to take any of the companies of saints meeting in private fasting and prayer, and the success of the trial against the traitorous Lord Deputy of Ireland and the subsequent downfall of the bishops were all evidence of divine mercy obtained "by prayer."[115]

The correspondence was evidently resumed in the 1640's, and Cole wrote urging Nehemiah in apocalyptic terms to "watch and stand fast and . . . never be moved from the hope of the gospel, for He that will come, will come, and will not tarry and His reward is with Him." Cole anticipated that a further emigration of the godly from old England to the new would take place before the heat of the divine "indignation is overpast," and he hoped that if Nehemiah should be among them, "God will keep our hearts so together that what the one hath the other shall not want."[116] The last letter copied into the letter books is dated August 22, 1650, and is addressed to his "dear and loving brother Mr. Cole." Gone is the political optimism of his 1642 letter, for now "brethren goeth to war against brethren contrary to their covenant, and the prayers of God's people go cross against one another." In the face of such cross-purposes among the saints Nehemiah could only ask: "Oh Lord, what will become of thy great name, and how will the enemies rejoice and say 'aha! aha! it is now as we would have it.'" The only consolation he can discover is that "all things are possible with God." Yet for all his evidence of England's failure to benefit from God's great mercies, he can report that "truly, brother, I never did find more of God and heavenly joy than now within this twelvemonth; my heart is bent for God's glory and longs to be at home." Nehemiah confessed that he had not prospered in the world, and that he was still given to "unthankfulness and discontent" because of it, but as he writes to Cole, "let not you and I be troubled about the world." While "it is true that there are many temptations in poverty," it is nevertheless the case that "there are far many more temptations in riches," and Nehemiah hopes still to learn how not to "murmur and complain." On the whole this last letter reveals a man purged by the battles of a long life, ready to accept at last his imperfections and failures, looking forward to the inevitable end, and wishing only in the short time remaining to give brother Cole kind thanks "for your love and kindness always."[117] The staid and anxious Londoner seems to have little enough in common with the much more venturesome and daring New Englander, and yet the passionate godliness that had drawn them together as David and Jonathan in their youth cemented an equally passionate friendship that survived separation by both time and distance. Nehemiah's economic failure and political disappointments never quite soured what must have been a warm and affectionate nature.

Evidence of other friendships, though none as close as that with James Cole, appears in Nehemiah's correspondence. In 1644 he received a letter from his old friend and former neighbor Edward Brown, now of Ipswich, Massachusetts, who complained that he had had "no letter from you this year" (a statement that tells much about the length of time it took letters to be exchanged with friends in the New World plantations). Brown had emigrated by 1638, for when Nehemiah and his brother John were questioned before the Star Chamber in April of that year, Nehemiah on oath was able to implicate Brown in his crime, safe in the knowledge that his neighbor was beyond the reach of that court. Nehemiah was questioned closely about the distribution of Prynne's *News from Ipswich*:

Q: To whom have you dispersed any?
A: I did let one Edward Brown see one of them, but I sold him none, but being something timorous, I had it of him again and have burnt it.
Q: Where doth he dwell and what trade is he?
A: He did dwell in Little Eastcheap, a turner; he was my neighbor.[118]

In 1644 Brown wrote that they found themselves "much more comfortable" than might have been expected "in a wilderness," although they still lacked "that fullness which is with you in Eastcheap." However, if food and clothing were in short supply, "God doth much appear to us in the way of his pure worship." In a telling phrase that must have spoken volumes to any Englishman who had lived through the years of King Charles's personal rule, Brown explained that in the Bay Colony "the way of God is much sought out among us, both in magistracy and ministry, and wise men among us hath appeared to be but men, and God doth much manifest himself amongst us: this way the Lord keep us from abusing his goodness and our liberties."[119] Such letters from friends in the godly commonwealth across the Atlantic must have helped to prepare the conservative Nehemiah to be much less distressed by the execution of the king and by the creation of a republic than he was by the failure of godly reform. When Nehemiah replied in 1645, it was with news of the "uncivil war" and of "times turned upside down," but also with news of "our God" who was "sweeping away the trash and rubbish in his church, giving us ordinances in a more sweet, pure, and powerful manner than ever our forefathers knew." Nevertheless, Nehemiah was not able to report that Parliamentary England had become, like Massachusetts, a New Jerusalem. Although he can report that "his little grace the Bishop of Canterbury, that great enemy of God and his people, his head was cut off on a scaffold on Tower Hill," nevertheless "besides our sinful and wicked armies which are almost as vile as cavaliers, Oh London's pride, security, hypocrisy, and all manner of profaneness!" As a consequence, he feared that he would not be able to write again, "for though we seem all for a Reformation and took a covenant and a protestation and keep many days of humiliation, yet there is little or no reformation but the very power of godliness is hated with the most. And must not God be avenged of such a nation as this? I tell you, Brother, if the contrary and malignant party should but a little more get head, the stream would turn, and there were no way but destruction."[120] In the 1640's the high drama of politics had overwhelmed the personal element in letters among the godly, at least between Wallington and his friends, and this was true even in his correspondence with friends in England.

In his first mention of Francis Wilsmore, Nehemiah refers to him as "my loving friend Goodman Wilsmore of Nottingham," and in the first extant letter of Wilsmore recorded by Nehemiah, January 14, 1638/39, he signs himself "your poor yet loving brother in Christ." Evidently at some point they had met in London, for Wilsmore asks to be remembered to Grace Wallington and to Obediah Seeley, who had been Nehemiah's servant and then apprentice between 1627 and 1635. It also seems probable that Wilsmore was one of the provincial suppliers of wares sold in Nehemiah's shop, for in that first extant letter Wilsmore apologizes for the "hard bargain that you had of me (through the dishonesty of the chapman of whom I had the ware)." Wallington had also helped Wilsmore's son to an apprenticeship with a neighbor, and a second letter written two months later in the early spring of 1639 contains a message that Wallington was asked to give to the young apprentice, urging him to "wait at wisdom's gates" and "to walk on in the paths of righteousness." Yet, as the last injunctions suggest, the primary connection between Nehemiah and Francis Wilsmore seems to have rested less on a business relationship than on a shared concern for the fate of the godly cause. In the first letter Wilsmore sent thanks to Wallington for two books, by the reading of one of which (by the famous Puritan Thomas Hooker) "my soul . . . hath received no small comfort." In the second letter, in addition to the message for his son, Wilsmore sent along, in answer to Wallington's request, some suitably gruesome anecdotes concerning the fate of Sabbath breakers in Nottingham; he also asked that Wallington dispatch two shillings' worth of oranges and lemons by carrier for the "weak stomachs" of some of his congregation, including "our prophet," as Wilsmore refers to their preacher.[121] In December of 1641, frantic for news, Wilsmore wrote asking Nehemiah for word of "how it goeth with God's people and how the Parliament proceeds"; a year later he sent Nehemiah news of the fate of his sons, one of whom had been invalided home with three wounds ("but I wait still upon God, expecting a blessing on all my troubles or else deliverance, which way he pleaseth"); and six months later still, in June of 1643, a last letter gives news of his daughter's illness and asks for "word how things go with you and how the Lord doth reveal himself, since I was with you, both in his Providence for your own particular and for the Church of God in general, to the end that I might be strengthened in these evil times." To this last letter Wallington appended the following note: "A while after I did hear that this my loving friend and dear servant of God was with a bullet from the castle shot to death as he was in the town."[122]

Other friends and neighbors are briefly mentioned. In some instances their very proximity must have meant that little tangible evidence of the relationship survives. Nehemiah mentions writing a letter to his neighbor Alderman Adams in condolence on the death of Adams's daughter—"and he came and gave me thanks for it"— but the letter was never copied.[123] The letter must have been written in 1642 or later, for 1642 is the first year Adams appears in the precinct list as "Thomas Adams, Alderman," although he had been a neighbor of Wallington in the upper precinct when the first extant list was drawn up in 1634.[124] In October 1646 Wallington wrote to another neighbor, Captain Thomas Player, urging him to accept election as elder in the newly erected London Presbyterian classis. The formal and respectful tone, and Nehemiah's reference to himself as "your weak brother whom Christ died for," suggest that although Wallington and Player were neighbors, attended the same parish church, and participated in the same godly community, the social distinction between a mere artisan and an Oxford M.A. and captain of one of the London trainband regiments precluded any real intimacy.[125] Another letter to a neighbor, Constantine Waddington, implied a very different relationship. Written on December 26, 1640, as a "new year's gift," Wallington's letter is one of neighborly admonition: "now one sin that you live in openly in the face of God and man is the breach of the Lord's day in selling of your ware, which the Lord commands us to remember to keep it holy." Nehemiah then elaborates on a whole catalogue of moral failings: Waddington is to "take heed of deceit, for thus saith St. Paul, 'let no man oppress or defraud his brother,' for the Lord is avenger of all such things"; Waddington is also accused of lying; and "you and your wife should take heed of sleeping in church." In a passage that suggests how intimately neighbors knew each other's lives, Wallington wrote that "forasmuch as I have heard you many times at prayer and sometimes a reading, I do much marvel what comfort you can find in those duties, when your conscience (if it be not seared) cries guilty of many abominations you live in." Such officiousness was no more than one neighbor owed another—"and now neighbor, take this my admonition in love, for did I not this out of conscience in obedience [to] my duty to God and of my love to your poor soul"—which helps to explain, if explanation is needed, why Nehemiah welcomed the creation of the London classis system in 1646.[126]

Those outside the godly community who could be reached by brotherly or neighborly admonition were owed at least that gesture toward their spiritual well-being, but fundamentally Nehemiah doubted whether salvation was possible in practice outside the community of saints. And that community was both more extensive and more exclusive—because voluntary and self-selective—than the precinct or parish. In a letter written in 1642 that continues a conversation begun at Charing Cross with a friend, Goodman Cox, a devotee of the Book of Common Prayer, Wallington insists that the main fault of the service book is not that it was "the Mass Book translated into English, . . . a mingle mangle, linsey-woolsey" compendium (although he implies that that is bad enough), but rather that he "did never know that ever any were converted by the service book." Conversion required an awareness of our true state, a "sight of sin," especially of "our own particular sins," and that state of self-knowledge required much private prayer and the encouragement of powerful preaching. But growth in one's life as a Christian also required a community to discipline and nurture it, and Wallington's final gratuitous advice to poor Goodman Cox is to "use some means to grow acquainted with those that they call Puritans or (that new nickname) Roundhead, I say keep company with such, for with the wise and godly you will learn to be wise and how to please God and so get to heaven."[127] (The fact that Wallington thought that it was possible to learn to be wise, please God, and so get to heaven suggests how far preparationist thought had eroded orthodox predestinarianism among the laity by the 1640's.)[128]

Almost all of Wallington's connections beyond the most superficial and casual seem to have taken place within the godly community. It created a network of concern that stretched to Massachusetts and Connecticut on the one side and to France and Germany on the other. Hence, Wallington carefully copied Thomas Weld's long letter from New England to his old congregation in Terling, Essex, in 1633, a letter that proudly described the "precise rule" to be found in that exiled godly community on Massachusetts Bay. Wallington also carefully copied twice a vivid description of the "troubles and sorrows of the Rochellers," written on October 30, 1628, by Nehemiah's nephew, John Bradshaw, to his grandfather, John Wallington, Sr.[129] Even those relationships that seem at first glance to be the most businesslike turn out, on examination, to take place within the godly community. John Gace, a turner in the neighboring parish of St. Andrew's Hubbard, was evidently a trusted business associate. He, James Cole, and John Wallington, Sr., mediated the disagreement between Nehemiah and his journeyman Roberts in 1630; he replaced James Cole as one of the executors in Nehemiah's 1632 will after Cole left for America; and he appeared again in 1635 as one of the executors of the elder John Wallington's will. In the early 1650's he and John Wallington, Jr., appear as partners in several war contracts in which they were paid for supplying the army in Ireland with some thousands of shovels and spades. John Gace was also an elder in the Fourth London Classis.[130]

Ministers played a crucial role in the community, and Nehemiah both sought their counsel and offered advice and criticism on the way they performed their roles as leaders and teachers of the godly. In 1638 Wallington wrote a long letter in which he complained about his lack of spiritual progress, a letter addressed to his own minister, Henry Roborough. He recalled that he had in the early 1620's promised God that, if he were spared, he "would become a new man in the reformation of [his] life," but instead he had become "worse and worse." Two years later he wrote again, complaining that he had "gone about this twenty years to the Sacrament and yet could not tell of any good I got by it." However, Wallington's real problem was the perennial one of the conscientious saint. He reminded Roborough of the "heavy troubles of mind and many grievous temptations of Satan" he had suffered in the past two decades, but he also noted the "many comforts and consolations" he had experienced since his father's death. What he desperately needed to know, and what he somehow believed Roborough could correctly diagnose, was whether his "trouble and sorrow were a right trouble and sorrow," and whether his current "joy [was] a true and right joy." In short, he asked Roborough to examine him and to weigh up the state of his soul, and he put the request in writing because he knew that he would feel ashamed at making it in person and would "seek to put off time to do it." Whether such an examination ever took place cannot be known, but shortly after Wallington wrote that "as I am bound to praise God for you, so I give you most kind thanks for all your pains and instructions unto me, and I praise God I do grow in grace by your teaching."[131]

On the whole, Wallington accepted ministerial leadership in the church as right and proper—at least in the case of Roborough—both because he was the minister "whom God hath set over me for to teach and establish me in the ways of God," and because Wallington had come to trust his "judgment before any man's in the world." Nevertheless, this was not an unqualified trust but rather one tested by twenty years of acquaintance with his ministry. As Wallington remarked about the Westminster Assembly in 1643, "they be not only learned but godly, and when learning and godliness go together, I do much regard and reverence it."[132] Where one or the other was lacking, however, Wallington was quite prepared to criticize and to seek to correct what he regarded as ministerial failings.

On August 8, 1642, he wrote to Abraham Colfe, who had been the absentee rector of St. Leonard's since 1609, and who held the vicarage of Lewisham in plurality, that he was sadly remiss in his ministerial duties, for "I am persuaded if you had privately and publicly told your people plainly of their wicked ways, . . . then surely there would not have been so many ignorant, drunken swearers, mockers, and profaners of the Lord's day at Lewisham, as now there be." Wallington had been shocked when he was last at Lewisham on a lecture day to hear a woman swear "a grievous oath that there was a lecture at their church, but she said she was never at it." In fact, when the lecture was done there was "roaring in the alehouse, mocking and calling of Roundhead," and Wallington heard that all this went on with Colfe's encouragement, much to the offense and discouragement of the local godly community. In effect Wallington argued that it was the minister's job to respond positively to the sensitivities of the children of God, as a people for whom all ministers had a special responsibility—an attitude and an expectation that must have done much to shape the ecclesiastical peculiarities of Puritan parishes. "Oh Sir, I pray you, let not the difference of judgment of the Service Book make difference of affections, but bear with the tenderness of their consciences, and forbear as much as may be the reading of the Service Book, which is a goad in the side of God's dear children. Oh take heed you offend not one of those little ones, for woe to them by whom offense comes." Wallington also suggested that Colfe cease praying for the "lordly bishops," who were "the very limbs of Antichrist" and "the cause of bringing in of all those miseries and troubles in Church and Commonwealth which we have had, so that now they are odious and stink in the nostrils of all good men that love God." In 1642 Wallington saw the former acquiescence of the godly in episcopal government as owing to ignorance, "but now God would have you and I and all men come to the knowledge of the truth." Wallington recognized that Colfe might tend to slight a letter from such "a poor silly fellow," but Wallington reminds him that he does "but put you in mind of what God requires of you," and that the source is consequently of less importance than the content of the message. Wallington believed himself moved to write by the Holy Spirit, and on the basis of that high authorization believed himself excused for ignoring the normal deference due to a minister of God's Word.[133]

Wallington was equally critical of the Independents and, paradoxically, for very much the same reason. As he wrote to Matthew Barker, who became minister of St. Leonard's after the death of Henry Roborough in 1650, "some may sleep and lie snorting in their sins for many years and scarce be ever awakened by so sweet preaching as yours is." Wallington admitted that he personally had found it "very sweet and profitable," but he went on to remind Barker that "there is a foundation of humbling the soul in true and sound repentance, as well as a building up," and that "it is the brokenhearted undone sinner that prizes Jesus Christ." What was needed "in these wicked sinful days," Wallington wrote in early 1650 to another Independent, George Griffith, who often preached on fast days, was ministers who would "thunder out God's judgments against all horrible covenant breakers that promised reformation and never was such a deformation." Wallington's quarrel with the Independents was neither doctrinal nor really ecclesiological. Rather he thought them cowards who had lost their prophetic voice:

> Oh how doth pride abound . . . and the ministers afraid to tell them of it. Oh the profaning of the Lord's day, drunkenness, whoredom, the swearing and blasphemies, the errors and schisms, and neither the sword of magistracy nor ministry pulled out against them. What shall I say of the covetousness, the oppression, the cruelty and unmercifulness to the poor. Oh the contempt of the Gospel, the breach of protestations and covenants, and not a minister's mouth opened to reprove any of these sins except a few of despised Presbyterians as they call them.

Wallington never considered that the process of revolution and of lay assertion had weakened ministerial authority. Rather, he attributed the ministers' "sweetness" to a lack of backbone and to the Independents' tendency to "make the way to heaven easier than it is."[134]

Ideally, ministers were God's messengers, but messengers of a special kind. As Nehemiah wrote to his nephew Nathaniel Church in 1649, the model messenger was the prophet Ezekiel, "a watchman unto the house of Israel," summoned by God to warn Israel of its wickedness: "thou shalt hear the word at my mouth and admonish them from me. When I shall say unto the wicked, O wicked man, thou shalt die the death, if thou dost not speak and admonish the wicked of his way, that wicked man shall die for his iniquity, but his blood will I require at thine hand."[135] It was a heavy burden to lay on a young preacher, just two years beyond his bachelor's degree, but the ministerial charge was by its nature a heavy responsibility, "no less than the charge of souls." The first requirement was "a good understanding in the word of God," but it was equally important that "the power of godliness" be in "life and conversation," for otherwise, "if the blind lead the blind, they fall both into the pit." Wallington does not accuse his nephew of any dereliction in his duties, except that he gave "too much liberty to the vanity of youth, which is to jests, to rhymes and songs and other corruptions." As God's ambassador, a minister ought to be "grave and mild and not jocund." The example the minister set was important, and association with bad company was damaging, "for by that the power of your office, which is much grounded upon a reverent estimation, will be by company keeping many ways diminished."[136] By 1649 Wallington had come to realize that, lacking the disciplinary machinery of episcopal courts or the sanctions of a powerful presbyterian system, the minister had only his preaching and example to give force to his message. In his deepening pessimism about the ability (or indeed the desire) of the secular authorities to bring about moral reform, Nehemiah felt that the minister's role as Israel's watchman had taken on a new significance.

The role of the minister in the godly community was as obvious as it was crucial. Wallington saw his own letters of warning and correction as a necessary way to "discharge his conscience" toward these acknowledged guides. However, this by no means exhausted his responsibilities toward the godly community, in which he shared two much more frequent roles. The first was to participate with and call upon the godly as a community of prayer. The practice was perfectly illustrated on Friday, October 22, 1630, when Nehemiah's daughter Sarah was very sick: "on the Sabbath day we thought she would have died, and I sent bills to have the prayers of the church of God for her, and the Lord did hear the prayers of His children, His name be praised."[137] Wallington never saw prayer as a substitute for other means of self-help, but it was a fundamental and necessary means, even though communal prayer was not always answered as the petitioner wished. When his son and namesake was sick in the autumn of 1628, Nehemiah wrote that "we used all the means we could, both outward and inward, and made many bills and sent them to the churches and had the prayers of many of the children of God both public and private, but the Lord would not hear us, but took from us our sweet son Nehemiah . . . for causes best known to himself."[138] The practice apparently continued throughout Wallington's life, for in his old age he notes an occasion on August 22, 1654, when he attended a private day of fasting, humiliation, and prayer for a Dr. Austin's son who had become "distracted with overmuch studying."[139] If the Puritans had given up prayers for the souls of the dead, it had been not because in a providential and predestinate world such personal petitions were seen as without efficacy, but because the Puritans had ceased to believe in Purgatory. Instead, they turned this powerful collective act of prayer to the benefit of the living; and if, given the mysterious will of God, such prayers were not always answered as the petitioners wished, they must nevertheless have done much to give the embattled saints a sense of mutual involvement in each other's lives at a time when more practical acts of assistance—medicine and doctors in particular—were so lacking in real help.

Prayer, both public and private, was one of the first duties the saint learned, but in his middle years Wallington found himself thrust into another role in the godly community, that of adviser to the spiritually troubled. Doubtless he was sought out as a spiritual counselor because he himself had such a long experience of coping with his own morbid scrupulosity. At any rate, those who sought him out seem to have suffered from troubles similar to his own. A gentlewoman he counseled in November of 1643 appears through Wallington's eyes to be a sick parody of the saint, the Puritan as neurotic. At first he was "astonished to see her lie weeping and lamenting that she could do no more in the service of God, with many strange carriages and sweet speeches she had that I could scarce tell what to say to her." Indeed, "she spoke so understandingly and heavenly in affections with earnest desires to please God" that Wallington, baffled, could only wish himself in her place and confessed rather shamefacedly that he "received much comfort from her." However,

as her mother, being a godly woman, told me in her presence, which she could not deny, that she would go constantly to church and sometimes be all day forth and eat nothing and then go and spend two hours alone late at night in prayer after she came home, as also much abstaining from the good creatures of God (thinking she is unworthy) to the much weakening of her body, as also when she is at meals with her mother and five children comfortable together, on a sudden she will burst out aweeping and crying out (and falling upon her knees) with her hands and eyes cast up to heaven, saying, Oh Lord, forgive her that she either eat amiss or thought or spoke amiss.

These emotional outbursts frightened the children, who in turn "would fall aweeping and crying, . . . 'Ah, mother, what ails you, how do you do?'" Even Wallington, whose own temperament was so similar, realized that such outbursts revealed a religiosity lacking in any balance. "I told her God required no more of us than what we could do, and that our sweet Savior hath made up all our weaknesses and infirmity for us. And I prayed her to take heed of weakening her body, so that [it] makes her unfit for the service of God." Doubtless because it was advice both spiritual and practical that he had many times given himself, he concluded his account by noting that in "thus speaking to her I found some comfort myself."[140] However, the point, as he noted on another occasion, was not to find comfort himself but to "fasten" some "comfort" on the one troubled in mind. He was apparently not always successful as a physician of the soul, but he was himself so driven by religious scruples and so obviously wracked by religious anxieties that he must have seemed both a sympathetic listener and a fellow sufferer who had nevertheless survived more or less intact. Particularly after 1650, when he came to believe in the reality of his own election, he must have seemed a living symbol of hope to the religiously troubled in mind. At any rate, the last recorded incident in which he offered counsel evidently had a happy outcome. On November 29, 1654, he recorded that "upon tender search I find that this day, meeting with two that were afflicted, I did give them such counsel as I received of the Lord, which they thanked me for it."[141]

Wallington had come a long way from the suicidal youth who would not accept comfort either from his father or from his young ministerial friend Henry Roborough, and in part his own cure had come by means of his growing acceptance both of his own troubled soul and of his responsibilities toward his family, his kin, and the larger godly community. One of the last entries he recorded tells how "a gracious maid" gave him "many thanks for my prayers, saying she knew I prayed for her, she did find such workings of God upon her soul." Wallington concluded the entry in something of a tone of astonishment at his own accomplishment, that "it was true, for often she was in my prayers earnestly to God for her."[142] Such forgetfulness of self in a concern for another did not come easily to the introspective, self-absorbed saint, but in it he found at last that elusive sense of self-worth, and perhaps of self-love, that had escaped him in his years of fevered self-examination.

> *Believe always your estate to be the work of God, and vary not*
> *therein: for your humiliation, your consolation is the glory of God and*
> *the good of many others.*
>
> —Richard Greenham

5. The Particular Calling

In the spring of 1632 Nehemiah Wallington prayed God "to make me to remember . . . as I am a Christian, I ought to walk worthy of my vocation and calling; make me faithful in my calling and to remember that a day will come in which I must give account unto thee of all my actions done in this flesh."[1] Nevertheless, the process of getting and spending and the ethics of work were never major preoccupations, which may account in part for Wallington's comparative lack of economic success. Even in this prayer more is said about the politics of Protestantism—the fate of Gustavus Adolphus and the machinations of the Turk and the Pope—than about the prosperity, or lack of it, of Nehemiah Wallington as God's petitioner. For himself Wallington asks only that God "keep me that I fashion not myself to this world but rather imitate the fashion of the most godly in my calling."[2]

But if patterns of work and consumption and the ethics of getting and spending were subordinate to Wallington's major concerns with personal salvation and the fate of the godly community, nevertheless economic matters were a constant worry, a sore subject to which Wallington recurred over and over again in his writings. And how could it have been otherwise? Unworldly as Wallington may have been in most respects, he, like all artisans and small tradesmen, expected to spend most of his waking hours in pursuit of his livelihood. Normally up long before dawn, Wallington arose "at five, four, three, and sometimes two o'clock in the morning," and although he first went to his closet "in private prayer," he was usually "about my calling" by six and continued on the shop floor with time away for breakfast and dinner until sometime between seven and nine in the evening, a long day of work that he sometimes admitted he found tedious. As he wrote late on a December evening in 1654, "at night after examination how I have spent the day, after a chapter read I went to prayer with my family; then I went into my shop to my employment more out of conscience to God's commands than of any love I had unto it."[3]

By the time Wallington penned that sour note at the end of what must have been a most wearisome winter day, he had been an independent householder and shopkeeper for 34 years. He had been admitted to the freedom of the Turners' Company on May 18, 1620, by patrimony on payment of a silver spoon.[4] Both the patrimony and the payment were exceptional. The vast majority entered the freedom of the guild by apprenticeship (88 percent of the first 200 recorded in the company's book of apprentice bindings) and the payment of a fine of 13 shillings, 4 pence. Only 6.5 percent entered by redemption, and a mere 5.5 percent by claiming a son's right to his father's trade.[5] During the first twenty years for which records exist (between August 1, 1604, and June 1, 1624), 476 apprentices were bound to members of the company, only ten of whom were sons of turners (2.3 percent); of the ten, four were apprenticed to their own fathers.[6] During the years when John, Jr., and Nehemiah were growing up, the Slutter sons followed their father, Peter, into the family trade, but there were few such turner dynasties. Biological failure doubtless accounts for this in part, but the more ambitious survivors probably looked elsewhere for a potentially more profitable calling, for Wallington's long hours and modest gains were presumably all that most turners could aspire to.

The reasons are not far to seek. The turner's art was an ancient one—their guild was among those given the power of self-regulation in the early fourteenth century—but never a very prosperous or prestigious one.[7] A list of London crafts dating from 1422 shows the turners in the 75th place in a total of 111, and a precedence list for the Lord Mayor's Show in Henry VIII's reign places the turners 36th in a list of 60 guilds.[8] Turning, making articles of wood on a lathe, requires considerable skill, but the articles made were by and large humble household or industrial goods. The standard "proof piece" by which the newly admitted freeman demonstrated his competence in his craft was a simple stool with turned legs.[9] Turners produced chairs, wooden bowls, shovels, scoops, bushel measures, washing tubs, wheels, pails, trays, spools, pulleys, blocks, sheaves, deadeyes and other maritime tackle, wooden bandoliers for muskets, and other such commodities.[10] The variety was considerable, and as a consequence most shops sold goods made elsewhere as well as items produced on the premises. Yet the price of individual objects was small. For example, in 1616 the company ordered that "plain matted chairs" produced by strangers and foreigners (e.g., turners in Colchester) should be sold wholesale in the London market for only 6/– the dozen, and "turned matted chairs" for only 7/– the dozen. Even if the retail price were double the wholesale, turned chairs must have brought only about fourteen pence a piece, of which two pence represented the charges for the turning itself.[11]

Turner entrepreneurship was limited further both by the position of the company in the London guild system and by the desire of the guildsmen themselves to insure the survival of the marginal shop from undue competition. Within the guild system, the turners were prevented from expanding into the larger trade in wooden household furniture by the jurisdictional boundaries of the more powerful Joiners' Company, on the one side, and into the construction business by the even more powerful Carpenters, on the other. The consequence was, as the Turners' Court of Assistants complained in 1630, that "divers refractory and disobedient members of our said Company have heretofore and still do work and turn in the shops and other private rooms in the houses of Joiners within and about the City of London, and do teach and instruct Joiners in the art of turning . . . which doth greatly tend to the prejudice of our own Company."[12] The evident fear was that the turners would shortly become simply an adjunct to their more enterprising neighbors, and the Court of Assistants ordered all turners who failed on due warning to cease working in the shop of any joiner, carpenter, or coachmaker to pay at the discretion of the court a 10/– fine each week that they continued in such employment.[13]

The constraints of the highly structured urban market set limits on entrepreneurship, but the basic restraints on economic individualism were set by the very rules imposed on artisans and tradesmen by their own craft guilds. Doubtless such regulation was medieval in origin, but in the case of the turners (and a number of other London guilds that only achieved incorporation in the early seventeenth century) the rules of earlier times were found relevant and recodified as a consequence of the process of gaining a new charter. The patent of incorporation granted "at the humble petition of the freemen of the Society of Turners of London" was received on June 12, 1604; a new guild hall was begun on company property in Philpot Lane in the parish of St. Andrew's Hubbard in February 1605 (during the wardenships of Masters John Wallington, Sr., and John Peares); and new ordinances, having been approved by the Lord Chancellor and the Chief Justice of Common Pleas, were published on September 21, 1608.[14] Although these regulations did not attack business enterprise as such, they did set limits on the size of the unit of production and on the free play of competition—limits that effectively sheltered the household shop at least during Nehemiah's lifetime. Ordinary freemen of the company could bind only one apprentice at a time; liverymen could bind two on payment of a fine of five pounds; and the master, wardens, and assistants could bind three, the third only with permission of the Court of Assistants and on payment of a fine of two pounds. Equally as restrictive of the size of the shop, the new ordinances limited a master to hiring only one journeyman at a time and forbade the hiring of wage labor not free of the company. Finally, masters were forbidden to open more than one shop, to engross goods produced on the wholesale market, or to contract for goods produced outside London unless such goods could not be produced by a member of the company.[15] These latter rules suggest that the more enterprising capitalists among the masters had begun to experiment with economies of scale made possible by the growing market in London of free wage-laborers, as well as exploiting the older devices by which markets were engrossed, or cornered. But the new company ordinances firmly ruled against such practices, and the evidence suggests that the company was reasonably effective in enforcing these restrictions.

Although John Wallington, Sr., was named one of the wardens in the royal charter and was already a member of the ruling oligarchy of the Turners' Company from the moment of its incorporation, he does not appear to have sought to prevent his son-in-law, Richard Bradshaw, from being ordered to get rid of one of his apprentices when he had bound a third illegally in 1607.[16] The only gross use of influence seems to have been employed on behalf of Nehemiah himself. Nehemiah was made free of the company and fined to open a shop as an independent master in 1620, when he was 22 years old.

Theoretically, by a rule sanctioned by the London Common Council in Queen Mary's reign, all freemen must be aged 24—a reasonable enough regulation, since a seven-year apprenticeship contracted in the late teens would permit admission to the company's freedom at 24, and two years of mandatory wage labor as a journeyman would bring the young freeman to the age of 26 at least by the time of his full mastership.[17] Nehemiah's independent shop in Philpot Lane in 1620 violated both these rules, and one can guess that his father, who was master of the company that year, quietly arranged matters so that no record appeared in the court minutes that might suggest any irregularity. However, there is no evidence that the company oligarchy regularly stretched the regulations limiting economic advantage. When John Wallington, Sr., bound a third apprentice while master of the company, he was fined two pounds, the customary amount set out in the ordinances.[18] John Wallington, Sr., was a successful suitor for the Slutter loan fund of fifteen pounds on behalf of his son Nehemiah on January 19, 1625/26, and doubtless his influence on the Court of Assistants helped to place both sons among the nine freemen permitted to have stalls at Bartholomew's Fair in 1628. However, neither brother had been on the list of nine the year before.[19] Moreover, when the quarterly inspection of workshops turned up three chairs "deceitfully made" in Nehemiah's shop on October 9, 1645, the shoddy goods were routinely confiscated, and there is no indication that Nehemiah made on this occasion one of his frantic appeals to brother John for help, although the elder brother had by this time been on the Court of Assistants for over fifteen years and had served in both wardenships (he would shortly follow in his father's footsteps as master).[20]

To point to evidence that suggests the periodic enforcement of guild regulations proves neither that the regulations were never challenged nor that they were always enforced. At the court on April 15, 1630, the officers and assistants in what was clearly a fit of reforming zeal reaffirmed their determination to enforce their ordinances, which "hath hitherto been neglected," and among other things reiterated the order "to prevent the taking of many apprentices, which by experience is found very hurtful unto this mystery."[21] Yet the Court of Assistants was prepared to enforce the due subordination and "prenticelike" behavior of apprentices, and when Master Robert Audley complained of the stubbornness and long hair of his apprentice, "the apprentice coming before the Court with long hair and curled locked locks, a barber was sent for to the Hall, and so they were cut off in the parlor." The apprentice had been particularly provocative in wearing a "fair laced falling band" rather than a plain band, and this was confiscated and his handkerchief substituted around his neck. The whole procedure was obviously designed to humiliate the young upstart, and the effort was apparently success- ful, for "in the end he was compelled to submit and humble himself unto his master and to ask his forgiveness of the faults past and promised reformation and amendment of his conversation and car- riage."[22] A year later a general order was promulgated for the "de- cent appareling of apprentices," for Audley's apprentice was evi- dently not the only one who was no longer content to appear in public in canvas or fustian doublets with hair decently "round cut."[23] In the end fashion triumphed, not because apprentices got their way but because their masters no longer set an example of bourgeois restraint. On October 22, 1645, it was "ordered that for time to come the wearing of ruff or falling bands shall be left wholly to the discre- tion of each member of the Company."[24]

Fashions changed but the relative insignificance of the turners' trade and the relative poverty of their company seemed a constant. The company ordinances required that a sermon be given on the day when the master and wardens were elected in May, but an order of April 15, 1630, acknowledged that the sermon "hath hitherto been neglected because the company hath been poor and indebted." The sermon was eliminated twenty years later, "this company being greatly in debt."[25] All public bodies in this period regularly pleaded poverty, particularly when asked to take on some unwanted burden, but in this case the plea seems to have been genuine. In 1640 and again in 1642 the City of London raised substantial loans, the first for the king and the second for Parliament. A further loan was raised in 1643 for the defense of the City. In each instance the Turners' Com- pany was assessed to pay less than two-tenths of one percent of the total (.17 percent), a sum that suggests the mayor and aldermen shared the turners' estimate of their financial resources.[26] Individual turners seem to have prospered, but the generality must have found the war years in particular a difficult time. As Nehemiah explained in a letter written in 1645 to his former neighbor, Edward Brown, who had emigrated to Ipswich, Massachusetts, "it is sometimes hard with me, for our ware is dear, because workmen are gone and trading is dead and customers hard [to come by] and taxes great, yet trading is good with those that make things for the wars, and those that have places and offices do not want, but enrich themselves."[27] Nehemiah doubtless had his brother in mind, for in these years John Wallington, sometimes in partnership with John Gace, became a military contractor, supplying shovels and spades and other stores to the Parliamentary armies and navy.[28] Those who remained artisans in the retail trade, however, never seem to have got above a comfortable mediocrity.

What a comfortable mediocrity may have amounted to is not at all easy to determine. John Wallington, Sr., who was both successful and known to be charitable, apparently had given away most of what fortune he had by the time he made his will in 1635; the will notes the "many debts" owed by "many poor men," but urges John, Jr., as executor, not to press payment of any "not able to pay" and not "to trouble any by expenses or suit of law but upon great and urgent cause."[29] Clearly the Wallington patriarch did not anticipate that these desperate debts would ever produce sums worth bequeathing. The mystery about Nehemiah's own domestic economy arises not from his abject poverty but from his apparent lack of interest in money matters, or rather—since money was a source of constant worry—from his vagueness about the nature of his difficulties. For all his scrupulosity in leaving a written record of his many sins, an account book nowhere appears among the 50 volumes catalogued in his last extant notebook.

It is evident that at least early on he had no very precise idea of either his receipts or his disbursements. In 1630, after Nehemiah had been an independent artisan shopkeeper for a decade, he discovered that his journeyman for the past two years, one Roberts, had been systematically looting the business. What is startling is how long it took Nehemiah to uncover the fact and how informal were the financial arrangements to which the eventual discovery testified. "For," as Nehemiah confessed, "I found my estate to decay and run in debt very much, and I and divers others could not tell how, and we did wonder at it, being I had very good trading and great helps, but I and my wife had many reproaches and hard words, and we were judged to consume our estate ourselves." Any regular inventory and bookkeeping would have shown that someone was helping himself to the till, but Wallington had no suspicions until his journeyman set up shop for himself at the end of his period of service and sued for his wages, claiming he had been working for two years without pay.

Nehemiah did not dispute this, noting only that "he had scarce asked me before, neither did I offer him any till now," but he found to his dismay that he could only offer to furnish Roberts' shop with goods, for he lacked any cash reserves from which to pay the back wages.

It was only at this point that it occurred to Nehemiah's father and to his friend James Cole that the journeyman must have had some source of income during those years, for he had supported himself, his wife, his wife's sister, and another sister for half a year and had furnished a house besides. When confronted with these facts, the journeyman at first declared his innocence, offering his oath on the Sacrament that he had not stolen as much as a farthing. One of the Wallington maids then told Nehemiah that she had seen the journeyman put a customer's money in his purse "and offered to take her oath on it." When Nehemiah confronted the journeyman with this information and pointed out that if such a sin were "to come to the public view, it will abound much to the dishonor of God and to your own shame," the journeyman swore that "he was as clear as the child that is newborn." Nehemiah returned home baffled, for Roberts was evidently a Puritan and Nehemiah was as hesitant as his father to go to law against one of the children of God. However,

> within half an hour his wife came unto me weeping and said, "Oh, Mr. Wallington, I pray you come to my husband presently, for he is like Nabal: his heart dieth within him like a stone, and he saith that he will be gone presently and saith that he will give you all that he hath, even to his shirt on his back, so you will be contented."

When Wallington arrived Roberts took to his bed and refused to talk. For three hours Wallington and Cole urged him to confess, but the broken journeyman turned his face to the wall and cried. Finally, his wife urged him to "deal plainly, for if we confess and forsake, we shall find mercy, but if we hide our sin, we shall not prosper." Roberts then confessed that he had taken eighteen pounds, but by the next morning the amount had become only eight pounds. By this time Nehemiah was convinced that his journeyman had in fact stolen upwards of 100 pounds in the course of the past two years, but although he made a reasonable case for this figure, he never explained how he could lose 50 pounds a year without remarking it. Even more astonishing, neither his father nor Cole suggested how he might protect himself in the future from such depredations. In the absence of any such remedy, Nehemiah could only celebrate God's "great mercy . . . in bringing this to light" and express the hope that God will "restore unto me double and if it be for my glory and good." More practically, he asked that God "bless and sanctify this my poverty unto me."[30]

It may be that Wallington did keep accounts of some kind, or did at least in later life. In 1650, while ruminating on the spiritual advantages of self-examination, he commented that the "oftener and daily reckoning up of accounts makes it more easier at the end of the week than it will be at a month's or year's end, so this daily examination and making even betwixt God and myself, the work will be easier at the time of my death."[31] But it may also be that he did not follow his own advice. At any rate, after his house was robbed while he and the family were away at church on an August Sunday morning in 1641, he found that he could come to only the vaguest estimate of his losses: "they had taken out, as I think, about three pounds and a box (written on: this is the poor's box) with, as I think, about twenty shillings in it." Nehemiah's initial response was gratitude "that I had lost no more, for they might have broken into my chamber and have took that little plate and some other money that was there." Further reflection led Nehemiah to ask why God would permit theft from "his poor child," to which the obvious answer apparently was that "the Lord doth see the world is likely to steal away my heart; therefore he doth it in love to wean me from the world." This in turn led Nehemiah to wonder how he had gained the money, "whether I have not robbed others by lying and deceit."[32] A year later, after Wallington had scraped together twelve shillings to pay a creditor, he thought he had emptied his coffers only to discover another thirteen or fourteen shillings distributed almost miraculously about his pockets and in various drawers in his shop and chamber.[33] The lack of precision may in fact reflect no more than Wallington's perception that his posterity would not be or ought not to be interested in the precise details of his daily financial transactions. The spiritual meaning of such events was always of greater interest and concern than the events themselves.

It may also be that the very nature of the artisan's household economy defied precise accounting. Customers were waited on not only by Wallington but also by his journeyman and apprentice. At the same time, chapmen came to the shop door for payment for wares Nehemiah bought wholesale. The apprentice must have been sent out for beer as Nehemiah had been as a boy in his father's shop, and Grace must have been given money daily for the marketing necessary to keep a household of six to nine in victuals. Given that counting his pennies was never Wallington's favorite occupation, it is perhaps surprising that he was able to keep track of his finances as well as he did. Certainly he thought he knew at least what his gross income was, for after Cromwell's army entered London in 1647, following the abortive Presbyterian revolt, "then my trading in my shop failed me very much." For once he is quite precise about his losses, for he writes that "whereas I did take the first half year in 1647 three hundred and twenty-three pounds, fourteen shillings, the next half year, 1648, I did take but three hundred and twenty pounds, but the third half year I did take but two hundred and five pounds and that was very small gain."[34] Why an artisan whose gross income might in a good year in the 1640's reach to 640 pounds should have lived such a hand-to-mouth existence is a puzzle, and the missing piece is obviously an account book showing expenditures.

In the absence of such a key to the artisanal economy one can only speculate on the basis of the odd scraps of information that Wallington provides. First of all, he faced certain fixed expenses. What rent he actually paid on his leasehold and what relation it bore to the fine he paid on renewal is unknown, but his rector, Abraham Colfe, estimated his rent for tithe purposes in 1638 at twenty pounds per annum.[35] All servants—maids, journeymen, and apprentices—presumably received wages, although the Roberts incident suggests how casual and imprecise such arrangements could sometimes be. On at least one occasion, in 1637, Wallington registered with the Turners' Company the terms of service of a journeyman, Obediah Seeley, as indeed the ordinances of the company required: the terms were recorded as "eight pounds per annum and meat and drink, etc."[36] What wages the apprentices received is unknown, and the Turners' Company book of apprentice bindings does not record the premiums individual masters charged either. Wallington presumably bargained for a premium larger than twenty pounds from at least some of the nine apprentices he bound between 1621 and 1655, for in urging Zachariah Rampaigne's widow in 1647 to send her son Charles to the Wallingtons to raise, Grace Wallington had written that she would persuade Nehemiah "to take but twenty pound," a sum she clearly implied was a special favor offered to induce that errant widow to dispatch the boy to the Wallingtons' safely Protestant household.[37] For all their evident importance, rents and tithes, wages and premiums were peripheral to the economy of the shop itself, and it is that mystery that remains largely impenetrable.

What is clear is that a daily income of 35 to 40 shillings (545 to 624 pounds per annum) seems to have been adequate, whereas 26 to 27 shillings a day (410 pounds per annum), the income he received in the latter half of 1648, was at least by the 1640's and 1650's "very small gain" indeed. What complicated these calculations and induced an almost constant state of anxiety was, on the one hand, the daily fluctuations in income and, on the other, the lack of substantial cash reserves. On August 15, 1643, Nehemiah found that he had not taken in a "full two shillings the day, which I never can remember I did take so little on any working day." Two years earlier on August 27, 1641, he had reported with some amazement that "the Lord did send me such trading that I took above nine pounds that day."[38] Obviously both these days were exceptional. So, too, was January 11, 1641/42, when despite the fear that there would be fighting in the streets of Westminster, the shop took in "above twenty shillings . . . which did make me admire at this great mercy of God." A week earlier, "a troublesome day" when shopkeepers in fear had shut up their windows and doors, "yet so good was my God that he sent in customers that I took in almost forty shillings."[39] For all that Nehemiah wrote as though these fluctuations were a result of political anxieties, it is clear that they were a constant in the life of a shopkeeper. On October 18, 1654, when the peace of London was not disturbed by rumors of the actions of armed men, Wallington "did take but little money, as about two shillings," although he was able to console himself with the thought that "God hath given me better than money, which is peace of conscience."[40] Five weeks earlier, on a good day, he had taken "above forty shillings."[41] However, when he managed to take in from two to five pounds daily for a whole week in May 1642, "in a dead time," his richer neighbors "looked on" him.[42] An occasional day that brought in five pounds might be a "great mercy," but a regular income above the two-pounds-a-day norm apparently excited neighborly attention.

When shop income dropped, as it evidently did with regularity, Wallington found himself without cash reserves. With much of his capital tied up in lumber and wares, and with fixed labor costs that could not be cut in bad times, Wallington constantly found himself lacking liquidity. Wallington paid his tithes during Easter week and would have found himself financially embarrassed but that "for three or four days I had extraordinary great trading."[43] On another occasion he suddenly discovered that his lumber merchant would deliver "three loads of wood" on the morrow.[44] In particular, the irregularity of supply and the unpredictability of income made coping with debt an extraordinarily precarious and nerve-racking business. On March 8, 1641/42, Wallington noted that "I was much called upon for money, I having upon promise to pay the [Turner's] Hall 15 pounds and 6 pounds to another, besides many other debts coming on me to pay, and having great want of some sorts of ware fit for the springtime as pails and troughs, and at this time very dead trading; these things did very much trouble me."[45] The wholesale purchase of already manufactured wares to be sold in the shop involved Wallington in a continuous round of petty debt. On Saturday, June 9, 1637, he promised a friend to repay a borrowed five pounds on the following Monday or Tuesday. However, on Monday a chapman came with three pounds worth of wares. A loan of 30 shillings from his father plus some unexpected customers sent by "the Lord in the midst of my cares" enabled Wallington to pay the chapman and in fact to lend him 15 shillings more. That evening when he and his servant had gone out, leaving Grace in charge of the shop, a customer came who by Grace's "care and diligence" in the end purchased three pounds and 15 shillings worth of goods. "So on the next day, being Tuesday, I did pay the five pound to my friend, which I did promise, thanks be given unto God." In the next sentence he admits that he was in "the like straits" the following Friday.[46]

How much Wallington borrowed at any one time or in the course of a year cannot even be estimated, but it is evident that survival rested on a network of small creditors who sustained him. On a Thursday evening in June 1643 one of these asked for repayment of ten pounds that Nehemiah had borrowed, and Nehemiah, who had less than twenty shillings about the premises, promised him 5 pounds within two days. The following day he did enough business to pay the five pounds promised, as well as another 50 shillings to two chapmen who brought him wares—"thus good is my heavenly Father." Wallington does not mention the fact, obvious to the reader, that only a miraculously successful day of business enabled him to meet his more pressing debts and even so left him still owing five pounds.[47] There is no evidence that he was ever completely out of debt, and in the autumn of 1643, as trade decayed in the face of civil war, he was only saved from insolvency by an old widow who was about to leave for New England and who not only returned his bill for two pounds borrowed earlier but loaned him another five pounds. She made Nehemiah promise to repay the loan if she sent for it, but, she said, "it may be I will never ask you for it again, for I am glad I can any way pleasure you." As Nehemiah concluded, "this I take to be an exceeding great mercy of God."[48] Nevertheless, mercies were scarce that autumn. On September 6, a market day, he noted that "I did not take six pence all that day, for I sold but a sack bottle, two pence, a pair of nipples, three pence, and a top, a half penny, and all in brass farthings, so that I took no silver all this day."[49] By December he was desperate, for only desperation would drive him to borrow from his brother, the cost of whose loan was "some tart words" concerning his own incompetence. John in these years was a lender, not a borrower, whereas Nehemiah judged himself too poor even to enter the livery of the Turners' Company. It was clearly with a sense of great relief that Nehemiah was able to record that "within two days I paid it him again."[50] As Nehemiah consoled himself on one bleak occasion in 1642, "any epicure can rejoice, when all things go well and think that God loves him, when thus he prospers, but none but God's child will love him in time of adversity."[51] Nehemiah's life as an artisan and tradesman gave him ample opportunity to test the truth of that saying.

Part of the responsibility of a child of God was to observe the proper hierarchy of values and priorities and to discipline his feelings so that he not only acted aright but did so with rejoicing. On the whole Nehemiah found the intellectual process easier than the emotional, and even in his mature years he observed that "my murmuring and discontent with my calling . . . is a great project of the devil to bring me to misery."[52] Yet he had had from his youth a pretty accurate theoretical sense of the proper place of economic activity in the life of the godly. In the list of New Year's resolutions to which he added annually during the early years of his marriage, he did not express any concern with his livelihood until the 47th article, where he noted "that I take not the least pin nor anything else from anyone and that if I do, then I restore it fourfold and [give] one farthing to the poor." He then resolved to put his "trust in God more than in riches, wisdom, strength, or anything else," not to stand "idle at any time nor negligent in my calling," not to "conceal the faults of my ware, nor speak words of deceit," nor to "take any more for my ware than it is worth." Then, having made a final resolution not to envy "the prosperity of my neighbors," he turned to more general resolutions, promising that "before I drink one drop of drink or eat a crumb of bread . . . I lift up my heart to God" and that "I be thankful to God for the least of his blessings." Of the 77 resolutions recorded in the course of a decade only four were remotely connected to economic activity, and the relative importance he attached to them can be seen in the trivial monetary fines he imposed on himself when he broke them. Whereas he promised to pay a penny to the use of the poor should he look "after a woman to lust after her in my heart," negligence in his calling seemed worthy only of a one-farthing fine.[53]

That sense of priorities, that conviction that the calling was important but not as important as other demands upon the conscientious Christian, remained with Wallington essentially unmodified by all the experiences of a long life. Late in October in 1654, when he set out a list of five ways that "we order our actions to God's glory," the fifth read: "Be diligent, faithful, and cheerful in the duties of thy particular calling. God is glorified when a man is in his shop and about his business."[54] The trouble was that Wallington's experience of work seldom corresponded to his intellectual conviction. As he wrote on one occasion in 1642, "many times . . . I have gone down to my shop with these thoughts and holy resolutions: now will I go about earthly things with an heavenly inside; I will neither buy nor sell, but I will send up joculations [sic] unto my God, and I will deal justly and uprightly, speaking the truth as in the presence of my God." However, all too often, "when I come down, all this is forgot . . . and I begin to be a dead man again."[55] The problem was not a lack of diligence. For all his lack of worldly success, he was not in any ordinary sense a lazy man. Even the most innocent diversions from the task at hand were noted and checked. In the late winter of 1642–43 he observed with evident dismay that despite his resolutions made on the Sabbath, he had on the following Monday spoken "idly" and had delighted in one who did so, too, "so misspending my precious time in laughing" when there were clearly other duties to perform: "This sin of mine did grieve me."[56] The trouble was not that Wallington preferred frivolous amusements to work, but that he found much of his work so worrying and wearying. Only his daily spiritual exercises seemed to bring him any regular sense of satisfaction and emotional peace.

Nonetheless, he knew that hard, regular work was a divine bless-

ing, not only because it was the chief means by which man was enabled to "glorify God in the place and calling wherein God had set
him," but also because work at one's calling was in so many instances
the chief antidote to sin. Plagued by a sense of his own propensity
to succumb to the sins of sloth and spiritual dullness, he saw it as a
particular mark of "the love and kindness of God in giving me six
days [to work] and taking but one for himself." Lust, which he
thought a besetting sin of his young manhood, was a result of
"much solitariness," and so "I set up shop, only thinking that would
help me."[57] However, work was only a relative good, and the man
who was "up early and late, very industrious and careful and painful
in use of all means, taking hold of all times, seasons, and opportunities" was not the industrious saint but the worldly-wise man. For
why should men "pinch their backs and bellies for that which will
not ease them upon a sickbed, neither comfort them at their hour of
death?"[58] If these attitudes seem closer to those of the medieval moralist than to the work ethic of Weber's Protestant saint, it may be that
the ethics of getting and spending had as yet changed little, and that
when change came, it was not at the hands of the Puritan artisans
and craftsmen.[59]

For Wallington, work, though a good, was a subordinate one.
When he "proposed by God's help to make more speed and redeem
the time," he was not proposing to work longer and harder at his
lathe. Rather, he was vexed that he overslept till "it was past five
o'clock" in the morning on a fast day, when he had proposed to arise
early in order to go up to his study to pray.[60] First Table duties—those
divine commands given to Moses on the first tablet of stone—always
and of necessity had priority, for they were duties owed to God, and
the task of the scrupulous moralist lay in sorting out the inevitable
conflicts between the demands of the particular calling and those of
the general calling of all Christians. Normally Wallington went to
prayers and sermons with alacrity. On one occasion he noted that he
had attended nineteen lectures in one week, and although he worried that he was no better than "a proud pharisee" for so doing, had
he done that very often he certainly would have been a very poverty-
stricken one. However, on April 20, 1641, a Tuesday fast day, he
found himself "very backward," for instead of attending the fast "I
had many excuses: how it was a drying day, and my wife wanted to
be forth adrying, and I had great want of money which moved me to
be more diligent." He convinced himself that he only wanted to go

to the fast in order to say self-righteously that he had been there.[61] Yet the significant fact is surely that he knew that these rationalizations were but excuses, however legitimate each might be in isolation. Later, on a Friday (July 22, 1642), God confirmed the priority of the general calling with a providential act. Wallington had intended to close up shop in order to hear John Goodwin preach, but considered that, if he did, "I must all that afternoon be out of my shop, which I must and ought to attend." Having thus excused his religious laziness, as he thought, by invoking the needs of his calling, he decided to "tarry at home"; but God, of course, saw through his feeble rationalization and caused him to drop a heavy pail, which cut his shin. Wallington concluded his description of the episode with the rueful comment: "I dare say my sin troubled me more than the punishment."[62]

In general Wallington did not question that "the chief care of a child of God is and must be still to glorify God in the place and calling wherein God hath set him." If he wished to succeed in his trade and calling, he should first "seek the Lord" before setting to work: "his heart upon his God, then is his business like to prosper."[63] However, although diligence and persistence in the exercise of the particular calling were prerequisites of prosperity, prosperity was not a necessary consequence of persistence and hard work. Wallington may have been a moralist, but he was not a fool, and he knew too much about artisanal life to suppose that hard work was necessarily rewarded with worldly success. On the contrary, he was all too aware that prosperity was frequently purchased by other means:

> many fear not to lie, deceive, and to use divers such like things, . . . only to purchase the outward means unto themselves. . . . Others think that they cannot [succeed] in this wicked and crooked generation . . . unless they cozen, falsify wares, break God's Sabbath. Is the Lord become so weak that his children should not be helped, but by such devilish practices? God forbid! Tis nothing but our weakness and unbelief that causeth us so to think.[64]

When it came to the ethics of the marketplace, Wallington invoked not the God of mercy but the strict God of justice that Israel's prophets knew. The Christian buying and selling did not obey one law, and dealing privately obey another. "God is set upon justice in another manner than you think of," Wallington insisted; "the Lord stands much upon the observing of the law and upon obedience to it."

Therefore, "thy justice is thy trading, this must be made up one way or other; either thou must pay eternally for it, and so justice made up, or else it must cost the blood of Jesus Christ." What particularly horrified Wallington were those godly hypocrites who followed the law of commercial expediency in their business dealings. "To see one who professeth the Gospel . . . [but] will rather break the rule of justice than lose sixpence or a shilling . . . is this as becomes the Gospel?"[65] Hence, Wallington was skeptical of riches: they might be a blessing, they were certainly a responsibility, but they were not necessarily a sign of God's approval, and "poverty is no token of God's displeasure, . . . for, as it is no argument that the Lord loves a wicked man because he is rich, so it is no argument that God rejects the godly because they are poor."[66]

The point of a calling was not to gain riches but to be profitable and useful to oneself and one's family, church, and commonwealth. If wealth came, it came not as a reward but as an obligation: "we are stewards and have nothing but that we have received; we came naked into the world, and we must so again return shortly, [when] we must give account of our stewardship."[67] It was the obligation of the rich to relieve their "poor brethren," especially but not only in times of dearth. Hospitality and neighborliness may have been vanishing virtues in seventeenth-century England, but the demise of these traditional obligations was not owing to Puritan individualism. "Let us show that we have not forsaken the fear of God. . . . Let us refresh our brethren and not be ashamed of their poverty. . . . If we were poor, we would think it the rich man's duty to relieve us; the royal law is to do as we would be done by; this is the law of God, the law of Nature, the law of Nations; it is equity to do it; it is iniquity to omit it."[68]

Riches carried an obligation to use them well, but all too often, Wallington feared, riches were not a reward for honest labor but a consequence of sharp practice, of "lying and oppression," of "cruelty and unmercifulness to the poor." In writing in this way Wallington was not complaining about the treatment he himself had received, for although he grumbled from time to time about the failure of his trade to prosper, he never placed himself among the poor. Rather, he placed himself among the honest householders and tradesmen, the middling sort (although he did not use that term), far above the "rude soldiers and common people," and for that very reason in a position of responsibility toward them.[69] As he wrote to

James Cole and his wife in Connecticut in 1650, what disturbed him about the growing prosperity of London under the newly established Commonwealth was the way riches were corrupting the godly: "if you were here, you would see a great change in some men, for, lo, many . . . that when they were in mean condition, they were humble, and they were for God, but now they be rich! Oh, how proud be they and seek themselves." And in their pride, they had forgotten the poor: for "we have laid out our means on brave houses, fine apparel, or belly cheer, when the poor saints have perished in want of our help."[70]

There was at times a hard realism about Wallington's thought. Knowing so well the sins of the rich, he sometimes wondered whether he might not be able to avoid them, enjoying the benefit of greater prosperity without paying a moral price for it. Late in life he wrote, "I think that if I had a little more of the world, I could serve God [a] far deal better, for I should not so murmur and be discontent, and distrust, but spend more time in holy duties with doing good to the saints." But then he concluded more soberly that "surely I am deceived, for those natural sins will still remain . . . [and] besides I should grow more proud and earthly minded."[71] Many years earlier he had written that "I have often thought why the Lord should restrain . . . those outward things from me, he being a loving, kind, and merciful father," and concluded that God did so "to conform me to my Savior, Christ Jesus, and his Apostles which were . . . but poor men."[72] Admittedly, just as the rich were subject to the sins of "misgetting, miskeeping, misspending," so the poor were prone to "envy" and "grumbling"; but on the whole Wallington preferred the temptations of the poor to those of the rich.[73] Poverty was not to be sought, but if poverty came despite diligent labor, it should not be a source of dismay. If God brings his children into necessity, "it is but for the trial of their faith . . . : if he cast them into the fire, it is not to consume them but to purge and refine them. . . . Afflictions are their schooling, and adversity their best university."[74]

These values and attitudes were not entirely medieval in outlook, but neither did they aid and abet the entrepreneurial spirit. Poverty was not to be sought, and voluntary poverty was never praised as a Christian virtue. No legitimate calling was better than another, and all Christians were commanded to "believe always . . . your estate to be the work of God and vary not therein."[75] Yet successful enterprise seemed all too often to depend on "lying, deceit, oppression, bribery, usury, false weights, false measures, or . . . like iniquity," a hazard to one's eternal soul for the sake of vainglorious and temporary show, for "all naughty gain will have a naughty end."[76] If Wallington was suspicious of economic success, he was equally dubious about the moral worth of economic failure, and he alternated in explaining his periodic bouts of poverty between attributing them to his own "idleness and negligence" in his calling, and attributing them to God's attempt to wean him from an inordinate love of the world.[77] In any event he was confident that God would not ultimately forsake his own, and there is no reason to suppose that his confidence was misplaced. He knew he was reputed "to be a very honest plain-dealing man"; over the years he found evidence of "God's providence toward my soul and body."[78] If he never approached the success of his father or brother, he nevertheless paid his tithes and his taxes, served thrice on the grand jury of his ward, attended for a decade the meetings of the Fourth London Classis, and died full of years, a respected member of his parish and of the local Puritan community.[79]

If Wallington's values and attitudes neither preserved the past nor anticipated the future, they were nevertheless appropriate to his time and station in life. By the time he opened his shop, a century of inflation—during which food prices rose almost 500 percent while craft wages barely doubled—had eroded what measure of material prosperity the late-medieval craftsman had enjoyed.[80] The artisan who failed to pursue his craft diligently was courting economic disaster. But the structure of guild regulations militated against unrestricted competition and unrestrained entrepreneurship. Even in London, which was growing very rapidly, markets seemed inelastic relative to supply. Hence, guilds sought not merely to monopolize the production of their specialized commodities and to organize and rationalize markets, but to ration opportunity so as to prevent competition from ruining them all. Early in 1627 the Turners' Company called a meeting of masters who frequented Bartholomew Fair, "for that it is found by long experience by such of this Company as have [kept the Fair] that the gains which they get thereby do not countervail their charges by reason that so many of them do keep it together." The Court of Assistants proposed "that the one half of them might keep the fair one year, the other half . . . the next year after," a measure to which all but one assented.[81]

Even had guild discipline faltered, the very density of London neighborhoods, which made everybody's business public knowledge, worked against unrestrained competitiveness. In St. Leonard's Eastcheap there were 73 houses crowded into a parish of less than one and a half acres. In the years at the beginning of the century when Nehemiah was growing up, 27 of his neighbors were butchers. Had they engaged in competition with each other, that little parish would have undoubtedly resembled nothing so much as Hobbes's state of nature.[82] Under such circumstances everyone knew how his neighbor was faring, and the maintenance of a fair price was virtually a social necessity. Even Wallington, not the most worldly man nor the keenest of social observers, was aware of how his neighbors prospered, and he recorded on August 21, 1643, that his neighbor "took as many pounds as I took shillings." Again, on November 13, 1643, he recorded in some perplexity that "through need and the persuasion of some I sold the ware cheaper than I could afford. And I would have been thankful to God but could not tell how, by reason my ware was sold under the price."[83] Prices were clearly determined by known costs, and the artisan who undercut them was, as likely as not (as Wallington discovered), cutting his own throat. Wallington knew that the notion of a fair or just price was sometimes observed more in the breach than in the practice, sometimes even by himself, but he was never surprised when sharp practice turned out to be self-defeating. "I did not take God with me in my selling . . . , but multiplied more words than I need with some lying words. For what words can a man use after he is bid the price he can afford and take for his ware, but they must be sinful and lying words, and therefore just with God that I should lose my customer."[84]

Finally, it is evident that consciousness of being numbered among the godly, of being a member of the Puritan community, inhibited sharp practice and profiteering. As the popular preacher Paul Baynes wrote in a letter Wallington copied into his letter book, "the communion of the saints must be a point of practice, as well as an article of belief."[85] Although Baynes did not mention the fact, Wallington knew from experience that the practice of the saints reflected upon the whole community. Apparently some customers regularly sought to take advantage of the fact. After telling Wallington that when she got home, others would look over her purchases and tell her that she paid too much, "that she always goes to these Puritans, and they make her pay so dear," one such customer tried to get Wallington to name a lower price.[86] On another occasion, even more troubling, a gentlewoman had purchased some wooden trenchers from Wallington's shop and had been assured by Wallington's apprentice that they were made of maple, when in fact they were made of aspen. On her departure a neighbor's apprentice told her that she had been cozened, and on the following day she returned and confronted Wallington with the evidence of deceit. Wallington was clearly embarrassed, but what cut the deepest was her remark that "I partly know you for an honest man and that you have lived under a faithful minister for a long time"; for such a person "to lie and cozen" was, she said, "to bring a slander on religion." Wallington accepted the charge as true and returned the purchase price but confessed that, as for the wrong his apprentice had done, Wallington could "no way help it." However, the accusation rankled, and he went on to record in his journal that "it is a detestable thing to me, and it goes to my heart to think of it," for "it opens the mouths of the wicked to say: 'These Puritans! They will not swear, but they will lie and cozen!'"[87]

The morality of the marketplace, at least as Wallington tried to practice it, seems on the whole to have corresponded to that taught from City pulpits. When it was not, Nehemiah was mightily disturbed. Just after New Year's Day in 1650, Henry Roborough was buried at St. Leonard's Eastcheap; a friend and contemporary of Wallington's, he had been minister and lecturer in the parish at least since 1620.[88] In March Matthew Barker, a score of years younger than Wallington and, unlike Roborough, a prominent Independent, was placed in the living.[89] Within a month Wallington was writing in complaint, not of Barker's Independency, but because "I fear some may sleep and lie snorting in their sins for many years and scarce be awakened by so sweet preaching as yours is." For Wallington, the failure to create a godly discipline, the failure to use the political revolution to bring about a moral reformation, was by 1650 a scandal almost past understanding. Since obviously the gravity of the situation was not as manifest to Barker as it was to Wallington, the latter catalogued the various unchecked vices—"profaning of the Lord's day, drunkenness, whoredom, the swearing and blaspheming, the errors and schisms," but also "the covetousness, the oppression, the cruelty and unmercifulness to the poor."[90] The failure to bring an end to economic exploitation—to the conditions that created a poverty caused not by moral failure, laziness, or improvidence, but by the greedy pursuit of riches—was as disillusioning as the failure to bring the long hoped-for reformation of manners. Nevertheless, however much Wallington might bewail Barker's gentle preaching and decry the failure of the godly reformation in practice, there is no evidence that he and the Puritan ministers, whether Presbyterian like Roborough or Independent like Barker, differed in their understanding of that reformation's substance.

The Puritan ministers of Wallington's generation preached a social ethic appropriate to the majority of their congregations, the artisanal householders and small masters of Wallington's stripe. They did not address themselves primarily either to the almsmen or laboring poor or to the enterprising rich—the great merchant adventurers, the transatlantic shippers clamoring for free trade, or the small circle of City financiers who farmed the customs and enjoyed the privileges of crown creditors.[91] This is not to suggest that the preachers were merely self-serving hirelings, preaching what their auditors wanted to hear, but rather that when the preachers moved from the overriding questions of sin and salvation to the more practical ones of how to lead a moral life acccording to God's commandments, the moral problems they confronted were those of the middle orders of their society who filled the pews before them and not those of the very privileged or of the very poor. Questions about the nature of legitimate contracts, interest, and prices might lead the Puritan casuists into all sorts of subtle distinctions, but in the main their message was clear and unambiguous.[92] Central to all discussions of economic ethics was the concept of the commonwealth in which God is glorified by "everyone . . . helping others in some particular calling, for everyone hath received his talent, or some part of a talent from God to that end, which cannot be buried or hid without sin."[93] As the widely read William Perkins put it, "the common good of man stands in this: not only that they live, but that they live well, in righteousness and holiness and consequently in true happiness. And for the attainment thereunto God hath ordained and disposed all callings, and in his providence designed the persons to bear them."[94] Hence, economic enterprise was never seen as an end in itself, or as an autonomous sphere of life; rather economic activity was always properly aimed beyond itself to a social good and ultimately to the glory of God. As Arthur Dent paraphrased Matthew 6:24 in his *Plaine Mans Path-Way to Heaven*, a work from which Wallington quoted extensively, "no man can serve two masters, both God and riches": the moral man must always subordinate the economic means to the larger social end.[95]

Dent's *Plaine Mans Path-Way* is interesting not only because Wallington evidently read it with approval, but also because it is so difficult to discern any kind of "class" bias in the analysis it presents. Although its message made sense of an artisanal economy, an artisan like Wallington reading it would not have felt singled out as its proper or only audience. Dent does not discuss wealth or entrepreneurial attitudes in isolation; rather, getting and spending are dealt with piecemeal in the course of a lengthy analysis of the sins of covetousness and idleness, two of the "nine manifest signs of damnation." It was behavior and attitude, not social position and condition, that condemned the wicked and defined the good. Hence, though Dent could describe the "good rich man" as one who "keepeth a good house, relieveth the poor, ministereth to the necessities of the Saints, and giveth cheerfully and with discretion where need is," he also recognized the existence of the good poor, those who are "humble, lowly, dutiful, painful, ready to help, and ready to please." Dent even sketches out the middling sort, the "good neighbor" or "good townsman," who is pictured as he "by whom a man may live quietly, peaceably, joyfully, and comfortably." The point was that everyone, rich or poor, was exhorted to labor in his calling and to keep "his standing, his range, and his rank."[96] However, Dent, like Wallington, does not assume that such labor will necessarily be rewarded, at least here on earth: "God will not give us too much ease and prosperity in this world, for he knoweth it will poison us."[97]

It is not riches or poverty as such, but appetite that Dent condemns. The good rich man and the good poor man must both pursue their callings in order to provide for the legitimate needs of themselves, their families, and their neighbors. Dent was not suspicious of riches per se: lords, gentlemen, and merchants were rich because their ranks and callings by definition involved great wealth. Like most moralists of his generation, what worried Dent was not wealth but the pursuit of riches as an end in itself. "An eager and sharp-set desire of getting" is a sign of covetousness; it is not riches but the desire to gain riches "in all haste, by hook or by crook" that is destructive. And the destruction is as universal as the appetite. Unchecked greed is an evil, not because those made rich by it are necessarily uncharitable or their offspring invariably lazy and idle, but because for rich and poor alike greed perverts all just relationships:

"it marreth marriages" as well as "alms deeds," and it "woundeth our farmers" as well as "our gentlemen." Greed is the universal solvent, finally destroying "any sound comfort in God, for no man can serve two masters."[98]

Arthur Dent, "preacher of the word of God" (as the title page described him), viewed the world from the vantage point of the rural village of South Shoebury, Essex, some 40 miles east of London. It was still a traditional rural world, if nonetheless a busy one, where

> God allows none to live idly, but all, both great and small, are to be employed one way or another, either for the benefit of the Church or Commonwealth, or for the good government of their own households, or for the good of towns and parishes and those amongst whom they do converse, or for the succor and relief of the poor, or for the furtherance of the Gospel and the maintenance of the ministry, or for the good use of one another.[99]

Although it was not Wallington's world, it had much in common with it, for Dent's rural commonwealth, like Wallington's urban world of small tradesmen, was threatened by unrestrained economic appetite and entrepreneurial energy. There were similar guides to the perplexed "plain man" written from an urban perspective, but the values that informed such guides do not seem radically different—which is not surprising, since well over 90 percent of Wallington's fellow Englishmen worked with their hands at their callings, and it was they, and not the few great lords and gentlemen, whom the preacher saw before his pulpit month in and month out.

In 1613 Robert Hill, D.D., rector of St. Margaret's Moses in the City, published *The Pathway to Prayer and Pietie*, which contained among other things, "A Direction to a Christian Life." Like Dent's rural world, Hill's urban one is organized by distinct ranks and orders. In considering what clothes were appropriate to be worn, Hill argued that one must consider the ends for which clothing was donned, one of which was "for distinction, both of men from women, young from old, magistrates from subjects, the clergy from the laity, and the rich from the poor." In particular, one "must not look so much what I am able to do, as what is fit for me to be done, to imitate the most grave and sober sort of my rank, and to keep myself rather under, than above my degree." Again, like Dent, Hill insists that "even gallant and great ones have a calling," for so "all godly men had."[100]

However, some of Hill's strictures suggest quite plainly the ambience of the struggling urban artisan, familiar enough with poverty to have some sympathy for the poor, depending on cheap credit to survive and so fearing the usurious lender, hoping at best for what Hill calls "Christian frugality." The first rule to be observed is to be sure that one's "calling be such an honest calling, as that I be not ashamed of the very name thereof, as usurers are to be called usurers." Hill is quite specific about what honest labor entails. It is, of course, to be pursued with diligence, but also without fraud and with honest weights and wares. One is not to enrich oneself "by the labor of the poor," but rather to show "mercifulness and friendly dealing with the poor in buying of them their commodities, selling to them their wares, and laboring for them to their good. This is a good way to thrive." One is neither to forswear oneself in trading nor to commend one's "servants for deceiving any." The ideal is an honest householder's ideal: to give to the poor without reproaching them, to have a regard for one's kindred, and "especially" to be in a position to "give to the godly." A "Christian frugality" is not incompatible with a "thriving frugality," but the assumption of Hill's treatise is that a modest liberality and a modest prosperity are best. What is utterly condemned is a parasitic existence "of such as live only upon other men's purses and pains, devouring the good creatures of God, and living upon the spoil of others," for such people are truly "a burden to the earth, a bane in the Commonwealth, and the worst creatures in the world."[101]

Civil honesty and hard work may reasonably lead to a moderate prosperity, but Hill never forgot the propensity of even the godly to sin:

> The pampering of our bellies, the pride of our apparel, the negligence in our calling, the misspending of our time, our vain conference at table, our wandering eyes, our wanton lusts, our ambitious minds, our covetous desires, our ungodly speeches, our lascivious ears, our censoring of our brethren, our sin in recreations, our unwillingness to labor, our unfaithfulness in life, our forgetfulness in death, and our abuse of thy mercies, especially in Christ, do testify against us.

Inner sins were matched by outer calamities: life for the godly was a constant battle against the temptations of the one and the despair induced by the other. "The life of Christians," as Hill reiterated over and over again, "must be warfare upon earth."[102]

Wallington's writings testify to the incessant warfare that was the lot of the Christian pilgrim on earth, but there is little evidence that he perceived any change in the nature of the battle in the course of his long life. The forces of a market economy may have been gaining at the expense of the old regulated monopolies of the City guilds and companies, but if so, Wallington seemed scarcely aware of the fact, nor was there any reason why he should have been. Obviously guild regulation could not protect the small master from all the effects of the market; when trade was dead, the artisan suffered along with the rest of the urban population. Nevertheless, there is no evidence that either guild regulation or Puritan precept changed in any substantial way from the time of John Wallington, Sr., to the death of his son Nehemiah.

In 1657, the last year of Nehemiah's life, the Reverend John Ball's *The Power of Godliness* was published posthumously, a work as reinforcing of Wallington's values as the treatises of Dent and Hill published half a century earlier. It is familiar territory indeed. Particular callings are to be pursued with "diligence, faithfulness, and painfulness." The "outward comforts of this life" are to be used with "frugality and moderation," lest we be "oppressed with surfeiting and voluptuousness, and the cares of the world"; for only if they are sanctified to our use will these "outward comforts" not draw our hearts away from God. Wealth should be appropriate to status: "a nobleman hath need of a large allowance to maintain him according to his nobility." It is proper to pray for "all things needful to the maintenance and comfort of this life," but it is also necessary to pray for "contentment with our estate, though it be mean," for the providence of God is ultimately unsearchable. We may legitimately pray for relief from "beggary and extreme want," but poverty is of itself no more a sign of reprobation than worldly success is of election: "if we be in Christ, and yet poor, having in a manner nothing, we pray that God out of his secret love would minister to us, and make the fruit of his daily providence a contented portion unto us, be it never so little." Christians must both pray for this daily bread and labor for it "by just and honest means." Further, those "things well and honestly gotten" must also be "wisely and justly" used. Finally, wealth exists for the common good: "God hath made us stewards of his blessings to be disposed to the glory of his name, and the comfort of our brethren. . . . The good things which we have gotten by our honest labor, through favor of God, are not our own wholly; our poor brethren must share with us therein."[103] It may be true, as C. H. George has argued, that "from the publication in 1659 of Marchemont Needham's *Interest Will Not Lie, or a View of England's True Interest*, to Pope's 'That Reason, Passion answer one great aim / That true Self-Love and Social are the same,' the written record of England's completed bourgeois revolution becomes overwhelming."[104] Nevertheless, that new world where unrestrained appetite and ego and the absolute rights of property could be thought conducive to the common good seems totally alien both to the social world of the London artisan and to the mental world of the Puritan householder. At least in Wallington's lifetime, Puritan precept and artisanal practice seemed to go hand in hand.

However, it is also obvious that religious principle and social reality existed together in some considerable tension, even or especially for the godly, and Nehemiah's moral fastidiousness and social awkwardness made his life as a tradesman always something of a burden. Even an institution as essential to the artisan's life as apprenticeship seemed to Wallington of problematic benefit and a potential source of grave disappointments. None of his sons lived, but he must have witnessed the pained anxieties of his friend Francis Wilsmore with heartfelt sympathy. In 1638 he had helped Wilsmore place one of his sons with an Eastcheap neighbor. On March 9 Wilsmore wrote from Nottingham thanking Wallington and asking him to "remember my love to my son's master, and I and my wife do thank him for the tokens that he sent me." Wilsmore then went on to address a note to his son so full of commands and entreaties, hopes and dreads, that it still makes painful reading: "And now, my son, thou hast begun well; go on and God Almighty bless you. Wait at wisdom's gates. Walk on in the paths of righteousness. Hear my words, Oh my son; if sinners entice thee, harken not unto them. Let me hear no ill, for if I do, thou wilt bring my grey hairs with sorrow to the grave." A letter to Wallington written a year later notes that he has had no news of his son since the previous November, and the tone of the letter makes it clear that the last news had not been good. On December 28, 1640, Wilsmore wrote Nehemiah again, apologizing for his long silence on the grounds of his "great troubles . . . by reason of my sons that ran away from their master. And I was forced to seek them and found them in great misery within 14 miles of London, and I was so filled with perplexity that I could not come to London but made home with them as soon as I could." The parental agony is almost palpable: "As for my son that was at London, I look for nothing but rebellion from him. He is now at home with me. He will neither fear God nor reverence man. I know not what course to take with him." Two years later in December 1642 Wilsmore wrote again, this time with the news that both sons were in the army and one had been invalided home after receiving three bullet wounds. "I wait," Wilsmore wrote, "still upon God, expecting a blessing on all my troubles or else deliverance, which way He pleaseth." Deliverance it was to be, for in 1643 he was killed by a stray bullet fired from the Parliamentary garrison in the castle in Nottingham.[105]

None of Wallington's apprentices ran away, but even late in life he found the process of taking on a new apprentice and assuming responsibility for another servant a source of endless worry and anxiety. By the summer of 1654 his nephew Samuel Rampaigne's apprenticeship was virtually at an end, and Wallington was seeking a new apprentice, although not with any great enthusiasm. When a potential candidate, a youth named John, appeared on July 4, Wallington wrote of his misgivings: "my care is how he may be a servant of God, because I have spoiled so many; my care is so much the more for this by instruction and example." Since Wallington could not have been the jolliest company at the best of times, he must have been unbearable in his self-conscious role as the stern and God-fearing master. Three weeks later, on the very day that young John was to be bound—"and all his friends were willing to it"—"his mind did alter, and he said he did not like London, and he would be gone, and so he went his way." Wallington's only consolation was that he had given the young fellow "no just cause" to leave—or at least so he thought, for the would-be apprentice had told Charles Rampaigne the night before that he would never stay the seven years but would break his apprenticeship as soon as he came of age, excusing his departure to his mother on the grounds of Nehemiah's strictness. The episode left Wallington profoundly depressed: "and, Oh, now . . . am I discouraged, and all my hopes lie in the dust in that I want wisdom, and I cannot get ware nor help nor go to work about my calling, nor get out of debt as I intended, but still worse and worse."[106]

Early in August another potential apprentice came, but Wallington, unprepared, lost him "for want of wisdom in my words." Wallington then set about rehearsing what he would say to the next candidate, "and yet when he came, I was worse in a few words than I was before and could not tell what to say." This failure left Wallington in an absolute agony of shame, "not only for the loss of him, but also that others should see how weak and simple I am in my dealings." The next interview went no better, which "did so vex and terrify my mind that I know not what to do." It seemed little short of a miracle when William Heacock, despite the initial stumbling interview, returned the next day "upon liking." On November 1 Wallington bound Heacock apprentice for seven years, but on the 27th of the month he left, his brother never having paid the promised premium. Poor shy and tongue-tied Nehemiah, by this time a 56-year-old patriarch in his own right, did not finally succeed in binding an apprentice until the following February.[107]

The very process of buying and selling left Wallington continually a prey to frantic indecision and moral uncertainty. On one occasion a woman insisted, as the price of her custom, that Wallington give her a written quittance for a larger sum than she had actually paid. Persuaded against his conscience by his apprentice and another customer, Wallington reluctantly acquiesced, but "I dreamed that night that I had a great store of trading but little peace . . . , and as I opened my study door for to go to prayer, there was a thing like a man in black ready to destroy me, and I would have cried out, but I could not."[108] On another occasion Wallington found himself persuaded by others to sell ware under his costs, a process he knew was foolish and self-defeating. As he concluded, "these things puzzle me and are rubs in my comfortable walking to heaven."[109]

Deliberate sharp practice he found even more puzzling and disturbing. Late in November of 1643 Wallington found himself (as he so often did) short of coin and forced to borrow ten shillings on a day when custom failed to bring in even than small sum. To make matters worse, a chapman appeared at the door that evening who told Wallington "that he had brought me some pails, scoops, and measures which I had present need of, and I was glad of them, but he said he had promised two dozen of the scoops to my neighbor Martin, and I said if he had promised, I would not desire them from him. . . . So he promised to send me up this ware in a cart the next morning." Wallington spent the rest of the evening borrowing the sums necessary to pay for the goods, only to discover the next morning that the chapman had sold all the goods to his neighbor Robert Martin. When Wallington taxed the chapman with his duplicity, the chapman told him that, when he had told Martin that the bulk of his goods were promised to Wallington, Martin had said "he would have all." Wallington was understandably thoroughly "vexed," but "after I had digested it, I then was pretty well and did consider my God had a hand in it and did believe it was for my good," not because he could see any good coming out of such an unneighborly action, but "because it is said all things shall work together for the good of those that love God." If Wallington's faith did not always move mountains, it nevertheless enabled him to surmount any number of defeats.[110]

Even the handling of money was a constant source of rueful comment. On one occasion, "not minding my money, I did take a sixpence for a shilling." He was fairly confident that his customer had not cheated him deliberately, "but I am sure it is my folly in not minding what I did." On another occasion he paid out eightpence more than he owed, "which made me to call to mind of twelvepence at another time in like kind." After such transactions he found comfort in the thought that "when I wrong myself, it only redounds to myself, but when I wrong another, then God is dishonored, his name is blasphemed, and religion evil spoken of."[111] On one occasion the appearance of a brass shilling in his money box became the basis of a great moral struggle. The customer to whom Wallington had been paying out money in change discovered the brass shilling among the coins Wallington had given him. Wallington took it back and "put it in my box with the rest of my money, intending to pay it away another time," presumably to a less watchful customer. However, then "conscience did begin to chide me and said I had a thief in my box, a brass shilling which will canker all the rest. And now the battle begins and the flesh begins to baffle me, saying that being I took it [for good coin], I may pay it away again, and a shilling loss to thee is a great matter, it is more than thou will gain in a good while, . . . and many such like cavils the flesh did say to me." If the flesh was weak, the spirit of God was strong and supplied Nehemiah with three good reasons for not passing along the false coin, the crucial one being that to do so would "be to God's dishonor, for it will cause men to say, this is your religion! Men, see how he hath cozened and deceived me!" After another long internal debate, Nehemiah resolved to destroy the false coin at daybreak, but before he had time to do so a chapman came for payment, and Wallington had to warn him that among the coins was a brass shilling. But "the man said they were all very good." Overcome by this miraculous deliverance, Nehemiah took the other false coins in his possession—two brass half crowns and a sixpence—and chopped the half crowns in half and nailed the sixpence to the post. "And so all this trouble was at an end: all the glory be to God."[112]

Wallington never complained about his craft as such, and doubtless this essentially contemplative man found that working at his lathe was calming to the spirit. However, his shyness and awkwardness made dealing with customers and chapmen difficult and unsatisfactory, and his scrupulosity made the business side of his trade a constant moral battle. Briefly at the beginning of August 1654 he contemplated leaving his trade altogether. Though it was true that "the Apostle saith, let every man abide in the same vocation wherein he was called," Nehemiah also knew that God had told Abraham, "Get thee out of thy country and from thy kindred and from thy father's house unto the land that I will show thee." The question, as Nehemiah saw it, was whether he had a legitimate warrant from God to give over his vocation, and he wrote down eight criteria by which he would know that he should do so. Essentially, the eight reasons catalogued his failure as a London tradesman. He would know it was God's will that he leave his calling when he lacked customers or wares and when profits were smaller than expenses, leading him to "run further and further into debt to the prejudice and loss of others." It would be time to leave when "age and strength fails" and when "servants are gone and I want help to assist me." Finally and most pathetically, he thought that it would be time to give over trading "when the world grows crafty and I want wisdom how to deal with [it]." The fundamental problem, as he saw it—and it was implicit in the godly ordering of priorities—was that the particular calling hindered his general calling as a Christian. His father and brother had found some way to live productively with that tension. Nehemiah never resolved it: even what were essentially precapitalist market relations proved too much for his scrupulous conscience. One recognizes a real cry from the heart in his conclusion that "wanting inward peace, I had then rather give over, though with disparagement and contempt, and, faring hard with bread and water, with inward peace in assurance that God is my God, than if I had all the honor and profit the world could afford."[113]

Prayer hath a casting voice in all the great affairs of the
kingdom, and it doth order under God the great things of the world:
they are according to the prayers of the saints.

6. Politics and Prayer

When Nehemiah Wallington lifted his eyes from his lathe or his
books and pondered his position in the wider world beyond family
and friends and the exigencies of his particular trade and calling, he
saw himself primarily not as a citizen turner, a Londoner or Englishman, but as a member of a more select but less geographically or
temporally limited group—the children of God. On occasion he referred to them as "the people of the Lord" or simply as "His people,"
but "children of God" was the usual locution.[1] "Puritan" was a pe-
jorative that Wallington normally used only when quoting those
hostile to the godly who employed such expressions about them as
"puritans and rebels" or who called them "by the names of puritans,
schismatical, seditious, factious, trouble-states, traitors that speak
against Caesar, with many slanders."[2] Sometimes Wallington used
the expression "the children of God" specifically to denote the godly community in London, as he did when he recorded on April
10, 1640, that even though "so many of God's children did meet
together in divers places in fasting and prayer for the king's good
success in Parliament, then were many of those . . . pursuivants
abroad, yet I did not hear of any of us they took."[3] Yet among the
children of God were also coreligionists abroad; in a letter of November 28, 1628, Wallington's brother-in-law, Livewell Rampaigne, lamented the harsh fate that had recently befallen the French Protestants at La Rochelle, "the general report" of which "filled me with

much . . . sorrow of heart that the people of God should endure such great miseries scarce heard of in our age."[4]

The term did not have for Wallington a sectarian meaning. The enemies threatening God's people were papists and prelatists or the morally indifferent—the Midianites of the day who tempted the Israelites with sensual pleasures and the worship of idols—not fellow Puritans, even those with whom Wallington might differ widely on political or ecclesiological issues.[5] Although Wallington was eventually to become an active and conscientious participant in the Presbyterian Fourth Classis of London, he never saw the Independents and the sects as a gangrene on the godly commonwealth.[6] As he wrote in 1645 to a former neighbor and fellow turner, Edward Browne, who had emigrated to Ipswich, Massachusetts, "that which sads my spirit most of all is that God's people . . . are ready to devour one another." Wallington recognized that "in these times turned upside down" the "differences in judgments" were over issues of substance, and that from his orthodox point of view many of the godly had been led into "errors and schisms," but what he found particularly tragic were the "differences of affections, so that we are ready to destroy one another." The consequence could only be, he feared, to "provoke God and rejoice the enemies."[7]

Wallington neither sentimentalized the children of God nor confused them with the elect. He prayed in 1632 for "thy whole church and each member of the same," which he enumerated as the churches of England, Scotland, France, and Ireland, but he commended them to God's grace not because they were good or deserving, but because he was certain that, like Old Testament Israel, these churches were the embodiment in history of God's redemptive purpose. Like Israel, God's children tended to be forgetful and wayward and to suffer punishment for their very real sins, but for all that they did not cease to be His people. In part Wallington's certainty was unshakable because God's adversaries were to him so obvious. Thus he prayed God to "disappoint both Turk and Pope from encroaching on thine inheritance," and asked God to remember the "Prince Palatine; strengthen him that he may fight thy battles and restore him to his former inheritance"—for his inheritance was part of God's, a church lost to the children of God by the successes of God's enemies. But if the Prince Palatine seemed a broken reed in 1632, God's children had a new champion, the "little thought on and despised" king of Sweden, who, Wallington prayed, would "triumph over all thy enemies, even to the pulling down of that man of sin, that scarlet whore."[8]

For all that Wallington was given to endless and searching introspection, to constant worry not only about the moral rightness of his actions but also about the correctness of his motives and feelings, he was neither a medieval contemplative seeking mystical union with the Godhead nor a modern intellectual content to record the actions of his mind. Nor for all his worry about his election was the issue of personal salvation the be-all and end-all of his faith. As Paul Baynes, the Puritan preacher, wrote in a letter Wallington preserved in his letter book, "A goodman cannot tell how to go to heaven alone. The communion of the saints must be a point of practice as well as an article of belief. One candle lighteth another; even so, grace where it is will labour to kindle grace where it is not. . . ."[9] The life of a genuine Christian was of necessity a life to be lived in a community of the faithful, and, given man's general sinfulness, this meant inevitably a life of communal conflict between God's children and their enemies.

The Christian had two callings, a general and a particular, and though Wallington was occasionally dismayed by his failure to prosper at his trade, he was never in any doubt about the legitimacy of his calling as a turner. However, as he wrote on one occasion to Henry Roborough, the curate of St. Leonard's Eastcheap, "it is no easy matter to be a Christian," for "it is no reading of the Scripture or boasting of faith or Christ; though these be good . . . it must be conformity of life. . . ." It was this general calling to conform one's life to the Gospel, to be active in the world but not of it, that Wallington still in 1638 found so difficult. As he confided to Roborough, "it makes me wonder wherefore I came into the world, when I consider how weak and unfit I am for any employment, either for Church or Commonwealth."[10] Wallington's puzzlement is not entirely surprising, for indeed it is not clear what larger public role a seventeenth-century London turner might expect to play.

In Sir Thomas Smith's *De Republica Anglorum*, published in London just fifteen years before Wallington's birth, the "subjects and citizens" who were "participant of the common wealth" were divided into two categories: those "that bear office, the other of them that bear none: the first are called magistrates, the second private men." Smith was quite categorical in insisting that "all artificers" were to be included among the "sort of men" who "have no voice nor authority in our common wealth," but he nevertheless conceded that in cities and corporate towns such men might be impaneled for duty on juries and inquests and "be commonly made churchwardens, aleconners, and many times constables."[11] As a substantial householder and a citizen by reason of his freedom in the Company of Turners, Wallington clearly qualified for these humble offices, even if his membership in a lesser company and his failure to enter the livery excluded him from active participation in the government of London itself.[12] Wallington's father had served as one of the two churchwardens of St. Leonard's in 1599, but the loss of the vestry minutes and churchwardens' accounts makes it impossible to tell whether Nehemiah followed in his father's footsteps—although given his 35 years as a resident householder, it would be surprising if he escaped election to that important and onerous parish office altogether.[13]

The two precincts of St. Leonard's were part of Bridge Ward Within, a ward stretching north from London Bridge and including a dozen precincts all told. Wallington served as constable in 1638 and 1639 and is listed among the 36 grand jurymen in 1643 and again in 1645, 1649, and 1655. He presumably found service in the wardmote inquest congenial; certainly the bylaws of the inquest, agreed upon in 1627 and reaffirmed annually thereafter, had a properly rigorous and serious ring to them: fines were exacted on any erring questman who swore, gamed, or smoked during the sitting of the inquest, or, worse yet, who slandered or "depraved" (maligned) any of the company. But what Wallington actually thought of his service to the ward is unknown, for his years on the grand jury are never alluded to in his writings.[14]

What is evident from his writings is his commitment to a wide-ranging discipline that he was quite prepared to impose by friendly admonition even in the absence of office. His letter to his neighbor Constantine Waddington, previously cited, in which Nehemiah upbraided him for selling his wares on the Sabbath and for sleeping in church, suggests both his sense of personal responsibility and his willingness to act on it. Leviticus 19:17, which Nehemiah cited in justification, seemed to provide a general sanction for such meddlesomeness: "thou shalt not hate thy brother in thine heart, but thou shalt plainly rebuke thy neighbor and suffer him not to sin."[15] All the same, such acts of neighborly correction were plainly not adequate to the problem, and as late as 1645 Wallington complained that a fitting instrumentality had yet to be found. As he wrote to his former neighbor, Edward Browne, "for though we seem all for a Reformation and took a Covenant and a protestation and keep many days of humiliation, yet there is little or no reformation, but the very power of godliness is hated with most."[16]

In 1645 Wallington was "betwixt fear and hope"; within a year he was exulting in his conviction that God had embarked upon "a great work," and, although protesting his weakness and unfitness, he accepted election as one of the ruling elders in St. Leonard's. The erection of England's "Lame, Erastian Presbytery"—hammered out by the Westminster Assembly in 1645, but not authorized finally by Parliament until June 1646—led to the first local elections of ruling elders in July and the first meetings of the new Classes that autumn.[17] According to Wallington, both he and Captain Player had been nominated but not chosen in July, and the records of the Fourth Classis in the Province of London show that Wallington's brother John and Tobias Lisle, Common Councilman and Deputy, were the initial choice of the parish. However, as Wallington noted in a letter to Player, on October 11 both Player and Nehemiah were again nominated, and this time both were called "by the free choice of [God's] Children." Though confessing that despite having "lived this thirty years under the Gospel, yet I have more need to be taught myself than to instruct others," Wallington went on to assure Player (and presumably himself) that "God never called any to any place, but he fitted them in some measure one way or another for that place." It was certainly a doctrine to embolden the inexperienced, and although Captain Player was not persuaded by Wallington's plea—he was, according to Dryden, "A saint that can both flesh and spirit use, Alike haunt conventicles and stews"—Wallington and his older brother were both to give the Classis (and presumably their parish) loyal service for more than a decade.[18]

Whether the eldership and the classical system of discipline as a whole met Wallington's initial expectations is less certain. There is no reason to suppose that Wallington as a layman objected to the Erastian nature of the presbyterian system authorized by Parliament. He evidently was anxious that the full synodical system set out in a Parliamentary ordinance of March 14, 1645, be put into effect, and he, his brother, and Tobias Lisle joined their minister, Henry Roborough, in signing a petition from the Fourth Classis on April 5, 1647, calling for the creation of Provincial and National Assemblies—measures seen as "very conducible to the preservation of religion and the worship of Almighty God" in the face of "a most dangerous inundation of horrid blasphemies, damnable heresies, and abominable profaneness daily increasing over the whole kingdom, all [of] which cry aloud for the speediest and most effectual application of the remedy of church-government."[19] Although the National Assembly never materialized, the Provincial Assembly of London began to function the following summer, and in October John Wallington was among those chosen as a delegate from the Fourth Classis to attend the Provincial Assembly meetings at Sion College. Both Wallingtons were among the delegates chosen in subsequent years—testimony to their conscientious service.[20] In fact, the two Wallingtons were present at more than 60 meetings of the Classis, a record of attendance only surpassed by William Wickins, minister of the neighboring parish of St. Andrew's Hubbard and the scribe of the Classis from its inception.[21]

Clearly all this activity had some consequences of moment. On December 22, 1646, the Classis thanked John Mould, ruling elder of St. George's Botolph Lane, "for procuring justice to be done on certain profaners of the Sabbath by tavern haunting"; at the same meeting the Classis ordered that all who wished to receive the Sacrament first be examined "by conference" on their "fitness." The following July the Classis took notice that "divers malignant ministers" were preaching about London and that the Book of Common Prayer was still in use to the contempt of Parliament, and the Classis was encouraged to be diligent in suppressing such enormities.[22] The Provincial Assembly also urged on the London parishes "a diligent course of catechism in all public assemblies," a measure that surely had Wallington's support.[23]

Nevertheless, the written record of the Classis suggests that less time by far was spent in backing local efforts to impose an effective parochial discipline than in examining and ordaining ministers, and it may be that ordination was the only task successfully performed by the Classis. Certainly its record in other respects was not very impressive. From the start the Classis found itself embroiled in a conflict in the parish of St. Michael's Crooked Lane between the parishioners and Mr. Joseph Browne, their minister since 1640. Although the Classis ultimately found that the grounds for objection alleged against Browne were neither sufficient nor substantial enough to compel his removal, the parishioners remained unconvinced and refused to join Browne in erecting a ruling eldership.

"The Browne business," as it came to be called, was first broached at the meeting of the Classis on January 18, 1646/47, but all efforts at mediation failed, and the Classis finally referred the problem to the Provincial Assembly more than a year later on April 10, 1648.[24] The failure in the Browne case—in part the result of a lack of effective sanctions to enforce the recommendations of the Classis—was symptomatic of the system's overall weakness. When the Grand Committee of the Province inquired about the state of the Fourth Classis in 1648, the latter body was forced to confess that two parishes (St. Benet's Gracechurch Street and St. Michael's Crooked Lane) lacked ruling elders, and two others (St. Margaret's New Fish Street and St. Clement's Eastcheap) lacked settled ministers—in effect serious deficiencies in the structure, to say nothing of the performance, of four of the fourteen parishes in the Classis. By the mid-1650's, half the London Classes were defunct.[25]

Wallington had no illusions about the performance of the London Classical system, but there is no sign that he willingly abandoned the experiment while life and breath remained. Man might fail—and by 1650 that failure was manifest—but the compulsion to carry out the disciplinary order commanded by God remained unchanging. On April 22, 1650, Wallington recorded a comprehensive indictment of disciplinary failure: "Oh, the profaning of the Lord's day, drunkenness, whoredom, the swearing and blasphemies, the errors and schisms, and neither the sword of magistracy nor ministry pulled out against them. What shall I say of the covetousness, the oppression, the cruelty and unmercifulness to the poor? Oh, the contempt of the Gospel, the breach of protestations and covenants!" What particularly struck Wallington was that not a voice was raised "to reprove any of these sins, except a few of despised Presbyterians, as they call them." He feared the vengeance of God "on such a nation . . . in these sad and declining times."[26] Wallington was not alone in his despairing assessment. Nine months later the Provincial Assembly, which Wallington attended, wrote to the London Classes that they "could not but easily foresee an utter dissolution of the whole frame of presbyterial government, unless some speedy and effectual remedy was applied." Nevertheless, even the Fourth Classis and Wallington's own parish proved unable to cope with the most basic of tasks. Henry Roborough, who had been curate and lecturer at St. Leonard's since 1620, was buried January 4, 1649/50. At the meeting of the Fourth Classis on April 29, 1650, it was ordered that "the business concerning the minister for St. Leonard's Eastcheap be taken into consideration at the next classis," but although the Classis met two weeks later, with both Wallingtons in attendance as usual, no more was heard about the ministerial matter.[27] In the meantime Matthew Barker, an Independent, had been appointed minister to St. Leonard's; he remained until the Restoration, never seeking admission to his living from the Fourth Classis or attending it, and leaving the two Wallingtons to soldier on alone at the affairs of that increasingly ineffectual body. Altogether the Classis had proved a thankless task; as Nehemiah noted, it had led to "mocks and scoffs with some charge and expense of time both of profit (in my shop) and pleasures abroad." Nehemiah attended the Classis for the last time on April 2, 1657, and was chosen delegate to the Provincial Assembly; he did not attend the November 10 meeting, the last to take place before his death the following summer.[28]

Although Wallington's sphere of action was largely limited to parish, ward, and classis, it would be wrong to suppose that his interest and concern were limited to the same narrow confines. For one thing, he had neighbors who did play active roles in the highest ranges of City politics: Thomas Adams, Alderman and Lord Mayor in 1646 (whose wife, Wallington noted, died of fright less than a week after the attempted arrest of the five members of Parliament early in January 1642); Thomas Player, who captained one of the City train bands; Richard Bourne, John Taylor, Richard Waring, Tobias Lisle, and Abraham Babington, all Common Councilmen in the 1630's and 1640's; and Stephen Estwick, a prominent City Puritan who sat on the Common Council from 1641 and became an Alderman in 1652.[29] In a parish of fewer than 70 households it is difficult to imagine that Wallington remained ignorant of the doings of his more prominent neighbors.

Even had he been incurious about his neighbors, he could not have been oblivious to the great events unfolding around him in the late 1630's and early 1640's. In early 1638 both Wallington brothers had been cited to appear before the king's attorney in Star Chamber in the bill that indicted Burton, Bastwick, and Prynne a second time for seditious libel. Although thoroughly frightened, Nehemiah was also "glad and joy was in my heart that I should be put among them and to be made a partaker of Saint's sufferings." Liberated by Parliament, Dr. Bastwick returned to London on December 7, 1640, in triumph. Wallington himself "went to Blackheath and did see many coaches and horse and thousands on foot with their rosemary and bays in their hands."[30] The following May 1, in the midst of the excitement occasioned by the Earl of Strafford's trial, it was rumored that the House of Commons was besieged by Papists who had set Parliament on fire, and Wallington "and abundance more out of the City and other parts went up thither with swords and other weapons," only to discover happily that the rumor was false. Two days later, on May 3, Wallington was among the crowd of citizens— 15,000 he suggested—who flocked to Westminster to petition the House of Lords to condemn the hated earl. "I never did see so many together in all my life," Wallington noted, "and when they did see any Lord coming, they all cried with one voice: Justice! Justice!"[31]

London was at the center of revolutionary change, and Wallington knew he was witnessing unprecedented events. When the remaining "idolatrous" and "superstitious" images were removed from city churches in October 1641, Wallington saved some stained glass fragments "to keep for a remembrance to show to the generation to come what God hath done for us, to give us such a reformation that our forefathers never saw the like."[32] But even had he had a less acute sense of historical significance, he could scarcely have ignored the fact that events of national importance were taking place virtually on his doorstep. On January 3, 1641/42, the king had impeached Lord Mandeville and the five members—Pym, Stroude, Hollis, Haselrig, and Hampden. On January 4, when the king attempted to arrest the five members on the floor of the House, fear that the king would turn his troops on the City was so widespread, Wallington noted, that "we were driven to shut up our windows and doors and to stand upon our guard." Two days later at midnight "there was a great cry in the streets that the enemy was come, and great knocking . . . at all our doors that we should stand at our guard."[33] A month later when petitions were brought up to Westminster in support of Parliament, those from south of the Thames came across London Bridge. On February 8 Wallington recorded that "these Kentish men I did see myself come up Fish Street Hill, many hundreds of them on horseback with their protestations sticking in their hats and girdles." A few days later the Sussex petitioners followed the same route, passing within yards of Wallington's shop door; he thought there were "three thousand of them in all," mostly on horseback.[34] By autumn the civil war had begun, and on November 6, the king's army approaching, "suddenly every man was to let his servant be tested to go forth in his arms with all expedition with his excellency, the Earl of Essex." William Grant, Wallington's apprentice since 1637, was enlisted and a week later on hearing news of the defeat of the Parliamentary forces at Acton, "suddenly drums struck up for our soldiers to go forth, and my man William Grant . . . went forth with the rest." All night and next day Wallington heard the wagons carrying shot and powder rumbling westward through the City.[35] In August 1643, London was again threatened by Royalist troops, new Parliamentary forces were hastily raised, and Wallington again noted that shops were ordered closed, "which did a little startle us at first."[36]

It would be a mistake, however, to suppose that Wallington first became historically conscious in a wider sense while watching Sussex petitioners ride up New Fish Street, or while watching City troops march off to Acton, just as it would be a mistake to suppose that he saw his own sphere of interest as limited to the world of parish and ward. One of Wallington's principal surviving journals, that entitled "A Record of the Mercies of God: or a Thankful Remembrance," was begun well before the Long Parliament was summoned to Westminster, and a second, an untitled collection of historical notices, was begun in 1640.[37] Both were intended to set forth God's glory by recording, in the first instance, God's mercies toward Wallington himself (all the more remarkable and glorious because he knew himself to be an undeserving sinner), and in the second instance God's mercies toward England or more particularly toward God's children in England. Both were written, at least in Wallington's eyes, under a profound sense of obligation: "it is . . . our duty to seek God's glory and the good of his church," twin goals that could be accomplished only by leaving an historical record of God's dealings with himself and with His people.[38] God had dealt mercifully both with Wallington and with the godly in England beyond their just deserts. To let those mercies pass unrecorded into oblivion was not only ungrateful but unwise.

To forget divine mercies was to deny God his due glory, and man's first duty as God's creature was at all times to recognize and glorify his Creator. God spoke immediately to man in His Word, but Scripture also demonstrated, at least to Wallington, that God spoke to man almost as distinctly in the historical process itself. It was, of course, the merest cliché that the created world revealed to the eye of the discerning the hand and intention of the Creator. Further, the intelligent observer might deduce that the ordered hierarchy of natural creation dictated an analogous ordered hierarchy of superiority and inferiority in human society, which would then be seen as natural, inevitable, and good. To Wallington, these arguments from natural law were true but trivial. He recognized that, in general, "the creatures of God . . . work . . . according to their own nature, which they receive of God at their first creation"—but only in general. Obviously man ignored natural laws at his peril: a man falling from a high place might reasonably expect, in the absence of a miracle, to break his neck. However, it was equally obvious that the Creator could change the operation of his creation at his "mere will and pleasure . . . whensoever it pleaseth him," and could make the creature "work both above and contrary to" its original nature. Wallington knew that such was the case, because Scripture provided obvious examples: "If it please God the creator, the sun shall stop her course . . . , Joshua 10:12, yea go backwards, 2 Kings 20:10."[39] Why God should will above or contrary to nature was in one sense both unknown and unknowable, for who could presume to fathom the inscrutable workings of God's secret will? However, in another sense the reason for providential interventions was obvious, even to a humble London turner, and it was recognition of these reasons that turned Wallington not only into an amateur psychologist in order to understand the workings of his own troubled mind, but also into an amateur historian to understand the workings of "all the mercies and deliverances," in particular "this great and miraculous mercy of God to us in England now of late years," which "(next to God's mercy in his Christ) exceeds all former mercies and deliverances that ever I heard or read of."[40]

Divine interventions were in one sense self-explanatory and self-justifying: "Thus the Lord maketh known himself every way to be absolute Lord of all." However, Providence is more than a constant reminder of God's fundamental omnipotence, for God uses providential events to teach mankind necessary lessons. First of all, Wallington saw many of the untoward happenings of the 1620's and 1630's as portents, warnings of the wrath to come. An account of the plague deaths in London in 1625, a great judgment, is followed by a complaint of how "idolatry crept in by little and little" and of how "cunningly and craftily hath the enemies of God's free grace brought in superstition," a complaint that is followed by an account taken from a letter of June 11, 1633, of how Dr. Collins, the Provost of King's College, "maintains transubstantiation and many points of

popery." All these are seen as "sins and abominations which provoke God to send his judgments among us . . . as the needle makes
way for the thread." The fire, for example, that burned most of the
houses on London Bridge on the night of February 11, 1633, was
seen as both a mercy and a judgment: a mercy, because the whole
city might have been consumed but was not; a judgment, because
any examination of its ultimate causes would lead to a consideration
of "the sins of the times which are now grown to their height," a
lengthy catalogue that ran the gamut from silencing of godly preachers—"God's prophets and servants"—to "the sin of buggery"
newly discovered to have been practiced for seven years by a group
of married men in Southwark.[41] Since sin was a prime cause of judgments, and since London was to the critical eye a veritable Sodom, it
was never difficult to find causes for visitations by fire or plague.
However, Wallington recorded such judgments because they were
also a warning and a portent that "we should not forget ourselves,
but we should declare it to all others, even to the generations to
come."[42]

There were other lessons to be learned from the correct reading of
Providence in addition to the obvious one that sin invites divine punishment. To Wallington's way of thinking, escape from such catastrophic judgments was not a sign of guiltlessness. Rather, it was an
unexpected mercy, at best a temporary respite, a gracious act of a
patient God to permit man to reflect and reform, for, as Wallington
writes of his own escape from the burning of London Bridge,
scarcely a hundred yards down New Fish Street hill, "we may not be
so unwise . . . that we should suppose that those that had their
houses and goods burnt upon the bridge were greater sinners than
all the rest of the City of London because they suffered such
things."[43] Judgments were a punishment for manifest sins, but they
also had their uses, their practical applications. To the wise, providential judgments were sermons written in the daily events of human affairs.[44]

There was a third lesson to be learned that was particularly crucial
for the children of God. For all that the godly were called Puritans,
Wallington, at least, was under no illusion that the godly were pure.
Calamities, then, were both a reminder of sinful mortality and a test
of faith. Moreover, persecution was the peculiar lot of the godly.
Suffering by fines and whipping, imprisonment and banishment au-
thenticated their role, for had not the "false prophets" always dealt

harshly with the true prophets? God's "people may seem to have cause to say with Gideon, if the Lord be with us, how hath this befallen us, and where are all the wonders which our forefathers told us, saying the Lord led us out of Egypt, but now hath the Lord forsaken us and given us into the hands of the Midianites." A weak faith was in this context a lack of proper historical perspective. The godly might be punished as a lesson in humility and a reminder of their common humanity, but the godly could not suffer ultimate defeat precisely because they were the children of God. On the other hand, God might sometimes use the distress of the godly to lull His enemies into a false sense of security, the more to confound them in the final confrontation. For Wallington, faced in the 1630's with the apparent defeat of God's people both at home and abroad, hope was all that remained. As he knew, "so soon as the people of God fell into any difficulty, their enemies out of spiteful mind begin to think that they are wholly gone, whereupon they begin to mock them and to prognosticate their utter ruin; they begin to shake the head at them and to put out the tongue, and to cry out, Aha! Aha! now they are perished." How comforting to know that such reverses were only temporary and that finally "the Lord raiseth up himself and turneth all the boasting of the adversaries of his people into a lie, and turneth also his people's case so that they hold up their heads in despite of all their enemies." Then "their woe is turned to joy, and their grief confounded, God glorified and his people comforted."[45]

History for Wallington was in effect the personal experience of the godly writ large. The biography of the true Christian was the story of repeated failure despite the ultimate promise of success, of a process of sanctification never completed in one's lifetime. The history of God's people, as Wallington knew from the Old Testament, was equally unpromising in the short run, for frequently the Israelites seemed chosen not for triumph, but for suffering. Yet if much of history was experienced as calamity, how filled it was with drama and meaning for those who could see and read. For the perpetual flux of events and the apparent interplay of chance and accident were actually only a backdrop against which the children of God played out their allotted role, confident that in the final act they would triumph because they knew the playwright and had read the script. Persecution by the wicked was no more than an evidence of the goodness of one's cause, an apparent success to lull the Adversary into false confidence, "for yet in a little while, . . . He that shall come, will come, and will not tarry, and the day of refreshing shall come." To suppose otherwise would be to doubt that "God liveth still; he loveth his Church still; he ruleth still."[46]

Beliefs such as these were not without consequence. As a not very successful London turner, Wallington's public role was limited to holding minor offices in ward and parish. However, as one of God's children, he saw himself as an observer and participant in an unfolding drama played out on a far vaster scale. The lesson he learned from history was "to be of good courage"—precisely the lesson needed to enable men born to be ruled rather than to rule to move from their traditional passivity as victims of the larger events that overwhelmed their communities to purposeful activity on behalf of a revolution they believed they must finally win. Hence, Wallington knew from the outset that in his public journal he must paint on the widest canvas, that he must record not only the burning of London Bridge but also "the miserable estate of Germany."[47] Almost the whole of the journal was written in the early 1640's, and by then Wallington knew he had witnessed in the overthrow of the Laudian Church a divine deliverance from a "hellish plot to undermine and overturn the gospel."[48] In early 1642 he copied the petitions sent up to Westminster in support of Parliament "for the generations to come, that they may see and behold what our God hath done in the stirring up of the people of all countries, and of all sorts . . . to go up to Westminster . . . with their petitions for the removing of those great obstacles that lie in the way [of] the blessed Reformation both of Church and Commonwealth, which we have so long hoped and labored for. This is the work of the Lord, and it is marvelous in my eyes."[49]

By early 1642 the task of assembling information for his public journals had become a major preoccupation. The editor of *Historical Notices* observes that Wallington "quotes or refers to more than three hundred of the tracts" in the Thomason Collection in the British Library in the course of his journal.[50] Wallington woefully commented that the piles "of these little pamphlets of weekly news about my house . . . were so many thieves that had stolen away my money before I was aware of them." However, although the expense occasioned some "sad thoughts," he recognized that when he came to "give account before the great God . . . how I have improved and laid out every penny," his journal would provide ample justification, for to God's glory it would enable "the generation to come . . . [to] see what God hath done."[51]

In February of 1642 Wallington was certain that "children unborn" who read his account would "stand up and praise the Lord and talk of all his wondrous works."[52] That note of high optimism was not one that Wallington had been able to sustain. The long volume had begun with "A Bundle of Mercies": with accounts of the defeat of the Spanish Armada in 1588, the failure of Gowrie's plot against King James and the Gunpowder Plot against the king in Parliament, Prince Charles's escape from a Spanish marriage, and London's escape from the terrible plague of 1625.[53] The volume ends 281 folios later with brief accounts of the burning of Bridgnorth, Shropshire, and Faringdon, Berkshire, by the Royalists who torched the villages to prevent Parliamentary forces from taking shelter there; news of these latest in a long series of wartime atrocities reached London and Wallington on April 9, 1646. Long before that Wallington had clearly lost his stomach for the dreary task. He had not lost his faith in a God who works through history, but precisely because he had not, he had ceased to look for any happy conclusions to the long and bloody civil war.

For despite Wallington's tendency simply to incorporate his sources wholesale into his text, he was no mere antiquarian, faithfully transcribing one account or diurnal after another in the hope that posterity would find some sense in it. He had an appreciation for the concrete solidity of facts; his accounts incorporate considerable detail. Plot after plot is lovingly uncovered; petition after petition is carefully catalogued. Nevertheless, certain themes are noted and certain lessons learned appropriate to the times. The 1630's were portentous years, filled with incidents warning of the wrath to come, for England's evident sins could not go unpunished. The years between 1640 and the outbreak of the civil war in the late summer of 1642 were years of incredible tension, for "the spirit of Antichrist is now lifted up and marcheth furiously," but "at this very time the delivery of his Church and the ruin of his enemies is in working." Despite the "forlorn" state of the Church, Wallington was sure that these were years of hope, that although "we shall have much opposition, yet . . . Christ's cause shall prevail, [and] Christ will rule."[54] By 1645 the optimism had vanished: "God hath done very much . . . , yet God's wrath is not turned away."[55] Wallington lost none of his interest in politics; he continued to read events as the farmer reads the coming weather in the evening sky; but by 1650 the future looked as grim as it had in 1630. "God doth house up many of his children from the storm that is coming, . . . I fear that judgment cannot be far off."[56] It was an assessment he saw no cause to change from 1650 until God came to house him up in the summer of 1658.

From the breakup of Parliament in 1629, when "no good thing is done and that abominable sin of Idolatry hath toleration," to the breakup on May 5, 1640, of the promising Short Parliament, after which "our proud prelates with the doctors sat still in their Convocation House . . . [and] made a most filthy, execrable book of Canons," Wallington saw little more than a series of catastrophes, personal as well as general, all of which gave warning of an impending national judgment.[57] By 1640 England was ripe for revolution, and Wallington thought he was ready for it.

What the children of God faced in the 1630's was clear enough; what to do about it was less obvious. For Wallington what was significant about the years between 1629 and 1640 was not the attempt by Charles I to erect a royal absolutism by ruling without Parliament, but rather the all-too-successful conspiracy by "prelates and papists" to bring in "popery little and little to the overturning of the gospel and the overthrowing of the Lord's day."[58] Although the reissuing of the Book of Sports in 1633 was perhaps the most dramatic move in the plot to bring in idolatry and suppress true religion, it was, nevertheless, only one part of a total program of subversion which included the licensing of heterodox books and the suppression of orthodoxy (the prelates "putting out and putting in what they think good"), the elimination from the Prayer Book of the phrase "Thou hast delivered us from superstition and idolatry," the suppression of weekly lectures, and the silencing of the "most godly, powerful, painful ministers."[59] The suppression of old orthodoxy was accompanied by the introduction not only of new and corrupt practices—witness "the high altar at Queen's College"—but also of new and erroneous doctrines, such as "that they that are baptized are truly regenerate," "that the ministerial power of forgiving sins is not merely declarative," and finally and most perniciously, "that the Church of Rome is a Church truly so called"—doctrines so at variance with reformed belief that they were final proof, if such were needed, that the prelates aimed at popery.[60]

If the 1630's had their obvious villains in the innovating bishops, they also had their hero-martyrs in Burton, Bastwick, and Prynne, "those three renowned soldiers and servants of Christ," a long account of whose trial in 1637 Wallington carefully copied into his journal.[61] In particular, William Prynne's impassioned speech from the pillory must have echoed Wallington's own fears and feelings:

> Alas poor England, what will become of thee, if thou look not the sooner into thine own privileges, and maintainest not thine own lawful liberty. Christian people, I beseech you all, stand firm and zealous for the cause of God and his true religion to the shedding of your dearest blood. Otherwise you will bring yourselves and all your posterity into perpetual bondage and slavery.[62]

By 1638, when *A Brief Relation*, the account of the trial of the three martyrs, reached Wallington's hands, he had had firsthand experience of the intimidating effect of a Star Chamber interrogation. In fact, although he does not mention it, he must have been aware of the earlier investigation in April, May, and June 1634, of Henry Roborough, his curate, and of his neighbors Thomas Player and William Adams, all of whom were summoned to answer articles under oath before the Court of High Commission.[63] Four years later social anonymity had ceased to be a form of protection, and the two Wallington brothers were themselves summoned to answer articles as part of a more general bill against Burton, Bastwick, and Prynne before the Court of Star Chamber.

The interrogation was an important part of Wallington's political education. If he learned concretely that the godly were "as sheep in the midst of wolves," he also learned that the bark of these wolves was worse than their bite. The two Wallingtons were summoned on the morning of February 5, 1637/38, to appear that afternoon before the Crown attorney, where they faced a lengthy attachment of 35 pages to the bill against Burton, Bastwick, and Prynne, in which it was charged that they "had long maligned the king's happy government and did vilify and defame his government, and that we had printed and divulged libelous books with other heinous crimes." On February 21 they submitted their written answers and were put on their oath, a process Nehemiah found more disquieting than any other, for in it he was forced to swear to testify to what he knew and believed both about himself and about others. Although his friends had assured him that he could lawfully take the oath, he was "much troubled" in his mind and conscience by this "devilish" and "exe-

crable oath," particularly in the light of his brother's strict examination by the court. He paid an attorney who promised to prevent his
having to appear, but to no avail. On April 20 he was compelled to
confess before the court that he had possessed and read Henry Burton's *A Divine Tragedy* and his *An Apology of an Appeale*, as well as
William Prynne's anonymously published *Newes from Ipswich*. He
denied having read John Bastwick's *Letany* or knowing anything
about the clandestine book trade and, what was crucial, managed
not to implicate any besides his brother and Edward Browne, a
neighbor and turner who had conveniently already emigrated to
Massachusetts. When asked whether he had had any letters from
the country requesting these books, he was happily able to reply that
"none in the country did know I had any of them," a clear admission
that he corresponded with godly friends outside London, a fact of
which the court was evidently aware. He left the court blessing God
that he had managed to escape with "a clear conscience." On reflection he realized that he had learned three important lessons: that
God kept those "promises he had made to those that trust him," that
these were indeed sad and grievous times, and, most importantly,
that sealed by the graces of God's spirit he was able to "stand for
God's cause." It was a lesson the government should have been more
reluctant to assist the saints in learning.[64]

There were other lessons to be learned in 1638. In a section of the
journal Wallington entitled "The Bitterness of War," he noted that
"in the year 1638 I had a book come into my hand of the miserable
estate of Germany, wherein as in a glass you might see the mournful
face of this our sister nation now drunk with misery." As with so
much else in the late 1630's, Wallington read it as a sign: "are there
no idolators and Sabbath breakers and drunkards, etc., but in Germany?"[65] The answer, he knew, was in the negative, for on the pages
preceding he had exhaustively catalogued both "the causes why the
Lord doth send a sword on the land" and the "signs that the sword
is coming on a land"; these causes and signs were already present in
the idolatry, the breach of the Sabbath, the hatred of the people of
God, and the persecution of the prophets of God. It seemed point-
less to Wallington not to profit by "God's long patience and trying us
with lesser judgments," but he knew his fellow countrymen had not
paid them heed, and he could only urge that the causes and signs
might "serve as a strong motive to stir us all up with speed to turn
unto God, that he may turn . . . from us this fearful calamity."[66]

Wallington anticipated war from the outset. When he recorded that "in April 1639 our king with his armies went against Scotland," he confessed that "we look for nothing but civil wars and that the sword should be sheathed in one another's bowels." It was nothing short of a "great mercy" that God "did spare us and sent our king in peace, and that not so much as one man slain, as I did hear of."[67] For the government, newly rescued by God's mercy from a fratricidal war with the Scots, to dismiss the first Parliament summoned in eleven years before any reforms were accomplished, and then to permit Convocation to continue to meet and to promulgate the hateful canons, seemed to Wallington so mad an act that he could only conclude that God had turned the "wisdom of the great Achitophels into foolishness."[68]

Peace was one casualty of the 1630's; trust in the fundamental soundness of the Stuart monarchy was another. Prelates and papists remained the prime enemy, the active agents at work against God's people. The king, however, had ceased to be a benign force in the state, a man whose fundamental goodwill could be depended upon however much his judgment might be perverted by the wiles of flatterers or by the insinuations of the wicked papists.[69] Wallington was never a radical, at least not by the standards of the Baptists and Levellers who were shortly to appear in the City. Yet there is no evidence that his "Presbyterianism" was ever accompanied by royalism, as it was so frequently in the later 1640's. Moreover, the one tract (among the hundreds he excerpted for his journal) that touched upon the powers of the monarchy and the rights of the subject in theoretical terms struck a remarkably radical note for the year 1640. The short title of the anonymous pamphlet, *England's Complaint to Jesus Christ against the Bishops' Canons*, gives an accurate sense of its focus but not of the full range of its contents, for in the course of a discussion of the third canon the author quickly moved from a consideration of the hypocrisy of the canon against popery to a consideration of monarchic power itself. Though prepared to admit that monarchy was divinely instituted, the author nevertheless argued for a contractual state: "The royal office is a sacred ordinance of God. And this ordinance of God comprehends in it not only the institution of the superiority of kings over their people, but their special office of government, as it is limited and established upon those laws and covenants and conditions agreed upon between the prince and the people." Such a definition of divine-right monarchy was one King James would have recognized, but the author then goes on to argue for a veritable right of revolution.

> If a king maintain a faction about him which go about to oppress his whole kingdom and people in their law and liberties and most of all in the true religion, so as he will not rule them by the good laws of the kingdom, but seeks to make all his subjects slaves . . . , is it not now high time for the whole state either to labour to heal the breach, or if necessary, when there is no other remedy, to stand up as one man to defend themselves and their country until the faction shall be utterly cashiered, and so the king reform himself and renew the convenant and conditions of the kingdom to the good and just satisfaction of the people?[70]

Wallington would doubtless have preferred a healing of the breach—he was scarcely a bloodthirsty fanatic—but it is clear that, given the continued machinations of "the Faction," he was prepared to see (and in fact anticipated) a general rising by the people "as one man" to defend themselves, their country, and in particular the true Church and the children of God.

The anonymous author must have struck a responsive note in 1640, but it was not a note sounded elsewhere in Wallington's writings. A letter that Thomas Weld wrote in 1633 to his former congregation in Terling, Essex, and that Wallington obtained somehow and copied into his letter book, undoubtedly described a polity and commonwealth Wallington found more congenial. In the New Jerusalem that Weld found on the American shore, "all things are done in the form and pattern shewed in the mount: members provided, church officers elected and ordained, Sacraments administered, scandals prevented, censured, Fast days . . . and all such things by Authority commanded and performed according to the precise rule." Here obviously was the ideal: an order commanded by God, backed by the magistrates who supervised a discipline already adumbrated in the Word and known and accepted by a godly people. "Here . . . our ears are not beaten, nor the air filled with oaths, swearers and ranters, nor our eyes and ears vexed with the unclean conversations of the wicked," for "here the greater part are the better part," and where the godly were in the majority, it was not surprising that "all things be so righteously, so religiously, and impartially carried." In New England, where the greater part was the better part, the majority at least could be assumed to have submitted voluntarily to a discipline recognized as desirable and good; coercion, so long at least as the ideal remained widely shared, would be at a minimum and the power of the state largely invisible. Hence, Weld could blandly assume that all "desire to breathe after perfection and to know what is the rule and to walk in it."[71] Even in old England, where the "better part" were a distinct minority, the 1640's nevertheless brought the defeat of the prelates and papists, but "the precise rule," the godly reformation, eluded Wallington and his friends, and discipline by the powerless Classes proved a broken reed indeed.

The two and a half years from the marching of the king's army to the north to meet the Scots in April 1639 to November 1641 seemed little short of miraculous to Wallington, years in which his soberest fears were falsified and his wildest expectations surpassed. He expected war in 1639, less because Scotland's Prayer Book rebellion inevitably invited English retaliation than because England's sins deserved such a punishment. When the war ended instead in a truce, "not so much as one man slain, as I heard of," Wallington could see in it only a sign of God's "great mercy and long suffering" patience.[72] Proof of God's special mercy lay precisely in the fact that the "adversaries" remained on the offensive, the "enemies of the godly" retained the initiative, yet their every move was frustrated and turned ultimately to unforeseen good. The wicked, fratricidal war against the Scots issued in an unexpected truce. The king returned and summoned a Parliament, "whereof our hearts were glad," but the Short Parliament "did break up presently and nothing was done."[73] Worse, oppression continued, the hated ship money taxation was still collected, Convocation met and drew up the scandalous new canons, and the king gathered a new army, which was marched north to York.

By September 1640 Wallington was drawing up a list of eight acts of the enemies of the godly, ranging from the very blasphemies uttered by the soldiers to prove that they were not "Puritans and Rebels," to the abuse of the Scots. The very fact that the English were spared some dreadful visitation was proof of God's continued "great patience and forbearing."[74] Yet before the year 1640 was out Wallington composed a new catalogue, this time showing the defeat of the wicked and the unlooked-for triumph of "His poor despised servants." For "whereas before ship money was paid, now I hear of none that would pay it"; "whereas before our Bishops were liked," now because of the new canons "they are in great detestation"; "whereas before our soldiers would go against Scotland, now not any that I know of in this land would go." Altar rails, erected the year before, were pulled down everywhere "by the rude soldiers and common people." Most importantly, although God had seemed deaf to the pleas of the godly when the Short Parliament was dismissed in May, now He was again listening to "His children," and a new Parliament was summoned in November. What else could one see in such a series of reverses but the "hand of Providence"?[75]

In the months that followed the assembling of the Long Parliament Wallington repeatedly saw the hand of Providence. On February 2, 1640/41, he noted the passage of the Triennial Act, "which was great joy to the Church of God." On May 1 he learned that the king had decided that the Earl of Strafford should not die, although proved a traitor, "which . . . did strike us all in a damp," but on May 12 Strafford, "this great Goliath," was executed "to the joy of the Church of God."[76] Finally, on July 5, Wallington copied an account of the abolition of Star Chamber and the High Commission and saw in the event "a very great mercy," for "these two terrible courts" had "undone so many thousands (and many of them God's children) . . . even till the time they were put down."[77] However, the destruction of these courts was chiefly important because it seemed to Wallington to usher in the first of a series of direct attacks on those "cunning Achitophels," the prelates, who were "the original cause of all the divisions and schisms in the church." When he noted the introduction of a bill against pluralities the following March, he commented that "thus the Lord doth consume our enemies (the bishops) and take away their horns, their strength and power by degrees." However, when the Root and Branch Bill was introduced for the utter overthrow of episcopacy, he was no longer sure that God "would not destroy the Canaanites . . . but by little and little." Although admitting that the bill had not yet passed the House of Lords, Wallington exulted that he that "hath an eye of faith may see . . . that Babylon is fallen, is fallen."[78] But if indeed Babylon had fallen, why did Israel wear such a troubled face?

On December 13, 1641, an old Nottingham friend, Francis Wilsmore, wrote to Wallington to discover "how it goeth with God's people, and how the Parliament proceeds."[79] What Wallington replied is unknown, but what he thought is evident from his journal. For Wallington that hopeful year had ended on a sour note, "for now the Lord hath suddenly turned our joy and cheerfulness into mourning and lamentation." There were four grounds for his pessimism: first,

Parliament had sat during the king's absence in Scotland and had heard many complaints against scandalous ministers, "but nothing [was] done to any purpose"; second, "many that were against bishops now began to . . . speak for bishops"; third, the news from Ireland was of successful rebellion and of the cruel and barbarous murder of the people of God; and finally, "on December the 23rd the Lieutenant of the Tower that was so just and faithful was put out and the next day that wicked, bloody Colonel Lunsford was put in."[80] Why the Lord should have apparently deserted His people at this juncture was not yet clear, but it is evident that Wallington was describing a revolution that had lost its momentum and that was about to give way to a counterrevolution.

During the winter and spring that followed, Wallington regained his certainty about the direction and meaning of events, but the rapturous optimism with which he had greeted the Root and Branch Bill—"Babylon is fallen, is fallen"—was not to return. However, he was soon reassured that God had not deserted His children. The king's horrendous blunder on January 4, first in attempting to arrest the five opposition leaders on the very floor of the House of Commons, and then in failing to make good their capture, was seen not as a singular act of political stupidity but, predictably, as a "great mercy of God . . . never to be forgotten to the world's end." The assurance that God was again prepared to deliver His servants was important, for in the terror that gripped London in the weeks that followed, "had not the Lord of his mercy stirred us up to bestir ourselves, it would have gone hard enough with us."[81]

However, more important than reassurance was understanding, and before the winter of 1641–42 was over Wallington understood two things—the significance of Ireland and the role of the king— that were to prepare him psychologically for war long before the king raised his standard at Nottingham on August 22. From the outset Wallington had claimed that all England's troubles were fundamentally owing to the prelates and papists, but whereas it was easy to point to the sins of the Laudian prelates in suppressing the godly and in introducing papistical innovations, in causing the war with Scotland and in promulgating the hypocritical canons, the role of the papists had remained more problematic. However, the Irish Rebellion made all clear. Noting that Sir Thomas Wentworth, the future Earl of Strafford, had disarmed the Protestant settlers, and that the Irish Catholics had stockpiled powder and shot and plotted to surprise Dublin Castle itself, he cited the "common" proverb: "He that will England win / Must first with Ireland begin." The point of the Irish Rebellion was not to free that troubled land of English rule—Wallington never entertained that supposition for a moment. Rather "all these plots in Ireland are but one plot against England," and in England the Irish and English Catholics had but one purpose: "to bring their damnable superstition and idolatry amongst us." The Irish Rebellion was a revelation for Wallington. From the Spanish Armada in 1588 and the Gunpowder Plot in 1604 to the Book of Canons and the Irish Rebellion, all of recent English history demonstrated irrefutably "how Antichrist, even those bloody-hearted Papists, doth plot against the poor Church of God."[82]

What seemed most pitiful to Wallington, "that it should make your heart bleed," was the failure of the English to rescue their coreligionists from the "tyrannical power" of the Irish papists. Worse, "we wicked hardhearted wretches . . . are so far from sending . . . help that those we do send rather take the rebels' part against them." Wallington knew what doom awaited such hardhearted folk. It was the curse on Meroz (Judges 5:23) "because they came not out to help the Lord, to help the Lord against the mighty." War was inevitable, and, although the English Protestants would ultimately triumph, their victory, or rather God's victory, would only come after "great troubles. . . . For the sins of the Amorites is not yet full, that the blood of all the prophets shed from the foundation of the world might be required of this generation, from the blood of Abel unto the blood of Zacharias which was slain between the altar and the Temple; verily I say unto you, it shall be required of this generation. Luke 11: 50–51."[83]

Wallington's assumption that all of politics could be reduced to a plot long in hatching by prelates and papists to overthrow true Protestantism, first in Ireland and then in England itself, may seem simpleminded indeed, but there was much material at hand to reinforce it. Among the many documents that he copied during the early weeks of 1642 was a letter, purportedly true, written to a Londoner urging him to "withdraw, lest you suffer among the Puritans." More ominously, it was this letter that contained the statement already cited (in n.69) that although "the king's heart is a Protestant, . . . our friends can persuade him and make him believe anything; he hates the Puritan party and is made irreconcilable to that side."[84] For the first time in these weeks the king appeared as an actor who rejected

the militia bill and associated increasingly with those whom Wallington now labeled as "papists and malignants," with those prepared
to say that "the world will never be good till there be some blood of
Puritans shed."[85] On July 20 Wallington noted that a letter from York
told of "divers commanders out of Ireland who left their employment against the rebels to come against us," and who "produce C. R.
for their warrant." The king was, in fact, preparing to wage "war
against his liege people and best subjects." Even before the first blow
was struck, Wallington was certain that the king was the aggressor,
and although the king's actions increasingly carried new and dire
implications, Wallington did not view the coming war with any enthusiasm: "it is a sad business; the Lord of his mercy help us."[86]

As late as June 1643 Wallington could still pray that "the Lord
would change the heart of the king and . . . bless the Parliament,
knitting hearts together and giving them wisdom, encouragement,
and zeal for the cause of God," but he no longer really expected any
change of heart on the part of the king.[87] Wallington tended to see
politics in stark black-and-white terms, not because he was simpleminded but because he saw politics fundamentally in moral terms,
as a struggle between good and evil, ultimately between Christ and
Antichrist. By the summer of 1642 he was convinced that "the spirit
of Antichrist . . . marcheth furiously," and among the evil incarna-
tions of this malign force were papists and malignants and increasingly the king himself.[88] Wallington never took an explicitly antimo-
narchical position; he never, for example, identified the king as the
little horn of the beast in Revelation. However, it seemed increasingly evident that the cause of the king and the cause of Antichrist
were the same; the king was clearly guilty by association. As Wallington wrote late in the summer of 1642 in a letter to Abraham Colfe,
the pluralist absentee rector of St. Leonard's Eastcheap, "the lordly
Bishops . . . be the very limbs of Antichrist, and they have been the
cause . . . of all those miseries and troubles in Church and commonwealth."[89] And who were these proud prelates but appointees, creatures, and supporters of the king? A month later Wallington recorded what purported to be the Catholic Lord Paulet's "cruel
speech to his soldiers at Sherborne," in which that peer of the realm
was supposed to have advised his troops to "give no quarter to none
that wears the sword . . . ; deafen your ears and harden your hearts
against all cries and prayers for mercy. But if you meet with any of
their clergy, reserve them for more exquisite torments. . . . I intend

to have them flayed alive. . . . " Finally, "when you come to the Puritanical towns—Taunton, Crewkerne, Bristol, Dorchester, and Exeter—then let your swords cruel it without differences of age, sex, or degree."[90] Such propaganda was the more readily believed because soon backed by atrocity stories that claimed to be actual accounts of the behavior of royalist troops, and because nothing better could be looked for from the army of Antichrist.

From August 1642 on, Wallington's journal is filled with accounts of "pillaging and plundering," of "Marlborough's miseries," of "Prince Robber's [so he referred to Prince Rupert] plundering of Wendover."[91] Sandwiched between a copy of a letter of June 5, 1643, describing the "cruelty used to prisoners at Oxford" (the royalists' capital) and an account of the "most savage cruelties at Bradford and Leeds," dated July 1643, is a section labeled "cruelties in Ireland," at the end of which Wallington inserted an account of the killing of his brother-in-law, Zachariah Rampaigne, in October 1641. The juxtapositions in Wallington's manuscript at this point are revealing. The editor of the published version has sensibly moved the account of Zachariah's death to where it belongs chronologically, just as she has moved the brief account of King Charles's execution to the end of volume two. However, in the manuscript Wallington places the description of Zachariah's murder by Brian Maguire's forces in the midst of the grim news of 1643, presumably when the news finally reached him, and he concludes with an account of Zachariah's last words to his wife. After assuring her that it is better to fear God than man, he is then reported to have said,

> as for the rebels, God will raise an army in His time to root them out, that
> although for a time they may prevail, yet at last God will find out men
> enough to destroy them. And as for the king, if it be true, as these rebels
> say, that they have his commission . . . to kill . . . all the Protestants
> . . . , if it be so, then surely the Lord will not suffer the king nor his
> posterity to reign, but the Lord at last will require our blood at their
> hands. . . .

Wallington concludes the account by noting that "it was not long after . . . that one of those men that had a hand in killing my brother . . . was killed, and I make no question but the rest are, or will be, in God's time." At the bottom of the page Wallington later drew a pointing finger, followed by the terse statement: "January the 30, 1649, at about two o'clock was King Charles beheaded on a scaffold at Whitehall."[92] Six years earlier Wallington had accepted the inevitability of the king's death. If one looks for an explanation for why Wallington, the moderate Puritan and Presbyterian disciplinarian, did not, like so many Londoners, become a Royalist in the later 1640's, the answer may well be found in the juxtapositions on this page. The ally of Antichrist, the man of blood, could never again command Wallington's allegiance.

By mid-1643 Wallington had come to understand the ultimate fate of the king, but what was to become of the kingdom and the children of God was less and less evident. The actual politics of these years— the endless and fruitless negotiations with the king and the conflicts in Parliament among the various groups and factions—held little interest for him. Nor did he include any excerpts from the Leveller tracts that began to appear at London booksellers long before he broke off his journal in mid-1646. Instead, Wallington copied account after account of obscure military skirmishes, of the latest atrocity committed by "Prince Robber," stirring and sifting through these accounts like tea leaves, searching for evidence of the hidden will of God. The reader of the journal—a journal that was, after all, written deliberately so that posterity might understand God's dealings with His children—would never suspect that by 1645 Parliament's armies were clearly ascendant and that the long First Civil War was almost at an end. On the penultimate page of the journal, Wallington wrote that on "April the 8, 1646, we received a letter from Rutland of most barbarous, bloody, cruel exploits," but this time the doers of these bloody deeds "were our own soldiers." Wallington concluded by asking: "if this be not punished to the full, can England ever look for a blessing, or that God should ever end her troubles? Hereafter, it is like, you may see the tragedy at large." On the next page he recorded that "we had intelligence of two most cruel and barbarous acts of the enemy"; with their recording, the journal breaks off.[93] Clearly Wallington had no stomach for unrelieved tragedy, undoubtedly because it signaled the end of any real hope for the joint fate of England and God's children.

Despite the grim military picture in 1643, Wallington had still been able to find some slim grounds for hope. Two years later, despite Parliamentary victories in the field, Wallington could only observe that "yet God's wrath is not turned away."[94] In mid-July of 1643 Wallington rather perversely found a basis for optimism precisely in the repeated Parliamentary defeats. As he explained to his wife, he was convinced that, despite appearances, God was "preparing us for deliverance." Had we not, he said, "at first hope and trust in the Earl of Essex with his great army?" And note "how little hath he done." Similarly at one time trust had been in "worthy Lord Brooke," in "Captain Lesly" [Leslie], the Scottish general, in Lord Fairfax, in Sir John Hotham, and in Sir William Waller, "and now the Lord hath turned all our joy to heaviness, and yet all for the best." All for the best, because, having run out of generals, in whom could the godly now place their trust but God himself?[95] At the end of July Wallington heard news of the surrender of Bristol, and at this point even his own previous rationalization failed to give satisfaction. As he recorded in his diary, the "great loss so discontented me that I could not settle about anything, nay, I could neither write, read, nor pray."[96]

Nevertheless, two weeks later when it was rumored that the fall of Bristol would be followed by the Royalists' capture of London itself, Wallington found new cause for optimism. As he well knew, "in a time of destructions, God hath and doth promise to leave a remnant," and although he quickly admitted that not "all God's people shall be spared," he did find comfort in the thought that "the Lord will leave a little number of them."[97] As he knew and had heard in a sermon preached at a fast day held at St. Mary's Abchurch in early August, the real problem was that the pride of Londoners provoked God. Even the godly had failed. "The enemy was but God's axe to hew his people," an instrument not of destruction but of correction. "Let there be a thorough reformation and then as soon as ever God hath done all his work on Mt. Zion, Oh! then woe to these rebels!"[98] What was needed, then, was some means to hold the children of God to the discipline they knew was commanded and to force by that means the long overdue reformation. The obvious mechanism was a covenant, for "a right covenant" was not only "a means of reformation" but also "a means of quenching the fire of the Lord's wrath." After the fall of Bristol that fire was very hot and near. On October 1, Wallington wrote that he "took the Covenant at our church before God and the congregation with the rest of the people of God."[99]

If two years later Wallington felt defeated, despite the coming of Parliamentary victories, it was because the promises the godly made in the Covenant had not been kept, or at least not kept by one of the contracting parties. For surely God had kept His part of the bargain:

"his little grace, the Bishop of Canterbury, that great enemy of God and his people," had been executed on January 15, 1645, and much of the "trash and rubbish" in the Church had been swept away, "giving us His ordinances in a more sweet, pure, and powerful manner than ever our fathers knew." If God's wrath had not been turned aside, it was conspicuously because the people of God had broken their covenant, "for besides our sinful and wicked armies," besides "London's pride, security, hypocrisy," the worst betrayal was in the divisions among the godly themselves, "so that we are ready to destroy one another."[100] Within a month of taking the Covenant Wallington wrote to Henry Roborough, seeking his advice about "some differences of judgment about church government," and noting that while he was prepared to await the judgment of the godly Assembly of Divines, there were others "whom I reverence" who "were going about settling a church by themselves."[101] By 1645 the differences had led to an open breach in the Westminster Assembly itself, and by 1646, when Wallington was elected a ruling elder, not only were the gathered churches outside the Classical system, but the New Model Army had become the guarantor of the safety of the Independents and the sects alike, and there was no hope of healing the widening breaches among the children of God.

Wallington was always of two minds about the New Model Army. Not that he ever disavowed "our Army," any more than he did the Independent preachers whom the army protected, but after the Presbyterian revolt in London brought troops within the City, then "there was a change of government, for many honest men was put out of . . . the Common Council." The problem was not so much that good men were replaced by evil either in London or, after Pride's Purge, in Parliament, but rather that these purges brought in "a loose liberty," a toleration that permitted "a flood of errors and schisms" to break forth. After witnessing the emergence of Baptists and Ranters, True Levellers, Fifth Monarchy Men, and Quakers, Wallington was prepared to see the Cromwellian "liberty of conscience" as a source of "national sin." As Wallington saw it, the curse of religious toleration lay not merely in the spread of error, but more seriously in the endless jarring of theological controversy. The result was much "brain knowledge" and a readiness "to discourse, but little or nothing of holiness of life."[102]

Yet for all Wallington's great disappointments, he never abandoned his religious leadings. He continued to believe, like Cromwell, that the godly must be one in affections, if differing in judgments, and although he willingly accepted the duties of a Presbyterian ruling elder, he did not see this as incompatible with profiting from the godly preaching of the local Independents. Goodwin, Peter, Caryl, and other Independents appear as often in his notes on sermons as Ash, Roborough, Cross, and the other City Presbyterians.[103] Wallington hewed to his own line in secular politics as well. In a letter he addressed to his old friend James Cole, who had gone to New England more than a decade before, Wallington wrote of the victories of the Parliamentary armies at Marston Moor and Naseby as "our victories": "there was God seen."[104] Despite his conviction that the Scots were "God's people," and despite his loyalty to the Covenant signed in 1643, which had cemented the political and military alliance with the Scots that Pym had forged before his death, Wallington was not a blind partisan of the Scottish Presbyterians. When the Scots allied with the Royalists in 1648 and precipitated the Second Civil War, Wallington saw them as hypocrites and their claim that they fought to maintain the Covenant and godly reformation as a "pretense." Of Cromwell's victory over Hamilton's Scottish forces at Preston, Wallington wrote, "Oh, how did God scatter them and give us a great victory over them with a small number."[105]

A victory over an invading army was a great mercy of God, but a war of "Brethren . . . against Brethren" could only be seen as a disaster. For Wallington, writing in the midst of the second war against Presbyterian Scotland and less than a fortnight before Dunbar, the great blasphemy was not that Cromwell had again come to blows with the Scots, but that "the prayers of God's people go cross against one another." He had heard that the Scots on their fast days prayed that "God would destroy this army of Sectaries (as I believe some doth the like here with us)," while in England the "Independents . . . pray that God would bless our army . . . to destroy all the enemies that rise up against them." Convinced that "there be of God's dear children both in Scotland as also in our Army," Wallington could only see this war as evidence that God was no longer heeding his prayers and that a fearful "judgment cannot be far off."[106]

Not only was a war of brother against brother wrong, but for Wallington the great struggle between Scottish Presbyterian Royalists and the English sectarian army was diversionary as well. Eight months earlier, on January 4, 1649/50, the House of Commons had published the Engagement and had ordered all adult males to take it in support of the newly constituted Rump Republic. That very day a powder magazine in Tower Street had exploded, killing several people and destroying the surrounding houses and church, "an emblem of the great day of Judgment." Wallington learned from a friend that the Commons' Declaration, announcing the Engagement, had been "torn all to pieces" by the explosion, whereas the old Covenant, affixed to a pillar since 1643, remained undamaged. Needless to say, Wallington saw a lesson in this "great and wonderful judgment," but it was not the obvious one that a regime that had executed the king and defeated the English and Scottish Presbyterian Royalists had earned God's wrath. The Engagement was a minor peccadillo; the real sin was "that we do not keep our Covenant." And for Wallington the Covenant meant principally two things: respect for the spiritual leadership of "the ministers of Jesus Christ," and the imposition of a rigorous moral discipline. Along with the Covenant, the parish whip for drunkards had survived the terrible explosion, and Wallington saw in this a warning "that if we will not execute justice on drunkards, then He will do it himself."[107]

There is no evidence that Wallington ever believed in *jure divino* Presbyterianism, but he did believe in parish discipline. That is what he thought the Covenant was all about. His objection to the gathered churches of the Independents and the sects was precisely that such bodies of Saints abandoned the task of disciplining their sinful neighbors; it was precisely to take on that necessary responsibility that Wallington had become a ruling elder in 1646. God had spared His English Israelites for a special purpose. "If we sin, we sin under special mercies. . . . We are under a special Covenant. We should show our Reformation." So Wallington had written in summary of a sermon heard on Christmas Eve in 1643.[108] Wallington found the Commonwealth and later the Cromwellian Protectorate wanting, not because they were enemies of the Presbyterians, but because they were godly regimes that nevertheless failed to bring the long-looked-for reformation. In a series of fires that devastated London in late 1654 and early 1655 Wallington saw a series of judgments on a City that provoked God by its toleration of "many strange, false forms of worship," by "Sabbath profanation," by "our cruel oppression of the poor," by "our impudent pride," and by the "contempt of ministry." It was a comprehensive indictment; it was also one Wallington had made many times before. The "rebellious City" had failed in carrying out the First Table duties, symbolized by the profanation of the Sabbath; it had failed in its Second Table duties, symbolized by the oppression of the poor. In its contempt of God's ministers, Wallington saw evidence of a City that had ceased to listen to its prophets and that was therefore bound to have lost its way. Wallington's solution to the universal failure he saw around him was not to petition the Lord Protector or even the London Common Council; that had never been Wallington's way, for these were merely instruments in the hands of Providence. Instead, Wallington advised a return to fundamentals: "First, beg of God that he would sprinkle this sinful land . . . with the blood of Christ. . . . Secondly, pour upon these flames the tears of repentance."[109]

There is something strangely modern in the picture of Wallington hurrying out to buy the latest news sheet and diurnal, constantly aware of the great events of his time but participating in them only vicariously through the media. Puritanism is supposed to have created active citizens out of passive subjects and to have welded these citizens into factions and parties for common action based on a common ideology and goals. However much Wallington was aware of belonging to the children of God, his actions nevertheless seemed limited to secreting himself in his study where, surrounded by his latest collection of pamphlets, he copied out the "principal heads" of the most recent news into one or another of his journals. His apprentice was marched off to the wars; his friend Francis Wilsmore was shot to death at Nottingham in 1643; but Wallington remained throughout the apparently passive observer and recorder of other men's actions.[110]

So much is obvious, yet Wallington would not have recognized such a portrait, for in his own eyes he was vitally engaged and involved in the actions he recorded. When he came to analyze the lessons to be learned from the many plots against God's people brought to light in the summer and autumn of 1642, he concluded that "we should labor . . . to come under Christ's sweet and victorious government, for though we shall have much opposition, yet if we strive, he will help us." It is laboring and striving that are rewarded; God helps those who help themselves.[111] However, such a catchphrase does not convey the full content of Wallington's conviction. For all that he was prepared to discover evidence of God's direct providential intervention in human history, particularly in the heady days of the early 1640's, such divine intervention was in no way incompatible with human agency or responsibility. As a general principle, Wallington knew that "the wicked always hate the godly and plot against them"; such malignancy was a manifestation of Antichrist in the world and had been part of human history since Cain's plot against his brother Abel. That God's "poor despised children" escaped at times "from these hellish and devilish plots and designs" could only be viewed as the consequence of "God's great and wonderful mercies." Nevertheless, what had made the early 1640's such a hopeful time was the discovery and defeat of these "devilish designs" owing to the "vigilancy of those who were well affected."[112] In fact, for Wallington it was evident not only that God and Antichrist carried out their perpetual conflict by means of human agency, but that the godly and well affected had a special obligation to act, and this was never more true than in the apocalyptic struggle of the early 1640's when, Wallington noted, "We are under a special Covenant. We should show our Reformation."[113]

If "the blessed Reformation both of Church and Commonwealth" was something the covenanted had not only "long hoped" but also "labored for," it is nevertheless not entirely evident in what sense Wallington, scribbling away in his study, was a laborer in that vineyard.[114] Part of the answer presumably lies in the fact that Wallington did labor long and hard to erect that godly discipline which the reformation of Church and State was intended to bring about. Wallington always hoped that others more able than he would act in his stead, but in the absence of such action this shy and awkward man faced his responsibilities and acted as best he could. In 1654, in an incident whose comic possibilities Wallington blessedly failed to perceive, that worthy launched a one-man campaign against the sin of long hair. Having often in prayer "desired that God would stir up some to speak against this sin of pride," Wallington finally took it upon himself to do so, bought a number of copies of a tract titled *The Loathsomeness of Long Hair*, appended to each an epistle of his own composition, and began to distribute them, "first in shewing and speaking to ministers whom it chiefly concerns, and so to professors." On September 25 he presented a copy to his neighbor Colonel Player, then Chamberlain of London, "desiring him to do what lies in his power to suppress this sin of long hair in youth and apprentices." He then proposed to present his book and read his epistle at the next meeting of the provincial synod at Sion College, and although that meeting turned out to be thinly attended and nothing came of his initiative, Wallington had the consolation of knowing that he had "done my duty."[115]

Wallington may have regretted that the classical system lacked disciplinary teeth, that its participants could do little more than investigate, expose, and exhort. For people of the Word, that little was, nevertheless, not to be despised. As Wallington noted in a letter to Abraham Colfe, the incumbent at Lewisham and the absentee rector of St. Leonard's, "surely, Sir, I am persuaded, if you had privately and publicly told your people plainly of their wicked ways, as here the Lord commands you (you having so long lived at Lewisham, as you have done), then surely there would not have been so many ignorant, drunken swearers, mockers, and profaners of the Lord's day at Lewisham as now there be."[116] It was precisely this capacity to preach and teach, to exhort and admonish—to use their rhetorical skills, in short, in behalf of their prophetic function—that justified the clergy's leadership role among the godly in Wallington's eyes. However, had Wallington felt any need for self-justification, he would not have limited his defense to pointing to his active participation in the Fourth London Classis.

The particular form that the activism of the well affected took was defined and limited by talent, opportunity, and vocation. Wallington's apprentice marched off to fight in defense of Parliament; Wallington, already in his mid-forties, stayed behind to labor at his lathe. Nevertheless, all the godly united in one essential activity, that of prayer. Prayer was the activity that undergirded all else. It was prayer, that gift of God, that "stirred us up to bestir ourselves," and without that divine mercy "it would have gone hard enough with us" in the aftermath of the abortive attempt by the king to arrest the five members on the floor of the House of Commons early in 1642.[117] Prayer in the dark days of 1629 after "Parliament . . . broke up and no good thing is done" became the means by which commitment to the godly cause could be renewed: "therefore, I do promise by thy assistance, Oh Lord, to be more watchful over my ways and diligent in good things and to double my service unto thee, and to spend one hour in reading and prayer in the morning and one hour in the evening. . . ."[118] Prayers in 1639 prevented the first Bishops' War from leading to the anticipated bloodshed.[119] Prayer in the fateful days of 1643 became a way of articulating the hoped-for politics of the godly party: Wallington prayed "that the Lord would change the heart of the king and . . . bless the Parliament, knitting hearts together and giving them wisdom, encouragement, and zeal for the cause of God;" he also prayed "that God will remember desolate Germany and almost lost Ireland," that "our navy at sea . . . God would prosper, . . . our armies . . . that fight His battles, . . . God would give them joyful victories," and "that God would purge his Church of all things that displease him."[120] Prayer led to the defeat of the bills to abolish tithes in 1653, which "under pretense of religion would destroy all religion by putting down both ministers and ministry and so rob us of the gospel of Jesus Christ."[121] Because he had failed to enter the livery of his company, Wallington lacked the vote, but he was equally certain he could influence an election by prayer, and so on July 13, 1654, "when others were at the Guildhall holding up hands for choice of Parliament men, I would be in my closet holding up my hands to the God of heaven for such choice who were men according to God's hands."[122] And who could doubt the potency of such prayers, for "God never said to the house of Israel, seek ye my face in vain."[123]

Prayer was in fact the most basic activity of the godly, for it was fundamental to a right relationship to God. Prayers of humiliation acknowledged both the sinful condition even of the children of God and their utter dependence on the Divine Father. Prayers of thanksgiving acknowledged that "God of His mercy kept us, that it was not so bad as we feared. His name have all the praise!"[124] The source of victory must be acknowledged in prayer; but even defeat, so Wallington suspected, was intended as a spur to prayer, for, "although for a time the Lord may suffer his enemies to have the upper hand of his dear children . . . , for some reasons best known to himself," such defeats should lead "his people to fly to him in holy prayer." Indeed, "God many times brings his people into great troubles . . . so that He might have the more honor and praise in their deliverance."[125] Scripture gave access to the divine Will and Word; prayer gave access to the living God, "for prayer is a key that will open any lock, a medicine that will heal any wound, a weapon that will prevail in any place."[126]

Hence, human action properly began and ended in prayer, and the efficacy of such activity was, to Wallington, beyond question. At the end of 1639 and 1640, those "praying years," Wallington asked his readers to "take notice how God hath accepted of the poor endeavors of His poor despised servants, and hath accepted of their humiliation, and granted their prayers in many particulars." There followed a precise catalogue of what Wallington believed prayer had accomplished: whereas before the king refused petitions and a Parliament, now he had granted both; whereas before ship money had been paid, now there was a universal refusal; whereas before the bishops were respected, now they were held in great detestation; and so on and on through "fifthlys" and "sixthlys," to "ninthly, Oh how hath God of His great mercy heard my prayers with many more of His children that there is as many excellent and worthy good men chose again that we trust will stand for the cause of God and His children."[127] Prayer was the link that connected human action and the divine, indeed linked the two so closely that Wallington in his use of causal language frequently wrote of the actions of God and the godly interchangeably. Hence, he wrote in one letter that "on the Parliament side, our God hath done very much," and in another that "by prayer we have obtained a bloody war to cease; by prayer we have a Parliament; . . . by prayer we have got the overthrow of God's and our enemies, as the Deputy of Ireland."[128] Prayer was for Wallington the ultimate political act, for though it referred all to God, it specified temporal goals and encouraged the godly to work toward their fulfillment. And though much of the prayer Wallington recorded was uttered in the privacy of his study, his prayer was in a very real sense part of the common prayer of the godly that defined the community of the saints to themselves. Much as the saints were given to self-examination, even private prayer was not really an act of introspection, for it led outward to God and to the life of his children in the world.

In the end Wallington knew that his revolution had failed, that Christ's kingdom had not come. Early on, anticipation of its coming had been a source of confidence, for, as he noted, such an expectation "makes God's children undergo affliction more cheerfully."[129] By 1650 he had witnessed four wars, so he told James Cole: a prelatical war in 1639 and 1640 fought to maintain the wicked government of the bishops; a profane war in the years after 1642, fought by the king's army "to maintain all manner of wickedness and superstition"; a hypocritical war in 1648, "when the Scots did come under pretense of the maintaining of the Covenant and for a Reformation"; and finally in 1650 a war—"I know not how to term it"—that pitted God's people in Scotland against God's people in England. The enemies of the godly could not ultimately triumph; the godly could only defeat themselves. Wallington prayed "to God that the Lord would think upon his own children, which side soever they be," but such a fratricidal war could have no good end.[130] Wallington's letter to Cole on August 22, 1650, was the last recorded in his letter book; he evidently had no heart to write again.

Yet even in defeat there could be no surrender. When in 1655 Wallington analyzed the significance of a series of frightening fires that devastated London, he concluded, not unexpectedly, that they were to be seen as a divine visitation, a warning against London's continued sinning. The very familiarity of Wallington's dreary catalogue measures out the dimensions of the failure of his revolution. For, as usual, Wallington's fellow Londoners had provoked God by their "unthankfulness," and by their "distrust of the power, Providence, and promises of God," by Sabbath-breaking and oppression of the poor, by "impudent pride" and the "contempt of ministry." Nevertheless, the saint could not allow himself to despair. Rather, it was time once again to seek Christ's forgiveness and redemption by a public acknowledgment of London's manifest rebelliousness.[131] In short, it was time to turn again to prayer, for as Wallington had noted in other times of trouble, "Prayer getteth any of God's blessings, and thankfulness keepeth them."[132] And who was he to doubt that ultimately all was intended for the good of God's children, that there were "divers and weighty reasons" for their apparent reverses? The chief of these reasons was, of course, the sins of the godly, yet finally in His own good time God would turn "all the boasting of the adversaries of His people into a lie, and turneth also His people's case so that they hold up their heads in despite of their enemies, and that their woe is turned into joy, and their grief confounded, God glorified, and His people comforted."[133] Given such beliefs, despair was impossible; for defeat was no more than a temporary setback, a fatherly act of correction. The godly were perhaps better equipped to live with their failures than to exploit their victories, for failures taught a lesson whereas victories were a gratuitous act of a gracious God.

Nevertheless, by the mid-1650's, when Wallington's writings break off, the future seemed shrouded in darkness, for the godly had lost their way. The "hypocritical" war in 1648 had been followed by the fratricidal war against the Scots in 1650 and, in 1653, by a "war against our neighbor nation Holland." As he noted rather petulantly, "these wars I cannot find any warrant for them." England had lost its way in 1647 and 1648 and, as a result of "these seven years' windings and overturnings . . . , now God walks in the dark and His ways are hid from our eyes."[134] Much had been accomplished by the prayers of God's people, but there was much evidence that England had ceased to wait for an answer. As Thomas Goodwin had warned, "if God give you an answer, if you mind it not, you let God speak to you in vain. . . . Yea, you will provoke the Lord not to answer at all," and what else was the darkness that obscured the future in 1654 and 1655 but that cosmic silence?[135] Not that England's condition was obscure, for was not England a second Israel, and should not the English pray with Ezra (9:13–14): "Thou having punished us less than we deserve, and given us such a deliverance as this, should we again break thy Commandments, wouldst thou not be angry with us till thou hadst consumed us?" England, like Israel, had become a "backslider," and as all the godly knew,

> A backslider is like lukewarm water, having once been heated, which good men spew out, and evil men regard not; for what use can be made of it? "Like salt that hath lost its savor, it is good for nothing but the dunghill." . . . Such is the condition of those that fall away and repent not: You who have turned unto folly, and are not grown to a despising and despiting God's ways, "Return, Oh Shulamite, return." And you that have peace and communion with God, take heed you do not lose Him; you will never have such a God again.[136]

Nevertheless, the example of Israel was always ultimately a hopeful one, for no matter how often Israel transgressed, the Israelites remained God's Chosen People. History for the Chosen, like the life of the elect, must in the final analysis take the form of a divine comedy and have a happy ending. The lukewarm Protectorate, in which Cromwell, like a village constable, was content to keep peace among the warring saints, obviously could not be that high Jerusalem the saints sought, but in the end Wallington was sure that God was "bringing us through the . . . barren wilderness before He brings us into that pleasant fruitful land of Canaan that our rest might be the sweeter, and that we may see the more His wisdom and power, and He may have all the glory."[137]

Less than two years after Wallington's death the "Good Old Cause" of reformation in Church and Commonwealth lost in the Stuart Restoration what remained of its political reality. Wallington as a type became an anachronism; his godly manner and attitude came to seem the merest hypocrisy. The politics of prayer gave way to the more cynical and mundane politics of interest.[138] It may be that Wallington's politics always had a greater reality in the minds of the godly than in the affairs of men. Nevertheless, while that dream had at least the substance that came of its being widely shared by the members of the godly community, it permitted quite ordinary Englishmen to imagine a radically different world where the whole community would unite in disciplined work and mutual support, where elected leaders who shared their concern for the creation of a godly commonwealth would stand firm for God's cause, and where the whole community would voluntarily and naturally submit to the spiritual guidance of the prophetic and healing ministry of "God's ambassadors and messengers."[139] If it was hard to imagine London without its poor, its idle, its drunkards, and its profaners, the existence of Boston, Massachusetts, "wherein all things are done in the form and pattern shewed in the Mount," suggested that the realization of such an ideal godly commonwealth was not a human impossibility.[140] By any worldly standard Wallington was indeed, as he saw himself, too "weak and unfit . . . for any employment either for Church or Commonwealth." He was, moreover, experienced enough in his faith to recognize that "it is no easy matter to be a true Christian."[141] Yet for a long generation this rather unsuccessful member of a minor London craft guild knew that he was witnessing events of cosmic significance and, despite his self-doubts and manifest imperfections, was called to participate in their fulfillment. It was perhaps the first time in history that ordinary Englishmen were to have such an experience.

Oh God, thou hast taught me from my youth even until now;
therefore will I tell of thy wondrous works, yea even unto mine old
age and grey head. Oh God, forsake me not until I have declared thine
arm unto this generation and thy power to all them that shall come.

7. The Casting Up of Accounts

After the false start in which Wallington thought to give order to
his troubled life by numbering his sins—a process he soon found too
daunting—he set about drawing up New Year's resolutions, those
regulations for a godly life that became the first basis for that process
of self-examination he continued all his days. In the last pages of his
final notebook he recorded that he awoke "near three o'clock" on
December 26, 1654, and thought "how at this time of year many cast
up their estates and look over their books" to see "how far they have
increased in their outward estate." In an analogous fashion Wallington determined to examine his "inward condition, God assisting
me," a process that for the past 34 years had always involved a written record. Thus Wallington did more than continue the metaphor
of the account book when he wrote that he would begin the examination of his "soul's estate" by looking "over some books, even the
book of my conscience [to] see what increase of grace my book of
conscience will show me," for he then went on to fill four closely
written pages with a detailed analysis, not always very flattering, of
what his conscience would say.[1]

The impulse to bring order to chaotic experience by giving it the
objectivity and distance of the written word is historically limited
neither to Puritans nor to the seventeenth century. Thomas Mann,
another compulsive diarist, writing some three hundred years after
Wallington, set out his motives in terms that, for all their modern
idiom and secular tone, would nevertheless have been familiar to

that London turner: "These diary notes, resumed . . . during days of illness brought on by . . . the loss of our accustomed structured life, have been a comfort and support up to now, and I will surely continue them. I love this process by which each passing day is captured, . . . less for the purpose of rereading and remembering than for taking stock, reviewing, maintaining awareness, achieving perspective."[2] The heroic scale of Wallington's compulsion, which led him to fill 50 notebooks between 1618 and 1654, may well be unique, but in other respects it is the very ordinariness of his attitudes and sentiments, his motives and ideals, that make these writings so valuable a record. Other Puritan shopkeepers have left diaries—one thinks of Roger Lowe, the Lancashire Presbyterian—and other Londoners have left memoirs of lives that spanned the revolutionary decades—one thinks of William Kiffin, the Particular Baptist merchant.[3] Kiffin in fact justified writing his memoirs in terms virtually identical to Wallington's: "It was one of the charges which God gave his people of old, that those many great providences which they were made partakers of, might by them be left to their children, to the end that they might, from generation to generation, be the more engaged to cleave unto the Lord."[4] It is to this widespread conviction among that generation of godly Englishmen that even quite ordinary lives contained "remarkable passages" and "wonderful Providences" that we owe the rich horde of surviving diaries and memoirs. At the same time, the perception that one's life should be viewed from God's perspective and "not [be written] out of a vain affection of [one's] own glory," as Bishop Joseph Hall put it, gave these works an objectivity, a sense of standing outside even their authors' most personal and deepest feelings, that separates them from the diaries of a Pepys or a Boswell.[5] And this sense was achieved by describing those feelings in the highly conventionalized terms of the Protestant salvation process.

Such objectivity loses part of what is unique and personally idiosyncratic—neither a quality much admired by the Puritans—but it is not all loss. The advantage of such an objectivity and of a common religious idiom is that, regardless of the particularities of a life, the attitudes toward them can in most cases be taken as typical, as common not simply to godly shopkeepers and artisans but to the godly themselves as a community and culture, almost regardless of station or degree. As a consequence, there is hardly a response of Wallington's that is not echoed elsewhere. Thus, Lady Brilliana Harley, a woman born into Court circles far above Wallington's contact or ken, wrote in 1639 to her son Edward, a student at Oxford, in terms perfectly familiar to the reader of Wallington's works: "My dear Ned, keep always a watch over your precious soul; tie yourself to a daily self-examination; think over the company you have been in, and what your discourse was, and how you found yourself affected, how in the discourse of religion."[6] The discipline of the examined life may have been new when Richard Rogers began his diary back in the 1580's; it had become the veriest commonplace among both lay and clerical Puritans by the 1620's and 1630's.[7] Again, Thomas Scott, a gentleman who was twice M.P. for Canterbury in the 1620's, described the daily routine of family prayer in terms virtually identical to those Wallington used. On a weekday early in 1633 Scott noted that he spent "the evening with my wife, children, and family in hearing prayers." A reading of a passage from Acts preceded supper, and "after supper my wife readeth Doctor Preston his sixth sermon. . . . My daughter-in-law readeth line by line, and she and the rest of my family . . . sing the fifth psalm. After this I go into my chamber, and there serve God, alone, until my bedtime."[8] Again, Wallington's sense that the providential was to be found in the most trivial of everyday incidents was shared by Ralph Josselin, the Essex minister, who on September 5, 1644, recorded in his diary the following story without any sense that in so doing he was making himself ridiculous: "Stung I was by a bee on my nose; I presently plucked out the sting, and laid on honey, so that my face swelled not; thus divine providence reaches to the lowest thing. Let not sin, Oh Lord, that dreadful sting, be able to poison me."[9] Even Wallington's grim recognition of the problematic nature of his own birth under the iron law of original sin—"I, Nehemiah Wallington, had Christian parents. . . . Yet they could not derive grace in my soul, for . . . at five o'clock in the morning was I born in sin and came forth polluted into this wicked world"—was echoed in even more stark terms by Oliver Heywood, the northern divine who wrote in his autobiography:

> But though my parents were godly, yet my birth and my nativity was in sin, and so my conception, for they were instruments to bring me into the world not as saints but as man and woman. . . . Thereby I am by nature a child of wrath, a limb of Satan, exposed to shame and ruin, despoiled of God's image, having Satan's superscription and guilt with propensity to sin . . . incorporated in my primitive constitution.[10]

These examples could be multiplied many times over, for there is little that is original in Wallington's sensibility. Hence, much of the mentality that these writings reveal can be taken as typical, not to say stereotypical, of the Puritan saint of the time.

This should not surprise us. The Puritan saints were as self-conscious and self-disciplined a generation as can well be imagined, and conformity, not originality, was the hallmark of the disciplined life. Their angle of vision, the way they looked at the world and expressed what they saw, was anything but instinctual or idiosyncratic. Their culture was the product not only of deliberate learning but of literacy, and books gave them both a vocabulary and a set of conventions. The Puritans were the first people who could quite properly answer their children's questions with the injunction to "look it up." As Lady Brilliana Harley urged her son Edward, "if it be knowledge of any point, read something that may inform you in what you find you know not."[11] And in very much the same spirit, Wallington, when troubled by his inability to benefit from the Sacrament, went out and bought Daniel Rogers's *A Treatise of the Two Sacraments of the Gospel.*[12] If one is troubled by the sameness of expression and response, by the lack of an individual voice or sensibility, it is undoubtedly attributable not only to literary conventions but also to the fact that these first Puritan generations remained students all their lives, learning by rote and only gradually incorporating their literary understanding into their lives. Hence, surely, the repetitiveness of much of Wallington's reflections, the sense that he constantly needed to relearn the same lessons of patience and hope and assurance; hence, also, the need for constant reinforcement both by reading and by hearing the Word preached. It is no wonder that Robinson Crusoe is a generation away in imagination; a shipwrecked Wallington would have insisted on a library and a godly minister as prerequisites for creating a society capable of glorifying God. By the same token, if much of Wallington's writing now bores by its unremitting iteration, it also at times reaches surprising heights of eloquence, which must surely be owing to the constant practice of hearing and rehearsing sermons and, even more, to the constant reading of the Geneva Bible, whose cadences he made his own.

Imagination was neither a Puritan virtue nor Wallington's long suit, and much of the vividness of his expression was obviously rooted in the Bible rather than in the cultivation of a unique inner vision. Even his dreams tended to be conventional, or at least those he would admit to in writing. Dreams on the whole he dismissed as "lying vanities," part of the realm of subjectivity best ignored or repressed, but on one occasion he recorded a dream for the sake of the obvious lesson taught.

> [O]ne night I dreamed I was dead, and the day of Judgment was come, and I was raised and stood betwixt heaven and hell, but whither I should go I knew not. Heaven I did see was a glorious place, and as it might be to my apprehension a very spacious large room, and there sat in the midst of it our Savior Jesus Christ, [so] very glorious I cannot express it, and round about heaven sat all the saints that ever was. And on the left hand I saw hell, a large deformed place, only a kind of burning there, and the damned spirits facing one another. Then, thought I, Oh whither shall I go, and I thought I had one foot in heaven. One while I did think I should go into heaven, and another while I thought I should not, and Oh! that I would I were on the earth again, I would live better than ever I have done.[13]

On another occasion, when he had been particularly troubled by what he regarded as a dishonest practice forced on him by a determined customer, he dreamed that when he opened his study door to pray, "there was a thing like a man all in black ready to destroy me." On a third occasion he "dreamed a heavenly dream: that as I was in my shop amongst my baskets I was in meditation and conference upon Psalm 125: 'They that trust the Lord shall be as Mount Zion which cannot be moved . . . ,'" a dream so "sweet" that he found it inexpressible. Anyone who dreams so according to a predictable script must either have brought his unconscious well under control or have an imagination so patterned and limited by conscious concerns as to deal only in cultural clichés. Only once did Wallington record a dream that seemed to break the conventional mold. One Sunday morning he dreamed that "Lord Fairfax was to come to my house," and the wonder of that signal honor left Wallington on awakening with the happy thought that "if he were in my shop, what coming and looking there would be on him, saying this is the Lord Fairfax, this is he that won so many battles, and so what an honor it would be to me to have such a person at my house." However, even that piece of transparent wish fulfillment was immediately turned to pious uses: "these thoughts brought to my mind many sweet heavenly meditations [in] which I did much desire of the Lord that he would come to the house of my soul."[14]

Some years ago Joel Hurstfield argued that "all biography is distortion. However historically well founded his work may be, the biographer takes a man out of his context, and in so doing is forced to alter the focus of the age."[15] I have argued that Wallington's writings are important precisely because they are so largely and deliberately composed of "context," of a self-consciously learned language with all its riches of Biblical reference, of a studied set of community-determined norms and attitudes taught by the preachers and made habitual in their godly audiences through constant attendance at their sermons and repeated resort to their tracts and treatises.

Nevertheless, it would be a mistake to define Wallington's Puritanism in terms of the godly preachers. Wallington looked to them all his life for counsel and guidance; they were in an obvious sense the technical experts. Even as an old man Wallington turned to them for help in the conduct of a godly life. On October 16, 1654, he noted that "having sent to my cousin [the Rev. Nathaniel] Church for some practical rules how I may glorify God this little time I have to remain here, he did send them [to] me to my desire, in which this day I did much joy in them, as if I had some great estate given me."[16] For intellectual sustenance Wallington resorted particularly to the godly preachers, but more generally to the Reformed clergy—in his letter book he copied with obvious approval several pious letters of spiritual comfort by "Dr. Joseph Hall" (Wallington never referred to him as a bishop)—but his conception of the community of the saints, the children of God, was narrower than that. The godly shared their theology with Reformed Protestants everywhere, and that fundamental unity was not broken until the rise of Arminianism. However, the known "professors" had begun self-consciously to separate themselves from their "profane" neighbors long before that, to live in the world but be not of it.

Nehemiah Wallington had been conscious of his family's membership in the godly community from his childhood, and it had been his reluctance to hurt his father and his fear of how it would reflect on the children of God that had inhibited his early attempts at suicide. Yet that community had not existed when John Wallington, Sr., came to London in the early 1570's as a young apprentice and, finding no preaching in the parish of St. Andrew's Hubbard, spent the

Sabbath engaged in household chores. Sometime during John Wallington's years as a young master married to the godly Elizabeth Hall, that community, at least in south-central London, had come into being. In the early 1570's there had been only fifteen parishes in London with active lectureships; by the late 1580's, by which time four children had been born into the Wallington household, more than three times that number of parishes had active lectureships.[17] The presence of a preaching ministry was important, but regardless of whether a parish had an active preacher, the new catechisms had come to describe a religion centered not on the fallible parish but on the one social institution the godly could be sure of controlling even in the worst of times: the household itself. Guidebooks for such a household religion were available even before John and Elizabeth Wallington married in November of 1583. To the question of how best to "order and govern thy house in Christian religion," Christopher Shute had provided a ready answer in 1579:

> As Moses commanded the people of Israel, to teach their children the law of the Lord, that in all their affairs they might have an eye to the same; so I am careful that my whole family fear God and know his word by some daily exercise and meditation thereof, so as they may be better able to render a reason of their faith. They pray and give thanks together in all their doings. They make restitution to whom they have done wrong. And finally, whatsoever they do, they will do to the glory of God.[18]

Each household was to have its domestic Moses mediating God's commands to His chosen people, a "pastor over his family," as Robert Cleaver phrased it.[19] For all that the godly made a habit of "gadding" after their faithful preachers—Wallington always seems to have heard more sermons than those preached by Henry Roborough at St. Leonard's—they were not a priest-ridden people. The preachers had their necessary place, and woe betide Israel when Israel ignored its prophets. But at the center of the community was not the priest but the household head. "[Do you] instruct your wife, children, and servants in the true knowledge of God, and pray with them or no?" demands Theologus of the ignorant parent, Asunetus, for the father who fails to do so "is guilty of the Fifth Commandment, which commandeth all duties of superiors toward their inferiors . . . whereof prayer and instructions are a part."[20]

Apparently from the beginning the godly had recognized that Israel could have no traffic with other tribes lest God's chosen be polluted. When Bishop Grindal faced a dissident congregation of Londoners in 1567 and reminded them of St. Paul's saying that "to the clean all things are clean," they had replied that "it cannot be proved that the ceremonies of Antichrist, works of darkness, and the Pope's canon law, may be clean to the true Christian, for the apostle saith, 'there is no fellowship between Christ and Belial, light and darkness.' 2 Corinthians 6:14–15."[21] The consequence of this certainty was not necessarily separatism, the formation of independent congregations outside the ecclesiastical establishment. Wallington never considered such a step, if only because it would have defeated any attempt to bring discipline to the ungodly of the parish by means of the threat to withhold the sacraments from them. Nevertheless, there was a psychological withdrawal from those who did not share the common culture of the godly—an understandable response, perhaps, in those deliberately and self-consciously choosing a different life while yet remaining in the world as artisans, preachers, and magistrates. "While men live here among men, must they not fashion themselves like unto other men?" asks George Gifford in his *Catechism*, and answers "we must consider our high calling and walk worthily of it. We must have no fellowship with the unfruitful works of darkness. . . . We are commanded to separate ourselves and to come out from among the wicked, because there can be no fellowship between light and darkness."[22] The positive side of such a withdrawal was the injunction to love the saints. Wallington saw his affection for the children of God as one of the marks that he was himself God's child. "I love them," he wrote, "as the children of God, bearing God's image upon them . . . ; I love a godly man for his grace that have no other thing to commend him, neither friends nor riches . . ."; finally, "I love and delight in the fellowship and society of the Saints: I love their brotherhood, their company, their conference and Communion with them."[23]

Such a community was doubtless at times somewhat bloodless and abstract, less a group of like-minded friends than an ideological party or a voluntary association dedicated to a cause, and doubtless it was this very fact that led the godly to see in the love of the saints a mark of their identity. Initially it must have disrupted kin relations, although by Nehemiah's generation marriages seem normally to have taken place within the community of the saints so that kinship and community became mutually reinforcing. A generation later the

Quakers were to undergo a similar evolution, initially calling their recruits out of the larger society by convincement and later insisting that all marriages take place within the faith. Puritan distinctiveness was obviously known and recognized both by other Puritans and by their non-Puritan neighbors. Some customers clearly came to Wallington's shop in the knowledge that they were dealing with a Puritan artisan. The implicit assumption that the Puritan shopkeeper was more honest than his neighbor must have had considerable truth to it, for no self-selected minority claiming holiness of life could have afforded to be less than scrupulous in its business dealings. The charge that the saints were hypocrites was already a commonplace by Wallington's childhood, and the only convincing defense was public behavior that was beyond reproach, a realization that doubtless increased both the watchfulness and the paranoia that were such common attributes of the Puritan personality. Wallington certainly recognized that any charge of sharp practice laid at his door would reflect on the community of the saints as a whole.

At the same time it is not at all clear what the boundaries of the community were in practice. When Wallington's children sickened, bills were taken to the churches asking for the prayers of the faithful, but which churches and how they were selected is never made clear. Wallington and his family went to sermons and fast days held elsewhere in the City, but how far he would travel to hear a favorite preacher is not specified. When Wallington was a venerable old man, he was evidently sought after as an adviser by other saints troubled in mind. From Nehemiah's chance remarks it seems evident that most of those who came seeking counsel were women and that their number included gentlewomen, with whom Wallington would not in the ordinary course of things have engaged in social intercourse. The links across parish boundaries and social cleavages may well have been formed by the clergy. John Dane, the Ipswich tailor, tells an anecdote in his memoirs that suggests as much: "After a while that I abode with my father, Mr. Norton, coming to my father's, wished him to put me [out] to Mr. Barenton's. That was a very religious family, [as much so] as ever I came in. And I went thither and was butler; there I kept company with the choicest Christians."[24] John Dane's father lived in Bishop Stortford, Hertfordshire, just across the Essex border; John Norton was a Puritan divine soon off to Massachusetts; "Mr. Barenton" was Sir Thomas Barrington, the Puritan grandee whose seat was at Hatfield Broadoak, some five miles southeast of Stortford. Ministers, whose university degrees gave an imputed gentility, and whose professional friendships gave an acquaintance beyond parish boundaries, were logical figures to provide a communication network within the godly community.[25]

Nevertheless, as members of a conspicuous and vulnerable minority, even quite ordinary folk must have expended considerable energy in maintaining connections that could provide succor in times of need as well as place and patronage year in and year out. Wallington had kin and business connections in Essex and must have known something of the East Anglian godly community. When he sought out his close friend James Cole, the bankrupt who had fled to Ipswich, he promptly dragged him off to counsel with Samuel Ward, the famous godly preacher of that town, who evidently was a figure known at least by reputation to Wallington. Yet neither Wallington nor Cole seemed to have knowledge of the godly in the West Midlands, for when Cole turned up next in Warwick, he wrote to his London friends in some amazement about the godly congregations he found there under the protection of two "great men" (an apparent reference to Lord Brooke and possibly Lord Say); it was under the auspices of those Puritan colonizers that Cole subsequently found himself settling in Hartford, Connecticut.

What makes drawing the boundaries around the communities or establishing the connections linking them particularly problematic by Nehemiah's generation is not simply our lack of knowledge about the details of the lives of these ordinary Englishmen. Rather, their literacy had made such boundaries artificial to a degree. How Nehemiah met his wife Grace is unknown, but it is evident that the Wallingtons in London remained in correspondence with Grace's brothers Livewell Rampaigne, in his Lincolnshire livings, and Zachariah Rampaigne in Ireland. It is obvious that some news of New England reached Nehemiah by way of such public letters as that of Thomas Weld, which were evidently passed from hand to hand within the godly community and copied into letter books. However, Wallington also remained in correspondence with his former neighbor Edward Browne, who left for the Bay Colony in the late 1630's. How Nehemiah Wallington and Francis Wilsmore of Nottingham met is unknown, but they had some business relationship, and Wallington helped one of Wilsmore's sons to obtain a London apprenticeship. Yet it is obvious that a deep friendship existed between these two godly men, a friendship nurtured by correspondence only rarely supplemented by the occasional visit Wilsmore paid to the metropolis. Their literacy was in all probability the key that had freed these godly laymen from clerical dependence, as it did to a degree from patronage or kinship connections, much as these latter continued to be exploited in time of need.

Literacy must also have been a key element in Wallington's surprising view of politics. In a country where politics was still largely defined in terms of the relations of congeries of local aristocratic connections to one another and to the Crown, Wallington's view seems a distinct oddity. Wallington was largely an observer, but the politics he observed (and in fact followed with increasing attention as the revolution approached) was not limited to his neighborhood or shire community. Just as the modern citizen of the West is taught to see the world through the ideological lens of Free World and Communist, so Wallington had learned to see politics in terms of a Europewide struggle between the forces of Christ and Antichrist, a battle whose fate was determined as much by the fall of La Rochelle or by the appearance of the Swedish Lion on the plains of Pomerania as by events in London or Westminster. Furthermore, Wallington's passivity was in part deceptive. The English revolution was not in intention a social revolution, however much it may have had revolutionary social consequences. Further, Wallington did not belong to the revolutionary "left" of Levellers and Baptists. Since he was a citizen but not of the livery, he could not in any case cast a vote; instead, he prayed during City elections for the success of the godly. However, he did take the Covenant with alacrity. By the time war broke out he was in his mid-forties and too old to fight, but he sent his apprentice off in the London draft to Essex's army with as much enthusiasm as a humane and timorous man could summon.[26]

More importantly, Wallington was part of that minority that wished for revolution, and even in monarchical states public opinion counts for something. Even if it was Cromwell's Ironsides rather than Nehemiah's prayers that determined the outcome of the war, no civil war against constituted authority can succeed without the delegitimation of that authority and the backing of at least a minority of the country. For Wallington, the king lost his right to rule when it was discovered that Catholics claimed his warrant for the rebellion in Ireland and that he was behind the machinations of the "malignant" party in England. The revolution that ensued was not, as is so often the case, the one Wallington and his godly friends had prayed for in the early 1640's. Some of the consequences were all that could be wished: prelacy vanished, the Arminian clergy lost their pulpits, and the parish churches were purged of the last of those popish remnants that had troubled the godly since the Elizabethan Settlement. However, Wallington looked in vain in the religious chaos of the Protectoral toleration for that reformation of manners—an end to public blasphemy, drunkenness, sexual laxity, and the oppression of the poor—that had always been the social aim of mainstream Puritanism, and to which he devoted much of the last ten years of his life in his participation as one of the ruling elders for St. Leonard's in the Fourth London Classis. What seemed tragic to Wallington and almost past understanding was why the moral reformation already accomplished in Boston, Massachusetts—where the better part were the greater part—was not possible in London after the overthrow of Archbishop Laud and King Charles.

However, it would be wrong to infer from the fact that Wallington's revolution died virtually at birth that this very ordinary Englishman failed to understand the nature of the revolution he had long wished and prayed for. It is obvious that he had backed the First Civil War and Covenant with enthusiasm, and had done so because he thought they would bring that revolution about. To deny these Puritans their revolutionary impulse; to mistake their lack of class animus for political timidity; to suppose that as a consequence Puritanism was a conservative force, reacting merely to the triumph of aggressive Arminian prelacy in the years after Charles I came to the throne in a vain attempt to preserve an Elizabethan Protestant consensus—all this is to miss Puritanism's essential history. It is perhaps fundamentally to confuse the particular reactions of the Puritan clergy with the essential life of the godly community as a whole. When Thomas Hooker preached with extraordinary eloquence to his Essex followers in June 1631 to "look to it, for God is going, and if he go, then our glory goes also . . . , for England hath seen her best days, and the reward of sin is coming on apace; for God is packing up his gospel, because none will buy his wares (not come to his price)," it was actually Hooker who had packed up, preparatory to his departure for Amsterdam and eventually New England.[27] A minority of the godly followed their "Noahs" on this lengthy pilgrimage, but the bulk of the godly stayed behind; some, like the Wallingtons, thought the doctrine of the calling required that they stay at the place to which God had brought them, regardless of the consequences. For Nehemiah, the creation of the godly community lay in the recent past, at least in London, and the demands of that community were already evident in the compulsions of his childhood. The children of God had come into existence not as a backward-looking response to Arminian innovations—Arminianism had not yet appeared on their intellectual horizon—but rather as a positive response to the command to build a godly church, not of the elect, but of the obedient. Lacking episcopal leadership and facing an indifferent monarch in Queen Elizabeth, these "professing" Protestants found each other, as the Lollard "known men" had a century or more before, by their behavior patterns as much as by their attitudes and ideals; they found their prophets among the activist preachers and their guidebooks in the new household catechisms, a potent invention of the 1570's. The discipline and self-reliance learned in the godly household characterized a generation of the godly, but their efforts to extend that discipline from their households to their parish neighborhoods were constantly frustrated, except where the parish godly found support among their respectable neighbors and, even more importantly, as at Terling, Essex, among the local magistracy.[28] So long as the godly minority believed itself under divine compulsion to extend that discipline, to create not merely godly households but a godly society, so long did Puritanism remain an active, potentially revolutionary movement.

Nehemiah Wallington died before the disillusionment and repression of the Restoration completed the transformation of Puritanism to inward-turning Dissent, but in the disappointed bafflement of his last years can be seen the beginning of that process. On the one hand was the toothless Classical system, more concerned with clerical affairs than with parish discipline. On the other was the falling away of the saints grown prosperous—was Nehemiah thinking of his older brother, the war contractor? The work ethic had proved an admirable stay in a troubled century in which the artisan and small tradesman faced uncertain markets and constantly rising food prices. Was London's growing prosperity rendering the erstwhile worried saint fat and complacent? Wallington died before the boom times of the commercial revolution were more than a cloud on the horizon of economic possibility.

What is evident in these last years—and it is one of the genuine surprises of Wallington's record of self-examination—is how little real difference his late and hard-won confidence in his own election made in his life. Here is a man whose early conviction of damnation led to despair and to the not illogical conclusion that an early death would limit or at least mitigate the severity of the inevitable eternal punishment. Recurring bouts of depression continued into his middle thirties, and shortly after his thirty-fourth birthday he wrote out a will in which he recognized that self-destruction still carried for him a terrible attraction. "Touching my body, if I die in peace, I desire it may be honestly committed to the earth from whence it came (and to be buried in St. Leonard's churchyard where my three sweet children lieth); if otherwise, let God dispose thereof according to his pleasure." Wallington knew, of course, all the correct formulas: "First, therefore (and principally), I bequeath and resign my soul unto God and to his son Jesus Christ who by his precious blood hath redeemed me and sealed my said redemption by his Holy Spirit of promise." But confidence in that redemption was lacking, for though he could confess at one time "that now I fear not any of the temptations of Satan, either to lay hands on myself or to fall into any other gross sin," he also had to recognize that, as he put it, "I am a poor weak wretch, ready to be blown away by every blast."[29] It was not until another fifteen troubled years had passed that Wallington could finally write with conviction about his own redemption.

"In the year 1647 I did then begin to walk close with God in holiness of life, even now in the forty-ninth year of my age, [convinced] that the older I grow, the better I would grow, and in my old age to be more settled and quiet in my soul with rest in the bosom of my Savior, living the life of faith with true peace and contentment." Although still bothered by the "hags and terrors and continual chiding and brawling" of his conscience, the conviction grew of "God's mercy in electing me before the foundation of the world." As he wrote, "now [in] this latter part of my life, which is the year 1650, the Lord hath filled my soul with joy and comfort and put in my mouth new songs of praises." In that year he gave over writing on the assumption that it was time now "to strive to practice what I have read and written, and to set myself to live to God's glory."[30]

Nevertheless, two years later he had resumed writing, recognizing in it a necessary concomitant to the discipline he sought to practice. Yet peace, even then, eluded him. By the end of 1654 his troubles once more seemed to overwhelm him. "I have my troubles and cares with frowns of the world, my wife with a sore cough and shortness of breath, my son[-in-law] great losses and troubles, my daughter much sickness and weakness, and three of us reaching after death and seeking to die first." And once again his troubles put an end to his inward peace, and the old doubts returned. "I did make a little search in my heart for . . . I find my old sins stare me in the face, as infidelity and discontent. Oh, Nehemiah, where is thy faith and confidence now!"[31] For Wallington the discipline of casting up accounts could only end when Christ claimed him for his own. If Wallington was in any way typical of that troubled generation, uncertainty, examination, and the constant need of renewal must have characterized their whole lives. Life was a pilgrimage from which there could necessarily be no rest short of the grave. Wallington did finally learn that a pilgrimage is a process, not a terminus, and that habitual actions were a necessary part of the disciplined life: "I may and ought to accustom myself to holy duties, but not to do them out of custom." At the end of December, having cast up his accounts, he resolved once more not to buy more notebooks, but he then hastily added that such a resolve did not mean that he intended to give over the practice of daily examination or even of writing. He had an old notebook with many blank pages remaining, and there he determined "to write some of God's mercies and dispensations to me, even New Year's mercies as [a] return of old year's prayers."[32] The examined life and the disciplines of preparationism were no longer preliminaries to justification, to salvation, but had become the life-long preparation for eternity.

In the spring and summer of 1658, weeks before his death, he once again read over each of his notebooks, sometimes abstracting the volume in a new table of contents. With that last reading he noted that he "forbore to take any further notice of it, for at the present I am very ill in my body," and with those brief notations the journey came to an end.[33]

Reference Matter

Appendix: Wallington's Notebooks

The best guide to Wallington's writings is contained in the prefatory "To the Christian Reader" in his 1654 notebook (Folger MS. V.a.436), and is reproduced below. Of the 50 numbered notebooks listed there, only nos. 3, 5, 16, 18, 39, and 47 survive. (The exact makeup of one extant manuscript is a puzzle, as noted below, but chiefly consists of no. 16.)

The names of these books that I have written (some are but in part) are as followeth:

1. First, The Poor Widow's Mite, in which is some places of Scripture I had gathered and written out in the year 1620.

2. Another book which in the twenty year of my age, 1618, in the trouble of my mind I did begin to write down my sins, but after by the goodness of God, finding some comfort, I left that and began to write another book called

3. A Record of God's Mercies, or A Thankful Remembrance, wherein is set down my miserable and sad condition of my corrupt nature with some of the many mercies of God to my soul and body to the year 1630. [GL, MS. 204]

4. Another book with places of holy Scripture, which I gather against all manner of sins in 1622.

5. A Memorial of God's Judgments upon Sabbath Breakers, Drunkards and Other Vile Livers, 1632. [BL, Sloane MS. 1457]

6. The Traveler's Meditation, or the Traveler's Exercise, 1632 in part written.

7. The Marks that I am a Child of God, 1632.

8. Psalms I gathered out to learn to sing in the heaviness and trouble of my mind, 1634.

9. The History of Francis Spira, 1635.

10. The Complaint of a Sinner, admiring at the mercies of God.

11. A book with a black cover, which I have written many precious sermons, which I did give to my wife, 1636.

12. A book wherein I did write the cruel suffering of Mr. Burton, Mr. Prynne, and Doctor Bastwick under the prelates in 1637.

13. A book of places of Scripture which I gathered out to show the woeful estate of the wicked and the happy estate of the godly, 1637.

14. A book of some choice Psalms, which my father chose out; I did write and gave them to my wife, 1639.

15. A black cover book wherein I did write out some special graces for the preparing to go to the Lord's Supper, 1639.

16. Three paper books of the weekly passages of Parliament, 1640, 1641. [BL, Add. MS. 21,935]

17. A black cover book called A Bundle of Mercies in the beginning of Parliament, which book I was constrained to leave about the middle and write of the miseries that broke forth in Ireland, 1640.

18. Another black cover book of the benefit that I have by the Lord's Supper, which I call The Growth of a Christian, 1641. [BL, Add. MS. 40,883]

19. A little book, which I called my Bosom Book of Protestation and Covenant, 1641.

20. A black cover book called Bitter Cries and Complaints at the Terrible Grim Looks of Sin, 1644.

21. A book at one end I have written places of Scripture, how the Lord hath heard and helped his children in war, and at the other end are places in Scripture of a right Fast, and how such a Fast and prayer prevailed with God, 1645.

22. A thin paper book with a parchment cover, wherein I have written the names of all my books, with my will and testament, and sweet exhortation to my wife and child.

23. A black cover book called The Wonder-Working God, or The God that Worketh Wonders, wherein you may see how the Lord from Fast to Fast answers prayers and giving us many great victories in 1643 and 1644.

24. A black cover book called Cordial Promises, which I did write to comfort my soul in these staggering times, 1644.

26. A black cover book called A Record of Mercies Continued, or Yet God is Good to Israel, shewing how God answers our prayers from Fast to Fast in many victories, 1645.

27. A small parchment book called England's Plots, 1645.

28. A double book with a red cover: one called A Encouragement to Faith and Prayer to Pert Persons;

29. The other, An Encouragement to Faith and Prayer in that the Lord hath given a return of prayer to us in general good, 1645.

30. Another book, which I called Examples of God's Wrath upon Those that have broke His Commandments, The Thunderbolt of God's Wrath, and Mr. Vicker's Looking Glass, bound up with it, 1645.

31. Two paper books which I did write sermons, 1646.

32. A black cover book called A Touchstone of Comfort; at the other end I did write my trouble in being chose to be an Elder, 1646.

33. A book called The Mighty Works of the Lord, which is a Prop to Faith. I did give this to my wife, 1646.

34. Another book, which I did begin to write sermons in, I did give to my wife, 1647.

35. A book with clasps, called The Cry of Conscience, 1647.

36. A black cover book, called A New War sprung out of the Old; in it is shewed how we have had three sorts of war in these nine years last past: a prelatical war; 2, a profane war; 3, an hypocritical war, 1648; and I did intend to have written on a fourth war, which I know not how to call it: brother goes to war against brother, 1649.

37. A black cover book I did begin to write against the errors of these times, but because there were so many that hath done it far better than I can, I did give it over, 1649.

38. A little book with clasps I did begin to write, concerning the means I should use before I take the Engagement, 1650.

39. A book with a red cover and blue leaves, wherein is written the copies of profitable and comfortable letters, 1650. [BL, Sloane MS. 922]

40. A red cover book with yellow leaves and clasps called Great Sorrow Turned into Great Rejoicing, 1650.

41. A long book with a black cover and clasps, called A Day Book of my Sins, or Of Experienced Mercies, 1652.

42. A little book with blue leaves called Morning Meditations, 1652.

43. A book with a red cover and clasps called Experienced Mercies of Faith and Return of Prayers, 1652/53.

44. 45. Two books more with blue leaves called Experienced Mercies of Faith and Return of Prayers, 1653.

46. A book with a black cover, yellow leaves, and clasps called Eight Hard Lessons, and at the end, Experienced Mercies of Faith in the Promises and Return of Prayer, 1653/54.

47. And now this last book which I intend to write, called Extract of the Passages of my Life, or The Book of All My Writing Books. [Folger MS. V.a.436]

[On a loose page, located at p. 51, is the following:]

48. Another book which concerned the grace of patience, which I did write near twenty years ago, and I gave it to my Sister Patience.

49. A paper book I did write in the year 1640, concerning some articles to reform my life, and some directions how to hear and pray well and to live an holy life.

50. And now this year 1654 in April 1, I did begin to write another book with sermons I did hear at the morning exercise. This is the fifty book that I have written in. The Lord make me humble and write it in my heart.

There is no notebook no. 25. However, both no. 16 and no. 28 are multiple volumes. No. 9, on "Francis Spira," written in 1635, is a copy of a manuscript that was evidently circulated among the godly in 1635, and that was subsequently printed in 1638 as *A Relation of the Fearefull Estate of Francis Spira, in the year, 1548*. The preface is signed "N.B.," who is identified in the *Short Title Catalogue* as Nathaniel Bacon. Francis Spira is an English rendering of Francesco Spiera, a lawyer of Cittadella in the territory of Venice who was converted to Protestantism by reading Luther's works and was subsequently betrayed to the papal legate. In fear for his life, Spiera denied the truth of his new faith. The bulk of the treatise, which runs to 134 pages in the 1638 edition, recounts the conversations Spiera later had with Bishop Pier Paolo Vergerio and others at Padua, who tried to convince Spiera that his apostasy was not convincing proof that he was predestined to damnation. Although the treatise is intended as a "terrible example" for subsequent generations of Protestants, Spiera also says much that Wallington found edifying, such as the following, which one finds echoed in many of his writings: ". . . take heed of relying on Faith that works not a holy, unblameable life, worthy of a believer; credit me, it will fail. I preached it to others, I had all places of Scripture in memory that might support it: I thought myself sure, and in the meantime, living impiously and carelessly, behold, now the judgments of God have overtaken me, not to correction but to condemnation . . ." (pp. 114–15). For a modern account of the Spiera incident, see Anne Jacobson Shutte, *Pier Paolo Vergerio: the Making of an Italian Reformer* (Geneva, 1977). The "Mr. Vicker's Looking Glass" mentioned in no. 30 is John Vicars, *A Prospective Glasse to Looke into Heaven* (London, 1618).

The earliest extant notebook is no. 3, "A Record of God's Mercies, or A Thankful Remembrance," now in the Guildhall Library as MS. 204. Beginning on the second folio is a table of contents that runs for six pages. This is followed by three pages entitled "To the Christian Reader." The 517 pages of numbered text follows. The opening section, pp. 1–14, called "The mercies of God to me, in my troubled mind," contains autobiographical information on his contemplated suicide and his attempt to begin a new life; this is followed, on pp. 15–46, by a section called "The way I took to overcome my corruptions," which begins with specific sins and the remedies Wallington found for them, and continues, from p. 35 on, with a listing of his 77 resolutions or covenants made between 1619 and 1629. On p. 47 Wallington begins a section called in the table of contents "Of the troubled conscience"; from this section to p. 400 is the main portion of the volume, which is not concretely autobiographical but rather a series of reflections on matters of spiritual concern. After the section on what sins trouble a conscience come others on the threefold difference between "the saints' trials and the reprobates' despair" (beginning on p. 57), on "the misery of a wounded spirit" (p. 63), on "the excellent grace of Faith" (p. 72), and on the proofs "of a true living Faith" (p. 82); next we pass to a catalogue of God's promises "to his children" (p. 87), to motives to "help their poor brethren this time of dearth" (p. 107), to various kinds of repentance (p. 116), to "seven ways wherein a natural man is miserable" (p. 121), to "eight motions to dissuade a man from sin" (p. 125), to "twenty marks of a child of God" (p. 131), to "why the Lord sends afflictions for the benefit of his child" (p. 207), to "rules concerning the manner of well doing" (p. 248), to "eight remedies against sorrows" (p. 269), to "sixteen signs of a child of God in his humiliation" (p. 294), and on through six ways to pray correctly, five ways to show love to one's enemies, the benefits of poverty, and so on. On p. 401 Wallington begins a substantial section on "outward mercies" and "great deliverances," which is autobiographical and describes the births, sicknesses, and deaths of his children, the escapes of the household from fire, the episode of the journeyman who stole from Wallington and its outcome, and various spiritual uses to be made of these mercies and deliverances. On p. 437 an account of some economic difficulties occasioned by a small debt in early June 1631 leads Wallington to extensive reflections on business ethics in general. On p. 463 Wallington returns to an account of various events in his life from 1632 to 1636; on p. 469 he begins his account of his Star Chamber trial in 1638; on p. 470 (Wallington's pagination goes astray here and should read 477) he describes the robbing of his house and the spiritual uses of this incident; this is followed by several pages of news from Heidelberg and Amsterdam about the destruction and famine caused by the Thirty Years War, the news dating from 1636; this is followed by an unpaginated section (actually beginning on p. 486) called "A Faithful Memorial of my own Mother that is Deceased," followed by a catalogue on pp. 475–76 (actually pp. 490–91) of the date of birth of the twelve children born to his mother. On p. 479 Wallington begins an account of the fire on London Bridge; on p. 489 he begins a section titled "My Private Prayer" in gratitude for judgments escaped and mercies received; on p. 504 Wallington recounts the several suicides he had heard of in 1632. This is followed on p. 505 by "My Postscript to my Loving Wife, Children and Friends," in which he admits that his family and friends still fear that he will "lay hands on" himself, that he needs the help and comfort of his friends in these times of temptation, and that he has some confidence in his salvation. This introduction leads into his "will and testament," although he admits that he has little to leave his family except the precepts previously written. He closes with accounts of those who were killed or died suddenly in 1632 (pp. 512–14), and with a concluding analytic table of contents (pp. 515–17).

The next extant volume, notebook no. 5, entitled "A Memorial of God's Judgments upon Sabbath Breakers, Drunkards and Other Vile Livers," now in the British Library (Sloane MS. 1457), is a much less complex work. It contains 107 folios and was begun in 1632. It begins with an account of portents in 1621 and in 1623 when Prince Charles was in Spain, and then, beginning on folio 6r, recounts stories of suicides—"A Memorial of those that laid violent hands on themselves"—from 1632 to 1635. After an account of the house in Blackfriars that collapsed killing "almost a hundred persons" when Drury, the Jesuit, preached (fos. 9v–10v), Wallington begins a section (on fo. 11r) entitled "A Memorial of the hand of God upon those that break the Sabbath," stories that run from 1620 to 1644. This is followed by a section entitled "A Memorial of God's Judgments upon Drunkards," which runs from folio 18r to 24r. Folios 24r to 29v contain a miscellany of divine judgments on those who drink healths, follow whores, blaspheme, etc. There follow sections on "those that died suddenly" (fo. 30r) and "those that drowned" (fo. 33r), a variety of accounts of accidents and sudden deaths (fo. 36r), another account of the burning of London Bridge in 1633 (fos. 47r–50r), a "Memorial of a Great Storm" (fo. 56r), "A Judgment upon Organs" in

1644 (fo. 58r), stories of the destruction of altar rails by the English soldiers mustered against the Scots in 1640 (fos. 60r–65v), and again, a miscellany of judgments on a parish priest who used a surplice, on a man who cursed Burton, Bastwick, and Prynne, on those who set up a maypole, on those who mocked Roundheads, on those who joined "the Enemies of God" (i.e., the Cavaliers), and on a variety of "remarkable and wonderful things." The volume concludes with an account of various fires in London, which are seen as a punishment for London's sins, the last dated May 2, 1655 (fo. 99r), with an undated account of the death of a three-year-old child who drowned while her parents, Independents, had gone to church (fo. 103r), and with an account of the death of "the Emperor of Russia," dated 1645 (fo. 104r), and a table of contents.

The real puzzle in this catalogue is the identity of the volume that has come down to us as BL, Additional MS. 21,935. It is presumably a compilation drawn from several of the notebooks listed in the catalogue, principally nos. 16, 17, 21, 23, and possibly 26 and 27. However, the first ten folios, labeled "A Bundle of Mercies," are concerned with pre-1640 events and may come in part from no. 10; in any event, this prefatory material seeks to set the stage by pointing to England's manifold sins and to God's manifold judgments and mercies that should have warned the English of the impending troubles. Folios 11v to 15v contain a short treatise on the implications of the Canons of 1640. Folios 16r to 37r contain detailed accounts of judgments visited on sabbath breakers, the accounts beginning in 1633 and going on to October 1641. These accounts are followed (fos. 39r–65v) by a section called "Heavy Times with the Poor Children of God," which begins with Old Testament accounts and concludes with material on the trial of Burton, Bastwick, and Prynne. Folios 66r to 73v encompass a section titled "A Short view of the prelatical Church of England," which is followed by sections titled "The Causes Why the Lord doth Send a Sword on a Land, 1637 & 1638" (fos. 74r–75v), "Signs that the Sword is Coming on a Land" (fos. 76r–77r [there are two folios numbered 77]), and finally "Of the Bitterness of War" (fos. 77v–84r). On folio 84v begins a section "Of the Power and Force of Prayer," in which Wallington attributes the peaceful end of the first war with the Scots in 1639 and the defeat by the Dutch of the second Spanish Armada later in the same year to the prayers of the godly. On folio 88r begins a running account of political and military events, copied from newsbooks and diurnals, interspersed with commentary, beginning with an account of "the King going with his Army the second time against Scotland" (fo. 88v), and continuing through sections on the "exploits" of the soldiers of the various county trainbands in 1640 (fos. 89r–91r), on the petitions against the bishops (fo. 99r), on the articles against Archbishop Laud (fo. 100r–v), on Parliament voting the thirteen bishops to be delinquents (fo. 108r), on scandalous ministers (fo. 116r), on "cruel projectors with their letters patent" (fo. 131r), on Strafford's trial and attainder (fos. 133r–40r), on the Protestation (fo. 150r), on the king's attempted arrest of the Five Members (fo. 160r), on the miseries of the Irish Rebellion (fos. 164v–69v), and on the petitions against the attempted arrest of the Five Members (fos. 170r–74v). On fo. 180v Wallington begins a section entitled "The wicked always hate the Godly and plot against them," which begins with Cain's plot against Abel and continues with details of the plots of the papists in Ireland and the various plots, again attributed to papists, in England in 1641 and 1642 (fos. 180v–93v). There follow accounts of the various events of the summer of 1642, culminating in the report of "the setting up of the King's standard at Nottingham" (fo. 204r). Except for a brief account of the Irish Rebellion and the death of Zachariah Rampaigne (fos. 227v–29v), the folios from 205 to the end (fo. 281) are largely given over to battles and the plunderings of soldiers from the beginning of the war to April 9, 1646.

The fourth extant volume chronologically is the notebook, begun in 1641, entitled "The Growth of a Christian," which is now in the British Library as Additional MS. 40,883, and which is no. 18 in Wallington's catalogue. This, Wallington explains, is "the second book concerning the fruit and benefit that (through the mercy of God) I gain by the Sacrament, which I here take notice of it, that I and all others might be encouraged to go to it preparedly as often as occasion is offered" (fo. 4r)—the first being notebook no. 15, dated 1639. The volume is organized chronologically from January 1640/41 to the end of December 1643 (fo. 189r) and describes Wallington's reflections in preparation for the Sacrament or for a Fast or Thanksgiving day; he sometimes includes notes on the sermon or sermons heard on such a day, and the benefits obtained. Although spiritual rather than political or autobiographical in intention, the volume nonetheless contains much comment on his own circumstances and on the times.

The fifth volume, notebook no. 39, is equally straightforward. It is a letterbook of 209 folios, copied in 1650, "concerning many pious, holy, godly and Christian letters; some are to instruct and advise, some to reprove and admonish; some are sweet and comfortable and some are to stir up to praise and thankfulness. They be all very useful and profitable." The letters begin on folio 6r with a copy of the second Epistle of St. John; thereafter follow (fo. 7r) letters by Lawrence Saunders and other martyrs of the Marian persecution, all copied out of Foxe (see fo. 22v), letters by Edward Dering (fos. 23r–30v), a letter by Richard Greenham (fos. 31r–33r), letters by Joseph Hall (fos. 34r–51v), letters by Paul Baynes (fos. 52r–68v), and a letter by John Burges (fos. 69r–70r). The remaining letters are largely those by or addressed to Nehemiah Wallington: folios 71r to 84r contain letters from Livewell Rampaigne (fos. 76v–77v contain a letter of Wallington's nephew, John Bradshaw, to John Wallington, Sr., about the siege of La Rochelle); folios 85r to 86r contain a letter by John Wallington, Sr., to his grandson, John Bradshaw, dated March 5, 1631; folios 87r to 89v contain a letter by Nehemiah to his father "to have a special care in the matching of their beloved daughter," dated 1632; folios 90r to 93v contain a letter from Thomas Weld from New England to his "people" in Terling, Essex, 1633; folios 94r to 107v and 173r to 176v contain correspondence from and to James Cole from 1634 to 1650; folio 108 contains a letter from John Wallington, Sr., to John Allen, a nephew, dated March 31, 1635; folios 109r to 115v contain part of a letter from Anthony Thatcher in New England to his brother Peter Thatcher in "Old England" describing a shipwreck off Marblehead, Massachusetts, in 1635; folios 116r to 117v, 120v to 121v, and 126v to 128v contain the Francis Wilsmore correspondence; folios 118r to 120r, 122r to 126r, and 140r to 141v contain letters to Henry Roborough; folio 129 contains "A Letter from York to a friend at London of the sad beginnings of war," dated September 13, 1640 (this is found in *Historical Notices* [see Chap. 1, n. 6], vol. 1, pp. 127–28); folios 130r to 131v contain a letter from the inhabitants of Hull to the High Sheriff and others at York, April 30, 1642 (this also is found in *Historical Notices*, vol. 2, pp. 65–67); folios 132r to 134r contain a letter to Abraham Colfe, the pluralist and absentee parson of St. Leonard's Eastcheap, dated August 8, 1642; folios 134v to 138v contain a letter of admonition to Wallington's neighbor Mr. Waddington, dated December 16, 1640; folios 142r to 144r contain a letter of instruction to "Goodman Cox," dated 1642; folios 144v to 147v contain the Edward Browne correspondence; folios 153r to 154v contain a letter to Captain Player, dated October 13, 1646; folios 155v to 159v contain letters by Grace and Nehemiah to Zachariah's widow, dated March 29, 1647; folios 160r to 162v contain a letter of admonition to cousin John Wallington, dated July 19, 1648; folio 164 contains a letter from Tobias Lisle, a neighbor, to his daughter Susan, dated 1648; and folios 165r to 170v contain letters to the ministers Griffith, Barker, and cousin Nathaniel Church, dated 1650.

The last extant notebook chronologically, which Nehemiah catalogues as no. 47, is now in the Folger Library (MS. V.a.436) and is titled "An Extract of the Passages of my Life, or The Book of All my Writing Books." The organization is very straightforward: pp. 1–201 contain summaries, excerpts, and tables of contents of all his notebooks; with p. 201 begins a section of daily or almost daily reflections on his life, dated from April 1, 1654, including occasional sermon notes, and interrupted (on pp. 251–96) by a long excerpt copied from the works of Jeremiah Burroughs. The accounts of daily examination then continue to the final entry on p. 540, dated December 31, 1654.

Notes

Chapter 1

The epigraph is from *The Shaking of the Olive Tree*, in *The Remaining Works of . . . Joseph Hall, D.D.* (London, 1660), p. 1. Hall was an Emmanuel graduate, a moralist, and an orthodox Calvinist, whose writings before his defense of divine right episcopacy were much admired by Wallington and other Puritans, although he became a bishop in 1627.

1. For the geographic mobility of early modern Englishmen, see Peter Clark, "The Migration in Kentish Towns, 1580–1640," in Peter Clark and Paul Slack, eds., *Crisis and Order in English Towns, 1500–1700* (London, 1972), pp. 117–63; and Peter Clark, "Migration in England During the Late Seventeenth and Early Eighteenth Centuries," *Past & Present*, 83 (1979), esp. pp. 58–60, which summarize recent research on the period before 1640. For migration to urban centers specifically, see John Patten, *English Towns* (Folkestone, Kent, 1978), pp. 125–35, 235–43.

2. Peter Laslett, *Family Life and Illicit Love in Earlier Generations* (Cambridge, Eng., 1977), pp. 29–34, 44–45, 63; James Horn, "Servant Emigration to the Chesapeake in the Seventeenth Century," in Thad W. Tate and David L. Ammerman, eds., *The Chesapeake in the Seventeenth Century* (Chapel Hill, N.C., 1979), pp. 51–95; Roger Finlay, *Population and Metropolis: The Demography of London, 1580–1650* (Cambridge, Eng., 1981), pp. 66–67.

3. For the age of marriage of London males, see Finlay, *Population and the Metropolis*, pp. 18–19, 139; for comparative purposes, see David Levine, *Family Formation in an Age of Nascent Capitalism* (New York, 1977).

4. For literacy among London artisans, see David Cressy, *Literacy and the Social Order* (Cambridge, Eng., 1980), pp. 128–29.

5. Paul Delany, *British Autobiography in the Seventeenth Century* (New York, 1969), pp. 27–204; Alan Macfarlane, *The Family Life of Ralph Josselin* (Cambridge, Eng., 1970), pp. 3–11; Dean Ebner, *Autobiography in Seventeenth-Century England* (The Hague, 1971); Owen C. Watkins, *The Puritan Experience: Studies in Spiritual Autobiography* (New York, 1972).

6. For a guide to Wallington's writings and a brief commentary, see the Appendix on pp. 199–208, above. Only six of some 50 notebooks are extant, in the following collections: (1) Guildhall Library [henceforth GL], MS. 204, a notebook entitled "A Record of the Mercies of God," 517 numbered pages plus at least 15 unnumbered and misnumbered pages; (2) British Library [henceforth BL], Additional MS. 21,935, a journal of political comment of 281 folios, published in an edited version as *Historical Notices of Events Occurring Chiefly in the Reign of Charles I* [henceforth *Historical Notices*], ed. R. Webb, 2 vols. (London, 1869); (3) BL, Add. MS. 40,883, a spiritual diary of 198 folios kept from 1641 to 1643, entitled "The Growth of a Christian"; (4) BL, Sloane MS. 922, a letter book of 209 folios; (5) BL, Sloane MS. 1457, an untitled compilation of "remarkable judgments against Sabbath breakers" and others of 107 folios; and (6) the Folger Shakespeare Library [henceforth Folger] MS. V.a.436, a volume of about 566 pages (some misnumbered), which is given the running title of "An Extract of the Passages of My Life and A Collection of Several of My Written Treatises."

7. Folger MS. V.a.436, "To the Christian Reader" (unpaginated). In this and all subsequent quotations, I have modernized the spelling and punctuation but otherwise made no editorial changes.

8. The three overlooked titles are on a loose sheet inserted at p. 51.

9. Folger MS. V.a.436, "To the Christian Reader"; Wallington's productivity was a match for that of the prolific Puritan theologian William Perkins, 47 of whose works were in print in the early seventeenth century, not counting various editions of his collected works: see *The Work of William Perkins*, ed. Ian Breward (Abingdon, Berks., 1970), pp. 613–32.

10. Folger MS. V.a.436, p. 537. Wallington thought he had written 50 volumes, but in his catalogue there is no 25th. On the other hand, no. 31 is actually two volumes of collected sermons.

11. *Ibid.*, pp. 105, 107. Heydon was Lieutenant of the Ordnance. I am obliged for this identification to Professor Conrad Russell.

12. *Ibid.*, pp. 161–63.

13. *Ibid.*, pp. 187–88.

14. *Ibid.*, pp. 155, 158–59, 201.

15. Wallington quoted verses from the Psalms on two occasions. After noting that he had begun a volume on "God's wonderful works and fearful judgments" in 1632, he added the following verses:

> And lo, all such as thee forsake,
> thou shalt destroy each one:

> And those that trust in anything
> saving in thee alone.
> Therefore will I draw near to God,
> and ever with him dwell.
> In God alone I put my trust,
> thy wonders will I tell.

Later, after noting that he was chosen constable for the ward in 1637 for the two following years, he adds:

> All praise to him that hath not put
> nor cast me out of mind,
> Nor yet his mercy from me shut
> which I do ever find.

Both of these verses appear in Folger MS. V.a.436, pp. 30, 60. The first set of verses is from Psalm 73, the second from Psalm 66; both are accurate quotations from the very popular Sternhold and Hopkins metrical version: see *The First Parte of the Psalmes Collected into English Meter by Thomas Sternhold and others . . .* (London, 1564), pp. 155, 132. On one occasion Wallington mentions that singing psalms was part of family devotions. Folger MS. V.a.436, p. 512.

16. Folger MS. V.a.436, p. 188.

17. *Ibid.*, p. 5; for Wallington's purchase of newsbooks, see BL, Add. MS. 40,883, fos. 15v–16r.

18. GL, MS. 204, p. 16; Folger MS. V.a.436, p. 462.

19. Folger MS. V.a.436, p. 11; BL, Sloane MS. 922, fo. 118r.

20. Folger MS. V.a.436, p. 94. The "Dialogue" is one of the tracts published as part of *A Treatise Tending unto a Declaration* [?1588]; see *The Work of William Perkins*, pp. 362–85.

21. Folger MS. V.a.436, pp. 251, 296.

22. In GL, MS. 204, pp. 453–57, Wallington quotes scattered passages from Arthur Dent's *Plaine Mans Path-Way to Heaven* (London, 1601), pp. 122–34.

23. GL, MS. 204, p. 507. The will, which is in the form of a postscript (pp. 505–10), is dated May 21, 1632; it appoints overseers, and provides for the disposition of his body and property.

24. *Ibid.*, verso of the first unnumbered page in the notebook.

25. Folger MS. V.a.436, p. 425.

26. *Ibid.*, p. 9.

27. *Ibid.*, pp. 9–10.

28. *Ibid.*, "To the Reader" (unpaginated).

29. *Ibid.*, pp. 205–6.   30. GL, MS. 204, p. 45.

31. BL, Sloane MS. 922, fo. 2r.   32. GL, MS. 204, p. 493.

33. *Ibid.*, p. 405; see also p. 407.

34. *Ibid.*, "To the Christian Reader" (unpaginated).

35. BL, Sloane MS. 922, fo. 2r.   36. BL, Add. MS. 40,883, fo. 4r.

37. BL, Sloane MS. 1457, fo. 3r.   38. *Ibid.*, fos. 28v, 88r.

39. BL, Add. MS. 21,935, fo. 194r; cf. fo. 111r, where reflections on the piecemeal reforms of 1641 are prefaced with the title, "The Lord said he would not destroy the Canaanites before Israel altogether but by little and little."

40. GL, MS. 204, pp. 477–79, misnumbered as pp. 470–71.

41. BL, Add. MS. 21,935, fo. 193r. Wallington's straightforward report of the plot of December 19, 1642, is badly garbled in the printed edition (*Historical Notices*, vol. 1, pp. 63–64), and the passage quoted is omitted altogether. Wallington's simile—"the poor Church of God is like a woman with child"— may be an echo of a similar comparison that Edmund Calamy made in his famous sermon given on December 22, 1641, before the House of Commons, which was printed as *Englands Looking-Glasse* (London, 1642); there he states that "the Child of reformation is come to birth; but there wants strength to bring it forth. This is a sign, that there are some great obstructions in the Kingdom, that hinder the birth of this much desired Child" (p. 18).

42. BL, Add. MS. 40,883, fo. 83r.

43. *Ibid.*, fos. 97v–99v.

44. BL, Soane MS. 922, fo. 108v. The practice may have been a common one in Puritan circles. Dr. Edmund Staunton also kept a diary of "God's Mercies," as did those other Puritan divines John Janeway and John Machin. See Samuel Clarke, *The Lives of Sundry Eminent Persons* (London, 1683), Part I, pp. 167, 74, 90. John Wallington, Sr., also left a memoir of some kind, from which Nehemiah quotes a few lines about the lack of preaching in London in the 1570's. Folger MS. V.a.436, pp. 202–3.

45. BL, Sloane MS. 922, fos. 122r–23v.

46. Folger MS. V.a.436, pp. 334–35. It may well be, of course, that Wallington exaggerated his inarticulateness, for a day after he recorded his failure he notes that the young man "came again upon liking," which suggests that Wallington may not have failed to express himself after all: *ibid.*, p. 336.

Chapter 2

The epigraph is from Folger MS. V.a.436, p. 216.

1. A listing of the birth dates of all the Wallington children by John Wallington's marriage to Elizabeth Hall is contained in a memoir Nehemiah wrote in memory of his mother: GL, MS. 204, unpaginated [pp. 486–90]. Wallington's maternal grandfather, Anthony Hall, was dead by the time of Nehemiah's birth; see the indenture recording the sale of Hall's London property in St. Botolph's Bishopsgate to John and Elizabeth Wallington: GL, MS. 1418. Nehemiah never mentions any kin of his father's, presumably because none was resident in the City; since John Wallington, Sr., was evi-

dently not London-born, he may have lost touch with his family during his years of apprenticeship more than a decade before Nehemiah's birth.

2. Folger MS. V.a.436, p. 1.

3. Wallington was christened May 17, according to the parish register of St. Leonard's Eastcheap. GL, MS. 17,607, fo. 12v.

4. Folger MS. V.a.436, "To the Reader," and p. 187.

5. GL, MS. 204, p. 1.

6. Folger MS. V.a.436, p. 12.

7. For his freedom, see Turners' Company Book of Apprentice Bindings under the date of May 18, 1620: GL, MS. 3302/1, unpaginated. For his first journeyman, see Folger MS. V.a.436, p. 12; for James Weld's binding, see GL, MS. 3302/1, under the date of March 20, 1620/21. James Weld was the son of Edmund Weld of Sudbury, Suffolk, mercer.

8. Folger MS. V.a.436, pp. 12–13.

9. GL, MS. 204, p. 1.

10. Typically, Paul Baynes was converted while at Christ's College, Cambridge, where "it pleased God . . . to shew him his sins, and to work effectual repentance in him for his evil ways; so that forsaking his former evil company and practice, he became eminent for piety and holiness. . . ." John Preston was weaned from his study of astrology and converted by hearing a sermon preached by John Cotton at St. Mary's, Cambridge. Samuel Clarke, *The Lives of Two and Twenty English Divines* (London, 1660), pp. 27, 99. Equally revealing is the account of John Janeway's conversion: "The great and divine work of conversion was not carried on in his soul after that dreadful manner as it is upon some, who precedently have been very bad (as in the case of Rob. Bolton) . . . but the Lord was pleased, by gentle draughts to dissolve the stone and sweetly to unlock his heart by the exemplary life, and heavenly and powerful discourse of a young man in the college, whose heart God had inflamed with a love to this precious soul . . . for his awakening out of his spiritual lethargy. The rather, being accompanied with the profitable and powerful preaching of those two able and worthy divines, Dr. Arrowsmith, and Dr. Hill, together with his reading several parts of Mr. Baxters *Everlasting Rest*." Samuel Clarke, *The Lives of Sundry Eminent Persons* (London, 1683), p. 62.

11. See, for example, William Kiffin, *Remarkable Passages in the Life of William Kiffin*, ed. William Orme (London, 1823), pp. 2–14.

12. GL, MS. 204, p. 8. For a discussion of early-seventeenth-century perceptions of mental illness, see Michael MacDonald, *Mystical Bedlam* (Cambridge, Eng., 1981), esp. Chapter 4.

13. GL, MS. 204, p. 1. Wallington bought his first notebook in 1618, "in which I did begin to write down my sins. . . ." But "having not written it to my liking," he went on in 1619 to begin "A Record of God's Mercies or A Thankful Remembrance." Folger MS. V.a.436, p. 11. Wallington was not alone in finding that an attempt at a disciplined life produced suicidal de-

spair rather than the looked-for assurance. Similarly John Crook, a London apprentice in the late 1630's, found that "I continued professing and praying, and hearing and reading, and yet I could not perceive any amendment in my self, but the same youthful vanities drew away my mind when opportunities offered. . . ." Such religious duties became an obsession, "for I durst not leave off my duties, for then I thought the Devil will prevail over me, to make me destroy myself; for I was afraid to see a knife, if I was alone, or to have any in the room all night where I lay." *A Short History of the Life of John Crook* (London, 1706), p. 10.

14. GL, MS. 204, p. 5.

15. *Winthrop Papers*, vol. 1, *1498–1628* (Boston, Mass. Historical Society, 1929), p. 154.

16. For example, William Perkins's works were widely read, as evidenced in references in the *Winthrop Papers*, vol. 1, p. 156; in the *Letters of Lady Brilliana Harley*, ed. Thomas Taylor Lewis (Camden Society, old series, vol. 58; London, 1854), p. 24; and in Wallington's own notebooks (see Folger MS. V.a.436, p. 94).

17. *Letters of Lady Brilliana Harley*, p. 52; Folger MS. V.a.436, p. 229.

18. *Letters of Lady Brilliana Harley*, p. 20; Folger MS. V.a.436, p. 189.

19. Folger MS. V.a.436, p. 231.

20. Comment on points of doctrine seems uncommon even in the memoirs of Wallington's and Winthrop's more radical contemporaries, William Kiffin and Lucy Hutchinson, both of whom became Baptists; see, for example, *Remarkable Passages in the Life of William Kiffin*, pp. 13–14, 46, 62–63, 68–72, 89–90; Lucy Hutchinson, *Memoirs of the Life of Colonel Hutchinson*, ed. James Sutherland (Oxford, 1973), pp. 34–35, 166–67, 234.

21. Folger MS. V.a.436, pp. 94, 230.

22. *Letters of Lady Brilliana Harley*, p. 20.

23. Folger MS. V.a.436, p. 11.

24. *Winthrop Papers*, vol. 1, pp. 156–57.

25. *Ibid.*

26. Folger MS. V.a.436, p. 102. Analysis of the "marks and signs" by which one could come to know the condition of one's soul was apparently the preoccupation of a generation of godly preachers and laymen. Of the 1630's in London, John Crook wrote that "the ministers then commonly preaching by marks and signs, how a man might know himself to be a child of God, if he were so, and how it would be for him, if it were not so, which made me sometime to conclude I had saving grace, and by and by conclude, I was but an hypocrite. . . ." *A Short History of the Life of John Crook*, p. 11. Wallington filled much of the middle part of his "A Record of the Mercies of God" with conscientious and lengthy analyses of marks and signs: see GL, MS. 204, p. 82, "Four infallible proofs of a true, living faith in weak Christians, which have no feeling of it"; or p. 292, "The signs of election or the purified heart."

Cf. William Ames, *Conscience with the Power and Cases Thereof* (n.p., 1639), book 2, pp. 14–15, "The signs of true faith."

27. *Winthrop Papers*, vol. 1, pp. 158–60.

28. *Letters of Lady Brilliana Harley*, p. 47.

29. *Winthrop Papers*, vol. 1, p. 160; Folger MS. V.a.436, p. 236. As R. T. Kendall argues in a chapter on "The Experimental Predestinarian Tradition," a generation of divines from William Perkins to Thomas Hooker sought to construct a convincing logic of assurance. So Preston stressed "sincerity" and the mere "desire" for holiness, arguing that "inwardly to desire holiness for itself is an infallible sign" of true repentance. Hence, Kendall argues that "while Perkins makes sanctification the alternative ground of assurance if full assurance is lacking, Preston shows how far this option can be carried, especially when sanctification, or repentance, or a godly disposition is regarded as that to which the promise of grace is made. The result is that preparation for faith becomes *repentance*, which, in turn, assures." *Calvin and English Calvinism to 1649* (Oxford, 1979), pp. 123, 124. Kendall is doubtless right about the logic of preparationism in the hands of Preston and others, but one is struck by how little assurance such a logic produced in the likes of Wallington or Crook, who were the prime audience for their sermons and books.

30. *Winthrop Papers*, vol. 1, p. 159; BL, Add. MS. 40,883, fo. 76v.

31. *Letters of Lady Brilliana Harley*, pp. 69, 71.

32. Folger MS. V.a.436, pp. 285–86.

33. *Winthrop Papers*, vol. 1, p. 196. If a "gospel conversation" separated the "professors" from their worldly neighbors, it does not seem to have led the second generation to reflect often on ecclesiological matters, at least before the mid-1640's. In a letter of February 19, 1640/41, Lady Brilliana Harley wrote that she had "always believed that the Lord would purge His church from all these things and persons that have been such a hindrance to the free passage of His glorious gospel; and I trust now is the time." Two weeks later Wallington wrote that he "entreated the Lord to sweep His church of all trash and rubbish which hath crept in, all men's inventions and traditions, and that the Lord would be pleased to put into the ears of those (worthies) whom it doth concern to set up such a reformation among us as may be pleasing to His will that we might enjoy the gospel in purity and to have none but the Lord Christ to reign over us." (*Letters of Lady Brilliana Harley*, p. 115; BL, Add. MS. 40,883, fo. 20r.) Both Lady Brilliana and Wallington seem to have believed that once the bishops were out of the way the godly would experience little difficulty in discovering what the nature of the Church was that was commanded in the Scriptures. Wallington ultimately became a Presbyterian elder, but that decision appears to have been a consequence of his belief in the necessity of parochial discipline; there is no real evidence that he believed that a Presbyterian church was commanded in Scripture.

34. Folger MS. V.a.436, p. 116.   35. *Ibid.*, p. 187.

36. GL, MS. 204, pp. 1–2.   37. *Ibid.*, p. 3.

38. *Ibid.*, p. 5.   39. *Ibid.*, p. 6.

40. *Ibid.*, p. 4.   41. *Ibid.*, p. 6.

42. *Ibid.*, pp. 7–8. In the Geneva Bible, 2 Corinthians 5 is glossed as follows: "Paul proceedeth to declare the utility that cometh by the cross. 4 How we ought to prepare ourselves unto it. 5 By whom, 9 And for what end. 14–19 He setteth forth the grace of Christ, 20 And the office of ministers, and all the faithful." *The Geneva Bible* (a facsimile of the 1560 edition), ed. Lloyd E. Berry (Madison, Wisc., 1969), The New Testament, fo. 84r.

43. GL, MS. 204, p. 8.   44. *Ibid.*

45. *Ibid.*, p. 35.   46. *Ibid.*, p. 30.

47. *Ibid.*, p. 25.

48. For Nehemiah's allusion to his very brief servitude, see *ibid.*, p. 11. John Wallington, Sr., was Master of the Turners' Company in these years, which may well have helped with any irregularity. See Court Minutes of the Turners' Company, GL, MS. 3295/1, no foliation, entries dated May 15, 1619, and May 25, 1620. John Wallington, Jr., although free of the Company in 1615, did not open his own shop until 1626. GL, MS. 3201/1, August 3, 1615; GL, MS. 3295/1, February 16, 1625/26.

49. The average age of first marriage for men in the period varied with economic circumstance and status but was everywhere higher than Wallington's 23. In London in the first half of the seventeenth century, the mean age of first marriage for males was 28.4 (Roger Finlay, *Population and Metropolis* [Cambridge, Eng., 1981], p. 19). In the early seventeenth century, the average at Shepshed was 29.4 years, at Bottesford 29.2, at Collyton 26.8, and at Terling 25.9 (David Levine, *Family Formation in an Age of Nascent Capitalism* [New York, 1977], pp. 61, 113, 123).

50. GL, MS. 204, p. 15.   51. *Ibid.*, p. 14.

52. *Ibid.*, p. 17.   53. *Ibid.*

54. *Ibid.*, p. 16 and an unpaginated sheet inserted between pp. 16 and 17.

55. Folger MS. V.a.436, p. 11.

56. *Ibid.*, p. 3.

57. GL, MS. 204, an unpaginated section following p. 469.

58. *Ibid.*

59. Folger MS. V.a.436, pp. 6–7.

60. *Ibid.*, p. 3.

61. *Ibid.*; the parish register of St. Leonard's Eastcheap, GL, MS. 17,607, fo. 16r.

62. Folger MS. V.a.436, pp. 3–4.   63. *Ibid.*, p. 4.

64. *Ibid.*, pp. 7–8.   65. *Ibid.*, p. 10.

66. BL, Sloane MS. 922, fo. 122r.   67. *Ibid.*, fo. 104v.

68. BL, Add. MS. 40,883, fo. 38v.   69. GL, MS. 204, p. 505.

70. BL, Sloane MS. 1457, fo. 7r. See also GL, MS. 204, p. 504.

71. GL, MS. 204, p. 505.

72. The 77 articles appear in *ibid.*, pp. 35–44.

73. *Ibid.*, p. 43. This article (art. 43) is the only one that refers explicitly to the contemporary political scene. For an acute discussion of the fact that the godly community was based not on election but rather on a willingness to walk in obedience to God outwardly, see John Coolidge, *The Pauline Renaissance in England* (Oxford, 1970), pp. 62–76, 82–84, 87–92.

74. GL, MS. 204, pp. 44–45, and a sheet later interleaved between these two pages.

75. *Ibid.*, p. 45. This book is not included in the catalogue of Wallington's 50 notebooks listed in Folger MS. V.a.436, "To the Christian Reader."

76. BL, Add. MS. 40,883, fo. 44v. For a recent discussion of the Puritans and the sacraments, see E. Brooks Holifield, *The Covenant Sealed: The Development of Puritan Sacramental Theology in Old and New England, 1570–1720* (New Haven, Conn., 1974).

77. Folger MS. V.a.436, p. 64. The two works were Daniel Rogers's *A Treatise of the Two Sacraments of the Gospel* (1633), and Jeremiah Dyke's *A Worthy Communicant* (1636).

78. BL, Add. MS. 40,883, fo.4r.

79. Folger MS. V.a.436, pp. 273, 276.

80. *Ibid.*, p. 275.

81. BL, Add. MS. 40,883, fo. 122r. Nor did his minister, Henry Roborough, attempt to form a covenanted congregation within the parish. It was symptomatic of his position that he was an active member of the Fourth London Classis.

82. Folger MS. V.a.436, pp. 261, 263, 267. The statement that "faith comes by hearing" is from Paul's Epistle to the Romans, 10:17. Here Wallington seems to be quoting from the Authorized Version, which reads: "So then faith cometh by hearing, and hearing by the word of God." In most instances that I have checked Wallington quotes from the Geneva Bible, which, however, in this instance reads: "Then faith is by hearing, and hearing by the word of God."

83. GL, MS. 204, p. 48.

84. Folger MS. V.a.436, pp. 202–3. For the growth of preaching in London, see my earlier book *The Puritan Lectureships* (Stanford, Calif., 1970).

85. BL, Add. MS. 40,883, fos. 41v–42r.

86. *Ibid.*, fos. 84r–96v. For Henry Jurden, see John and J. A. Venn, *Alumni Cantabrigienses*, Part 1 (Cambridge, Eng., 1922), vol. 2, p. 489; for Knollys, see the *Dictionary of National Biography*, s.v. Hansard Knollys.

87. BL, Add. MS. 40,883, fos. 51v–53r.

88. *Ibid.*, fo. 61r.   89. *Ibid.*, fos. 91v–92v.

90. GL, MS. 204, p. 21.   91. *Ibid.*, p. 23.

92. Folger MS. V.a.436, p. 301. What Wallington could never admit, although it may well have been the case, was that many of the sermons he

heard were indeed dull and tedious. At times his rationalizations suggest as much. On one occasion when the parson of St. Leonard's had "gone into the country" and a substitute had replaced him, Wallington was sorely tempted to go elsewhere for the sermon. However, he argued with himself that the substitute, William Wickens, was indeed "an honest man," and further that he and other ministers had had "many discouragements; I need not to add more." Nevertheless, the clinching argument suggests that Wallington feared the worst in this instance. It also suggests why hearing the Word remained the crucial discipline for the conscientious Christian: "I go not to hear the word of a weak man but to hear the word of the great God that often doth great things by despised instruments and will manifest his power in weak means." *Ibid.*, p. 222.

93. BL, Add. MS. 40,883, fo. 44v; cf. Folger MS. V.a.436, p. 274 (misnumbered p. 276): "I should come to the Lord's Supper with a suitable disposition, a brokenness of heart, a sense of my sin, of that dreadful breach that sin hath made between God and my soul. . . . And whatever sin I find in my heart I must set against it with all my might, my soul must renounce it, and say, Lord, as ever I expect to receive any good by this body and blood of Christ . . . , so, Lord, here I profess against every sin that I have found in my heart. . . ." The reception of the Sacrament was never seen as a passive act.

94. Folger MS. V.a.436, p. 234.

95. *Ibid.*, p. 304.

96. *Ibid.*, p. 305. Presumably Wallington has in mind the early verses of Romans 7, which read, according to the Geneva Bible: "know ye not, brethren, (for I speak to them that know the Law) that the Law hath dominion over a man as long as he liveth? . . . So ye, my brethren, are dead also to the Law by the body of Christ, that ye should be unto another, even unto him that is raised up from the dead, that we should bring forth fruit unto God. For when we were in the flesh, the motions of sins, which were by the Law had force in our members, to bring forth fruit unto death. But now we are delivered from the Law, being dead unto it, wherein we were holden, that we should serve in newness of Spirit, and not in the oldness of the letter."

97. BL, Add. MS. 40,883, fo. 176.

98. Folger MS. V.a.436, pp. 453, 470. Cf. BL, Add. MS. 40,883, fo. 78v, where Wallington records that "on the last day of the week toward evening after I had been in private seeking the Lord in holy prayer, Oh, how did my God fit and enlarge my heart the better in duty with my family in preparation for the Lord's day." The work Wallington refers to is Richard Rogers, Richard Greenham, William Perkins, and George Webb, *A Garden of Spiritual Flowers* (London, 1610).

99. BL, Add. MS. 40,883, fo. 167v.

100. Folger MS. V.a.436, pp. 277, 279, 282.

101. *Ibid.*, p. 277.

102. *Ibid.*, p. 454. Ezekiel 3:17–18 reads in the Geneva Bible as follows:

"Son of man, I have made thee a watchman unto the house of Israel: therefore hear the word of my mouth, and give them warning from me. When I shall say unto the wicked, Thou shalt surely die, and thou givest not him warning, nor speakest to admonish the wicked of his wicked way, that he may live, the same wicked man shall die in his iniquity: but his blood will I require at thine hand." Wallington was quite explicit about the instructional function of family prayer: "This morning while I was teaching and instructing my family, I did teach and instruct myself how to walk circumspectly"— so he recorded of the preparatory services that preceded public worship on Sunday, September 10, 1654. Folger MS. V.a.436, p. 358.

103. *Ibid.*, p. 285.

104. *Ibid.*, p. 471.

105. *Ibid.*, "To the Reader" (unpaginated).

106. BL, Add. MS. 40,883, fos. 5r, 147v.

107. GL, MS. 204, p. 49.

108. *Ibid.*

109. Folger MS. V.a.436, "To the Reader" (unpaginated).

110. *Ibid.*, p. 238.

111. *Ibid.*, p. 242.

112. BL, MS. 40,883, fo. 148r.

113. Folger MS. V.a.436, pp. 231, 230.

114. *Ibid.*, "To the Reader" (unpaginated).

115. BL, Sloane MS. 922, fos. 174v–75r.

116. Folger MS. V.a.436, p. 235.   117. *Ibid.*, p. 357.

118. *Ibid.*, p. 372.   119. *Ibid.*, p. 237.

120. BL, Sloane MS. 922, fo. 175r.

Chapter 3

The epigraphs are both from Wallington's notebooks, the psalm quotation from BL, Sloane MS. 1457, fo. 3r (the Geneva Bible version reads "for he is come to judge the earth: with righteousness shall he judge the world, and the people with equity") and Joseph Hall's remark from a letter copied by Wallington into his letter book, BL, Sloane MS. 922, fo. 42r.

1. Thomas Beard, *The Theatre of Gods Iudgements* (London, 1612), Sig. A2^{r-v}. The first edition was published in 1597; Wallington evidently had access to the 1632 edition and quoted from it extensively in *Historical Notices* (see, for example, vol. 1, p. 49, which quotes from Beard, *Theatre*, p. 209). It was doubtless his reading of Beard that inspired Wallington to begin his "A Memorial of God's Judgments upon Sabbath Breakers, Drunkards and Other Vile Livers" in 1632. See BL, Sloane MS. 1457, fo. 2v; Folger MS. V.a.436, "To the Christian Reader," p. 3. For a perceptive discussion of how far Beard deviated from anything that can be considered orthodox Calvinism, see Ronald J. Vander Molen, "Providence as Mystery, Providence as Revelation:

Puritan and Anglican Modifications of John Calvin's Doctrine of Providence," *Church History*, 47 (1978), pp. 27–47; see also Barbara Donagan, "Providence, Chance, and Explanation: Some Paradoxical Aspects of Puritan Views of Causation," *Journal of Religious History*, 11 (1981), pp. 385–403.

2. Quoted in Vander Molen, "Providence as Mystery," p. 31.

3. BL, Sloane MS. 1457, fo. 3r.

4. Folger MS. V.a.436, p. 145. In terms of the contemporary debate between Godfrey Goodman and George Hakewill, Wallington's thought generally sided with the pessimistic Bishop Goodman, except for about a decade in the late 1630's and early 1640's when he became increasingly convinced that the millennium was about to break forth.

5. BL, Sloane MS. 1457, fo. 3r.

6. Folger MS. V.a.436, p. 145. This second collection was begun in 1645. It differs from the earlier collection chiefly in being focused more strictly on the Ten Commandments. It also contains a number of accounts of terrible judgments visited on Anabaptists.

7. Beard, *Theatre of Gods Iudgements*, p. 542.

8. BL, Sloane MS. 1457, fo. 3r; see also Folger MS. V.a.436, p. 146. Although this chapter discusses Providence as Wallington understood its workings, it should not be inferred from this that providentialism was in this period a Puritan monopoly; on this point, see Lotte Mulligan, "Puritans and English Science: A Critique of Webster," *Isis*, 71 (1980), pp. 462–65. I owe this reference to my colleague Lewis Spitz.

9. BL, Sloane MS. 1457, fo. 11v.

10. *Ibid.*, fo. 13v. The observed statistical correlation was doubtless due in modern terms to the "accidents" of the unskilled who ventured on the water on the day of rest. In his observation of regularities in secondary causation Wallington is very much the contemporary of Sir Francis Bacon and Descartes; however, like most moralists, Wallington is more interested in the meaning of human actions than in their means, in God as final cause, and in the moral end or object of human action, the higher drama of God's will and man's response, rather than the mundane field of secondary causation on which that higher drama was acted out.

11. Beard, *Theatre of Gods Iudgements*, The Preface, A4r.

12. BL, Add. MS. 40,883, fo. 33v.

13. *Historical Notices*, vol. 1, p. 20.

14. GL, MS. 204, p. 495, misnumbered p. 480. Cf. BL, Sloane MS. 1457, fos. 47r–51r, for a slightly different account.

15. GL, MS. 204, p. 498, misnumbered p. 483.

16. *Ibid.*

17. *Ibid.*, p. 499, misnumbered p. 484.

18. *Ibid.*, p. 495, misnumbered p. 480. The reference is to Jeremiah 17:27.

19. *Historical Notices*, vol. 1, p. 14.　　20. GL, MS. 204, pp. 444–45.

21. Folger MS. V.a.436, p. 152.　　22. GL, MS. 204, p. 442.

23. Folger MS. V.a.436, p. 152; *Historical Notices*, vol. 1, p. 14.

24. GL, MS. 204, pp. 446–47.   25. *Ibid.*, p. 490.

26. *Ibid.*   27. *Ibid.*, p. 449.

28. *Ibid.*, p. 493.

29. BL, Add. MS. 21,935, fo. 180v. This passage is omitted from the printed *Historical Notices*. The passage mentions the "declaration of the Lords and Commons in Parliament," dated March 9, 1641/42, and was presumably written after that date.

30. GL, MS. 204, p. 457.

31. *Ibid.*, pp. 449–50.

32. BL, Sloane MS. 1457, fo. 56r.

33. Folger MS. V.a.436, pp. 497–98. The strange ceremony Wallington describes was apparently all that had survived of the festival and marching watch on the vigil of St. John the Baptist, once celebrated not only with garlands on all the houses but with bonfires and feasting and a great marching watch with lighted cressets that went through the principal streets of the City. See John Stow, *A Survey of London*, ed. C. L. Kingsford (Oxford, 1908), vol. 1, pp. 101–2. The conduit was endowed by Lord Mayor Thomas Hill and begun in 1491: *ibid.*, vol. 1, pp. 110, 211. Little of the public ceremonial life of the City seems to have survived the Reformation, but Wallington seems to have been indifferent even to what little did remain. Saint's day festivals, Rogation Day processions, and the like were necessarily things of the past and in any event too tainted with Catholicism to interest a man whose religion was so focused on the Word. However, there remained the great secular pageants of the Lord Mayor's processions, written in these years by Thomas Dekker and Thomas Middleton, and the even more spectacular pageantry of the royal progresses and entries; for all these, see D. M. Bergeron, *English Civic Pageantry, 1558–1642* (Columbia, S.C., 1971). Wallington must have witnessed some of these events—he could scarcely have avoided them—but he has left no record of any such occasion or of his feelings about such displays.

34. Folger MS. V.a.436, pp. 302, 388.

35. *Ibid.*, p. 298.   36. BL, Sloane MS. 1457, fo. 12r.

37. *Ibid.*, fo. 16v.   38. GL, MS. 204, p. 421.

39. *Ibid.*, p. 427.   40. *Ibid.*, pp. 434–35.

41. BL, Sloane MS. 1457, fo. 52r.   42. *Ibid.*, fo. 16v.

43. *Ibid.*, fo. 36r.   44. Folger MS. V.a.436, pp. 312–15.

45. BL, Sloane MS. 1457, fo. 12r–v.   46. *Ibid.*, fo. 15r.

47. *Ibid.*, fo. 15v. Salisbury in those years had a predominantly Puritan magistracy. See Paul Slack, "Poverty and Politics in Salisbury, 1597–1666," in Peter Clark and Paul Slack, eds., *Crisis and Order in English Towns, 1500–1700* (London, 1972), pp. 164–203.

48. BL, Sloane MS. 1457, fo. 18r.

49. *Ibid.*, fo. 18v.

50. *Ibid.*, fo. 19v. Sabbath breaking and drunkenness were in a sense the cardinal sins, but Wallington also noted judgments against murderers (fo. 39r–v), adulterers (fo. 34v), whoremongers (fo. 24v), and thieves (Folger MS. V.a.436, p. 150).

51. BL, Sloane MS. 1457, fo. 33r.   52. *Ibid.*, fo. 36v.

53. *Ibid.*, fo. 38r.   54. *Ibid.*, fo. 37r–v.

55. GL, MS. 204, p. 512.

56. BL, Add. MS. 40,883, fo. 169r–v. In 1612 a horse ridden at a gallop had gone "clean over" Wallington in Long Lane, leaving him lying unhurt in the street. GL, MS. 204, p. 418.

57. The following account is from GL, MS. 204, pp. 417–18. Wallington's house was apparently two rooms deep, the shop and workroom being on the ground floor, a kitchen and parlor on the first, a "folks chamber" (bedroom) and front room on the second, and a garret and storeroom above that.

58. It is perhaps worth noting that Wallington's pronouncement that "there was nobody at all hurt" ignored his wife's miscarriage, which makes one wonder whether miscarriages were so common that only the occasion was worth noting.

59. *Ibid.*, p. 434. A year earlier a similar accident had occurred: Nehemiah's brother-in-law was chopping wood in the garret, and the hatchet head had come off and fallen three stories down the stairwell to the shop, again missing everyone. *Ibid.*, p. 427.

60. *Ibid.*, p. 436.

61. BL, Sloane MS. 1457, fo. 6v.

62. See the story, already told in Chapter 2, of the Essex yeoman, an "ancient professor," who on a Sunday morning went into his chamber to dress for church and cut his throat instead. *Ibid.*, fo. 7r.

63. *Ibid.*, fo. 7v.   64. *Ibid.*, fo. 7r.

65. Folger MS. V.a.436, p. 148.   66. *Ibid.*, p. 151.

67. GL, MS. 204, p. 513.   68. BL, Sloane MS. 1457, fo. 58v.

69. *Ibid.*, fo. 65v. Those who took advantage of the Book of Sports—"the book of liberty," as Wallington called it—to profane the Sabbath courted death as well. *Ibid.*, fo. 13r.

70. *Ibid.*, fo. 73r.   71. *Ibid.*, fo. 41r.

72. *Ibid.*, fo. 66v.   73. *Ibid.*, fo. 59r.

74. *Ibid.*, fos. 68r–70r.

75. *Ibid.*, fo. 70r–v. These two examples are followed by 21 others of God's punishments of those who mock Roundheads. Wallington's book "Examples of God's Wrath upon those that have broken his Commandments" contains a section on "Blasphemies that they use in their devilish healths in the King's army." Folger MS. V.a.436, p. 147.

76. BL, Sloane MS. 1457, fo. 21r.

77. *Ibid.*, fo. 23v. The second part of Wallington's quote appears in the

Geneva Bible as "They provoked him with strange gods; they provoked him to anger with abominations," and is from Deuteronomy 32:16.

78. *Ibid.*, fo. 26r.   79. *Ibid.*, fo. 29r.

80. *Ibid.*, fo. 27v.   81. GL, MS. 204, pp. 512–13.

82. Wallington recognized the existence of natural portents, such as the comet that appeared in 1618 and was thought to portend convulsions in Germany, but he was not very much interested in them. See BL, Sloane MS. 1457, fo. 3v; *Historical Notices*, vol. 1, p. 14.

83. BL, Sloane MS. 1457, fos. 99r–100v.

84. *Ibid.*, fo. 103r.

85. Wallington was aware of conflicts between good and evil and between the children of God and those of the world. What is virtually absent is any sense of conflict between social strata, although he recounts one incident of sudden death that suggests the possibility of such antagonism. On May 23, 1632, the wind blew the hat off a gentleman in a coach coming along Bow Street. The gentleman leaned out of the coach and said to an old man passing by, "Sirrah, reach up my hat." The old man answered, "I do not owe you so much service," at which the gentleman leaped out of the coach "and thrust the ancient man through with his sword, and so he died." GL, MS. 204, p. 512.

Chapter 4

The epigraph is a passage from a letter of exhortation from Edward Dering to Mistress K., February 28, 1575/76, as copied into Nehemiah Wallington's letter book, BL, Sloane MS. 922, fos. 29r–30v. For Dering, the famous Elizabethan Puritan preacher, see Patrick Collinson, "A Mirror of Elizabethan Puritanism: The Life and Letters of 'Godly Master Dering,'" in *Godly People: Essays in English Protestantism and Puritanism* (London, 1983), pp. 289–324. "Mistress K." is probably Mrs. Catherine Killigrew. *Ibid.*, pp. 316–18.

1. GL, MS. 204, "To the Christian Reader," unpaginated.

2. Folger MS. V.a.436, p. 528. Entry dated December 27, 1654.

3. *Ibid.*, p. 196.

4. John Wallington, Sr., wrote that he first came to London and was apprenticed in St. Andrew's Hubbard in 1572. Folger MS. V.a.436, pp. 202–3. The extant Turners' Company record of apprentice bindings does not begin until 1604, so his recollection cannot be checked. John Houghton, Nehemiah's son-in-law, was born in Bedfordshire, the son of a yeoman, and was apprenticed December 15, 1637. GL, MS. 3302/1, under that date.

5. GL, MS. 3302/1.

6. This recruiting pattern was to change. The Company continued to recruit apprentices from Cumberland in the far north and Shropshire in the west, as well as from Wales, Scotland, and Ireland, but by the 1650's, the last

years of Wallington's life, 23.8 percent of the apprentices were London born, and this percentage was typical of the second half of the seventeenth century: 28.7 percent of the apprentices were London born in the 1660's, 22 percent in the 1670's, 32 percent in the 1680's.

7. The parish register of St. Leonard's does record the christening of an Elizabeth Wallington, daughter of William Wallington of Bottell Oledon, Bucks., on March 12, 1586/87, who might conceivably be John's brother. GL, MS. 17,607, fo. 9v.

8. BL, Sloane MS. 922, fos. 160r–62v.

9. On Elizabeth Hall, see Nehemiah Wallington's "A Faithful Memorial of my own Mother," GL, MS. 204, pp. 486–90. Although Nehemiah was sent to his grandmother Hall's house in St. Botolph's–Without–Bishopsgate during the sickness in 1609, he never mentions his mother's brother, Anthony Hall, of Tottenham, Middlesex, who had sold the St. Botolph's properties to the Wallingtons in 1597. See GL, MS. 1418.

10. For the births of the children, see GL, MS. 204, p. 490; for their christenings, see the parish register of St. Leonard's, GL, MS. 17,607. Although bridal pregnancy was not uncommon in this period, John Wallington's and Elizabeth Hall's marriage was on November 23, 1583, and their daughter Anne was born on August 11, 1584, which makes bridal pregnancy unlikely in this instance.

11. Joan Hinde is recorded as from Sacombe, Herts., widow, in the parish register, *ibid.*, fo. 10r.

12. *Ibid.*, fo. 10r; BL, Sloane MS. 922, fos. 5r, 127v.

13. GL, MS. 17,607, fo. 16r.

14. For Alice's burial, see GL, MS. 17,607, fo. 23r.

15. Patience Wallington, for example, was not christened in the parish of St. Leonard's Eastcheap, and there is no reason to suppose that she was unique in that respect.

16. Elizabeth's, Mary's, and Dorcas's weddings are noted in the parish register, GL, MS. 17,607, fos. 10v, 12r, and 13v; Dorcas married a second time in 1640 to Thomas Jube, *ibid.*, fo. 15v. Nehemiah mentions visiting Sarah in Lewisham in 1625, GL, MS. 204, p. 408. For Patience and Henry Church, see BL, Sloane MS. 922, fos. 87r–89v, 108v. Nehemiah gives the date of his own marriage (June 18, 1621), but not the parish in which he and Grace were married, in Folger MS. V.a.436, , p. 12.

17. The will is in Lambeth Palace Library, MS. VH 95/2036. Dorcas Fawken, daughter of Mary Wallington and Thomas Fawken, is mentioned in the will, but Dorcas Fawken's older sister Mary is not.

18. For a summary of what is known about the impact of the plague on different age groups in London, see Roger Finlay, *Population and Metropolis: The Demography of London, 1580–1650* (Cambridge, Eng., 1981), Chapter 6, and esp. pp. 129–30.

19. For these calculations the year 1611, which had ten unknowns, was eliminated. Between 1602 and 1610, with the plague year deaths eliminated, there were 101 deaths recorded, 91 with the age of death given. The child mortality rates given by Finlay are calculated to age 15 (see *ibid.*, Chapter 5). In St. Leonard's, 47 percent of the deaths had occurred by age 15 if one includes the plague year, 46 percent if one omits it.

20. Finlay notes that London-born women married younger than migrants (*ibid.*, p. 138). For example, Elizabeth Hall married John Wallington, Sr., when she was 20 and he was 31; their daughters Elizabeth, Mary, and Dorcas married at 21, 23, and 26, respectively. Patience Wallington was probably about 25 when she married Henry Church, but the dates of her birth, marriage, and death are conjectural. She was alive on March 31, 1635, when John Wallington, Sr., mentions her in a letter (BL, Sloane MS. 922, fo. 108r), but she was not mentioned in his will dated July 30, 1635 (Lambeth Palace Library, MS. VH 95/2036).

21. GL, MS. 17,607, fo. 15r–v.

22. For sister Sarah, see GL, MS. 204, p. 408. Nehemiah mentioned his nephew John Bradshaw in a prayer in 1632, and his father wrote his grandson a letter of admonition in March of that year: *ibid.*, p. 498; BL, Sloane MS. 922, fo. 85r–v. Nehemiah excerpted part of a letter Bradshaw wrote, dated October 30, 1628, about "the troubles and sorrows of the Rochellers," especially Bradshaw's account of the terrible famine that accompanied the siege. GL, MS. 204, p. 422. Wallington makes no comment on the disastrous attempt to relieve the siege.

23. Wallington's letter to "cousin" John Wallington is in BL, Sloane MS. 922, fos. 160r–62v. The indenture concerns the property of Anthony's and Elizabeth's parents in Bishopsgate (GL, MS. 1418); the property was sold in 1602 (GL, MS. 1419).

24. For the Allens, see John Wallington, Sr.'s, letter to the Rev. John Allen, March 31, 1635: BL, Sloane MS. 922, fo. 108r–v; for the Cross-Hinde connection in Chelmsford, see *ibid.*, fo. 5r; for Nehemiah's letter to his cousin the Rev. Nathaniel Church, see *ibid.*, fos. 166r–68r; see also Folger MS. V.a.436, p. 153.

25. For Zachariah, see the memoir in *Historical Notices*, vol. 1, pp. 304–7; for Livewell, see letters in BL, Sloane MS. 922, fos. 71r–84v.

26. For a presentation of these generalizations in their full complexity, see Lawrence Stone, *Family, Sex and Marriage in England, 1500–1800* (New York, 1977), Chapters 4 and 5 (but note the important qualification on p. 207). See also Richard L. Greaves, *Society and Religion in Elizabethan England* (Minneapolis, Minn., 1981), Chapter 6, and in particular his statement (p. 297) that "Elizabethan authors were divided over the proper role of affection, and the division did not strictly follow religious lines"; Keith Wrightson, *English Society, 1580–1680* (London, 1982), Chapters 2–4; and Michael MacDonald,

Mystical Bedlam (Cambridge, Eng., 1981), Chapter 3, which provides empirical data as well as an important theoretical discussion of family relationships and stress in the early seventeenth century.

27. John Wallington, Sr., was named in the Turners' Company charter of 1604: GL, MS. 3800, p. 11.

28. GL, MS. 204, unpaginated memoir between pp. 473 and 475. Nehemiah's memoir should be compared with Lucy Hutchinson's recollections of her mother, which are remarkably similar, allowing for the social differences between Lucy's aristocratic mother and Nehemiah's urban middle-class one: Lucy Hutchinson, *Memoirs of the Life of Colonel Hutchinson*, ed. James Sutherland (Oxford, 1973), pp. 284, 286–87.

29. BL, Sloane MS. 922, fo. 104v.

30. GL, MS. 204, misnumbered pp. 484–85.

31. Folger MS. V.a.436, p. 16.

32. GL, MS. 204, p. 413.   33. *Ibid.*, p. 318.

34. *Ibid.*, p. 7.   35. *Ibid.*, p. 8.

36. For John Wallington, Sr., as master, see GL, MS. 3295/1, "The Turners' Company Court Minutes, 1605–33," May 15, 1619, and throughout. For the requirement that journeymen serve two years, see the transcript of the "Turners' Company Ordinances 6 James I, 1608," GL, MS. 3308, fo. 7r. For Nehemiah's freedom, see the Freeman's Admissions at the back of the volume of Apprentice Bindings, GL, MS. 3302/1, dated May 18, 1620.

37. Folger MS. V.a.436, p. 12. The passage is from Genesis 2:18, as quoted from the Geneva Bible.

38. GL, MS. 3295/1, December 15, 1622. For a discussion of company loan funds in this period, see W. K. Jordan, *The Charities of London, 1480–1660* (London, 1960), pp. 24, 172–77.

39. In early 1624 Fawken pleaded with the company to mitigate a fine because "he was a poor man and the times were hard." GL, MS. 3295/1, March 11, 1623/24.

40. *Ibid.*, January 17, 1625/26. The loan to Nehemiah was arranged nonetheless.

41. *Ibid.*, August 9, 1627.

42. *Ibid.*, April 15, 1629, October 18, 1632. It is perhaps significant that at the same company meeting in 1632 Thomas Fawken was forgiven six shillings of a ten-shilling fine.

43. GL, MS. 204, pp. 418, 428–30.

44. Nehemiah already had an apprentice at this time and could not take on another. GL, MS. 3302/1, February 12, 1628/29; GL, MS. 204, p. 434.

45. GL, MS. 204, p. 437.

46. *Ibid.*, pp. 438–39.

47. Lambeth Palace Library, MS. VH 95/2036.

48. GL, MS. 204, p. 469; Folger MS. V.a.436, p. 63.

49. Folger MS. V.a.436, p.14.   50. GL, MS. 204, pp. 407–8.

51. *Ibid.*, p. 439.   52. *Ibid.*, pp. 463–65.

53. *Ibid.*, p. 408. Lewisham is about five miles southeast of London Bridge. Presumably Wallington took the boat downriver to Deptford and walked south a mile inland to the village of Lewisham on the road to Folkestone.

54. BL, Add. MS. 40,883, fo. 83r. On two occasions Nehemiah notes that he went to Peckham alone at five in the morning: "Oh, what sweet meditations and prayer had I with my God" is his characteristic comment. *Ibid.*, fos. 144v, 150v.

55. BL, Sloane MS. 922, fos. 78v–79r. The first three of these letters also appear in GL, MS. 204, pp. 413–16, 419–20, 424–26.

56. BL, Sloane MS. 922, fos. 75r, 76r.

57. *Ibid.*, fo. 71r–v.

58. *Ibid.*, fo. 73v. According to Venn, Livewell Rampaigne became rector of Broxholme in 1625. John and J. A. Venn, *Alumni Cantabrigienses*, Part 1 (Cambridge, Eng., 1922), vol. 3, p. 416. This letter and the others written in 1628 and 1629 are dated from Burton, a village less than a mile north of Lincoln and about a mile away from Broxholme.

59. Venn claims that Livewell became vicar of Great Grimsby in 1637; Nehemiah wrote that Sarah came to live with them nineteen years before her death in 1654 (Folger MS. V.a.436, p. 307). "Sister Sarah" was certainly ensconced in the household by April 1636: see GL, MS. 204, p. 468. Since "Sister Rampaigne" was clearly a young widow when she arrived at the Wallingtons, I have not been able to reconcile her presence there with the information in Venn. For Sarah Rampaigne's two children, see Grace's letter: BL, Sloane MS. 922, fo. 159v.

60. BL, Add. MS. 40,883, fo. 64r.   61. Folger MS. V.a.436, p. 304.

62. *Ibid.*   63. *Ibid.*, p. 307.

64. For the account of Zachariah Rampaigne's death, see BL, Add. MS. 21,935, fos. 228r–29v; see also *Historical Notices*, vol. 1, pp. 303–8.

65. BL, Sloane MS. 922, fos. 155r–58v.

66. *Ibid.*, fo. 159r–v.

67. GL, MS. 3302/1, under the date of July 18, 1655. Charles Rampaigne was the only relative Nehemiah took on as an apprentice, so far as one can tell from the records, but John Wallington, Jr., bound his nephew, John Kiffet, as an apprentice on May 30, 1654.

68. For Dorcas's marriage to Thomas Jube, see the parish register of St. Leonard's, GL, MS. 17,607, fo. 15v. It is worth noting also that the presence of the Rampaigne relatives in the Wallington household would escape the attention of the historical demographer, for the presence of Sarah and her children is known only from Wallington's personal papers (Sarah's burial is not recorded in the St. Leonard's parish register, and even if it had been, the record would not reveal that she had been resident with her two children in

Nehemiah's household), and the only "public" confirmation of Charles Rampaigne's presence is in the admissions section of the Turners' Company book of apprentice bindings.

69. Lambeth Palace Library MS. VH 95/2036. The 1638 tithe survey, dated three months before John, Sr.'s, death, does not show him as an independent householder, although both John, Jr., and Nehemiah are listed. T. C. Dale, *The Inhabitants of London in 1638* (London, 1931), vol. 1, pp. 88–89. The two precincts do not correspond with any precision to the parish boundaries of St. Leonard's Eastcheap, and precinct lists for St. Leonard's, which are extant from 1634, note neither John Wallington, father or son: GL, MS. 3461/1.

70. Folger MS. V.a.436, "To the Christian Reader," unpaginated.

71. GL, MS. 204, p. 437.

72. Folger MS. V.a.436, p. 159.

73. GL, MS. 204, p. 68.

74. *Ibid.*, pp. 418, 463. The latter miscarriage evidently ended Grace's childbearing.

75. BL, Add. MS. 40,883, fo. 138v. Nehemiah was surprised but not put off by this show of political concern, for he added that it "did my soul good to see her so to lay to heart the dishonors done to our God, and I shall love her for it the better as long as I live." *Ibid.*

76. GL, MS. 204, pp. 39, 425. 77. *Ibid.*, p. 401.

78. *Ibid.*, pp. 407, 410. 79. *Ibid.*, pp. 408–9.

80. *Ibid.*, p. 409. Wallington assumed that mothers loved their children, and at least on one occasion used that assumption as a means of illustrating the nature of divine love: "Oh, then my soul, be thou persuaded that thy God loves thee as well now [in adversity] as a mother loves her child, as well when she gives her child physic, even bitter pills, . . . nay, she is more tender over it than in time of health. How much more is my God loving and tender over one in adversity." BL, Add. MS. 40,883, fo. 34v.

81. GL, MS. 204, p. 409. 82. *Ibid.*, p. 404.

83. *Ibid.*, p. 417. 84. *Ibid.*, p. 412.

85. *Ibid.*, p. 419. 86. *Ibid.*, pp. 421–22.

87. *Ibid.*, pp. 431–32. As this incident suggests, Nehemiah did summon doctors on occasion, but clearly regarded doctors and apothecaries as a last desperate measure, a predictable expense for no predictable benefit. On a cold September day in 1643 Nehemiah considered what a mercy it was that they all had their health, "for the Lord might have struck some of us sick this hard time, when so little money is taken with so little gains, and we might have great expenses with doctors and apothecaries, with fire and candles all night and day, with hiring some nurse to look to them and watching by them . . . and at last have took an only child or else the pleasure of the eyes. These thoughts did keep [one] from murmuring." BL, Add. MS. 40,883, fo. 149r. The Puritan objection to the ready resort to wise or cunning men or women

has been explored at length by Keith Thomas in *Religion and the Decline of Magic* (London, 1971), esp. pp. 263–67. William Perkins even argued with a certain logic that the good witch—wise man or woman—was worse than the bad: *The Work of William Perkins*, ed. Ian Breward (Abingdon, Berks., 1970), p. 598. Wallington's resort to Mrs. Mason must, then, have been a real act of desperation, although he may have believed that he had summoned her only for her knowledge of folk medicine, not of magical healing. For the difficulty in making such a distinction in this period, see Thomas, *Religion and the Decline of Magic*, p. 189; cf. Michael MacDonald, *Mystical Bedlam* (Cambridge, Eng., 1981), pp. 13–32.

88. GL, MS. 204, pp. 435–36.

89. *Ibid.*, pp. 467, 436. It should be noted that Livewell Rampaigne in one of his letters to his brother-in-law Nehemiah suggests that the problem for parents was not a callous or crushed indifference, but rather inordinate grief, and that a kind of balance must be achieved, which required an act of will. To grieve at the loss of a child was, of course, understandable, but "to mourn overmuch is to murmur and repine against the decrees of the Almighty." Hence the godly Christian parent must intervene actively in his own grief: "Nature must not be suffered to take its own time for an end of lamenting; time is heathen's physic that wears out the greater griefs"; but for the godly "grace must restrain and limit inordinate sorrow and apply comforts to our fainting hearts." *Ibid.*, pp. 413–14. Nonetheless, there is no reason to posit any special sensitivity toward children in the godly community. Rather, the crucial difference in this society was doubtless whether the mother nursed the child or put it out to be wet-nursed. A child put out in infancy and dying soon after may have occasioned little emotional response from its parents. Yet Grace Wallington nursed four of her five children, and even Samuel, who was eventually put to nurse and died away from home, had wasted away for six months at home before that desperate measure was resorted to. Nehemiah was criticized not for feeling grief but for permitting it to overmaster him.

90. *Ibid.*, p. 470.

91. BL, Sloane MS. 922, fo. 164r–v. The letter is headed "T. L. to his daughter Susan Lithal" and was probably written by Wallington's neighbor, the Common Councilman Tobias Lisle.

92. Folger MS. V.a.436, p. 154.

93. BL, Sloane MS. 922, fos. 87r–89v. By the same token Nehemiah was convinced that a "cross or crooked yokefellow" was a "rod" of chastisement for choosing a spouse for "some by and sinister end, as for lust, or riches, or beauty, or honor, some by-end or other, not aiming at God's glory nor choosing for the best things as grace or virtue." Folger MS. V.a.436, p. 196. Although Wallington mentions having bought William Gouge's *Of Domestical Duties* (London, 1622), that lengthy treatise seems not to have been the model for this letter. Gouge does treat the subject in a section titled "Direc-

tions to parents in providing marriages," and writes that "they do offend, who for outward advantage match their children to such as by nature are unfit for marriage; to idiots, to idolaters, to profane persons, or they care not whom. . . . Many mischiefs ordinarily fall upon such marriages." *Of Domestical Duties* (2d ed., London, 1626), pp. 316–17. Nehemiah's letter seems rather to be closer to the concerns of Robert Cleaver, who writes: "For if parents and householders shall perform no further duties to their children and servants, than to provide them meat, drink, and apparel, . . . then Papists, Atheists, yea Turks and Infidels, do yield their duties as well as they." Cleaver goes on to say in a section on the duties of parents to children that "one of the principalist duties that belong to parents . . . is that they be very wary and careful that their sons and daughters do not match in marriage with such as are ungodly, wicked, and void of true religion," and, a few pages further on, that "parents must not match their children only for carnal respects." *Godlie Forme of Household Government: For the Ordering of Private Families, according to the direction of God's Word* (London, 1600), Epistle Dedicatory, A3ʳ, and pp. 313, 320–21. However, even though most of the points Nehemiah makes in his letter can be found in Cleaver's popular treatise, it is not obvious that Nehemiah copied, or even paraphrased, that work. The tone of Wallington's letter is much more passionate in its immediate concern, and the rhetoric is his own. It is probable that the ideas themselves were commonplace among the literate godly by the 1630's.

94. GL, MS. 3302/1, entry dated December 15, 1637. The marriage took place at St. Leonard's (GL, MS. 17,607, fo. 15v).

95. Folger MS. V.a.436, p. 172.

96. GL, MS. 3295/2, minute dated December 7, 1649.

97. GL, MS. 17,607, fo. 26r. One would have thought that the birth of twins three weeks apart was sufficiently unusual to elicit comment, but the parish register records the fact without comment, and Nehemiah apparently passes over the event in silence, because, as he notes, "I did then give over writing, intending to write no more books, . . . but now with help of God I will strive to practice what I have read and written and set myself to live to God's glory." Folger MS. V.a.436, p. 188. In 1652 he resumed his writing as a means of self-examination, "because I would be more careful over my ways." *Ibid.*

98. Folger MS. V.a.436, p. 213.

99. *Ibid.*, p. 301. The Psalm is from the extremely popular Sternhold and Hopkins metrical version.

100. *Ibid.*, pp. 323, 321, 329, 331.

101. *Ibid.*, pp. 331–32, 395.

102. *Ibid.*, pp. 418, 422. It should be noted that the greeting "God give you joy in your grandchild" gives public expression to the expectation that children were primarily a source not of dread or anxiety but of pleasure; evi-

dently parents and grandparents were expected to enjoy their children then as now.

103. *Ibid.*, pp. 431, 438, 441, 512, 432.

104. BL, Sloane MS. 922, fo. 98r. Cole evidently had three children—a son who was probably older than Nehemiah's daughter Sarah, a younger daughter, and a second son who was evidently an infant in 1634. See *ibid.*, fo. 95v.

105. GL, MS. 204, pp. 430, 506.

106. BL, Sloane MS. 922, fos. 98v, 104r, 97r.

107. *Ibid.*, fo. 99r–v.

108. *Ibid.*, fos. 94r–95v.

109. *Ibid.*, fo. 103r. "Place and calling" normally meant status and occupation; Nehemiah's father was evidently stretching that traditional injunction to cover geographical location as well.

110. *Ibid.*, fo. 101r.

111. *Ibid.*, fos. 99v, 101r, 102v.

112. *Ibid.*, fos. 101r, 97r–98r.

113. *Ibid.*, fo. 98v. Ipswich is almost seventy miles from London by road.

114. *Ibid.*, fo. 100r–v. One of the "two great men" was undoubtedly Lord Brooke (was the other Lord Say and Sele?), for whom see A. P. Newton, *The Colonizing Activities of the English Puritans* (New Haven, Conn., 1914), esp. pp. 65–67; and Valerie Pearl, *London and the Outbreak of the Puritan Revolution* (Oxford, 1961), pp. 160–70. For a sketch of the internal politics of Warwick, see Derek Hirst, *The Representative of the People?* (Cambridge, Eng., 1975), pp. 210–12.

115. BL, Sloane MS. 922, fos. 104r–6v. Wallington always refers to gatherings of the godly that are not parochial congregations as "companies."

116. *Ibid.*, fo. 107r–v.

117. *Ibid.*, fos. 173r–76v.

118. GL, MS. 204, p. 470 (the ms. is incorrectly paginated at this point and should read p. 475). Edward Browne bound an apprentice on February 2, 1635/36, and so was still active in the turner's trade at that date. GL, MS. 3302/1.

119. BL, Sloane MS. 922, fos. 144v–45r.

120. *Ibid.*, fos. 145v–47v.

121. *Ibid.*, fos. 5r, 116r–17r. Despite the shipment of oranges and lemons, a later letter informed Wallington of the death of "our dear and reverend pastor Mr. Coates." *Ibid.*, fo. 120r.

122. *Ibid.*, fos. 126v–28v. For an eyewitness account of the confused events at Nottingham in 1643, see *Memoirs of the Life of Colonel Hutchinson*, pp. 69–118. Wilsmore was probably killed by a ball fired by the Parliamentary garrison, an irony that Wallington would not have appreciated.

123. BL, Sloane MS. 922, fo. 4v. Mention is also made of another letter, to

a Goodman Prestland of Takely, Essex, which is also not included in the letter book: *ibid.*, fo. 5r.

124. GL, MS. 3461/1, under the dates 1634 and 1642. Adams does not appear on the 1646 precinct list and had presumably moved on to become Lord Mayor. For his history, see Pearl, *London and the Outbreak of the Puritan Revolution*, pp. 292–93.

125. BL, Sloane MS. 922, fos. 153r–54v; for his residence, see the precinct lists, 1634–46, in GL, MS. 3461/1; for details of his life, see the entry s.v. Thomas Player in the *Dictionary of National Biography*.

126. BL, Sloane MS. 922, fos. 134v–37v.

127. *Ibid.*, fos. 142r–44r.

128. Wallington did not, of course, actually believe that sanctification could come without justifying faith, at least not in any formal theological sense. However, the problem for the godly person who professed his faith but in his forties had still not undergone any kind of convincing conversion experience was acute: how was such a professor to gain assurance of ultimate salvation? Preparationist thought was an attempt to meet this very real pastoral problem, and one of the key figures in this development in pastoral theology was Thomas Hooker, a number of whose books—*The Poor Doubting Christian*, *The Soules Preparation for Christ*, and *The Soules Humiliation*—had gone through four or five editions by 1639. Wallington was evidently acquainted with some of Hooker's writings, as Francis Wilsmore's letter of thanks to Wallington for sending one of Hooker's treatises testifies. BL, Sloane MS. 922, fo. 116r (the letter is dated January 14, 1638/39). As R. T. Kendall points out, Hooker "is comforting to the soul who wants assurance as soon as possible that, however long the process, there is no danger the process can be aborted along the way. As long as one feels sorrow for sin, seeing that he is 'miserable,' his sorrow is sound. The consoling thought is that contrition is guaranteed to lead to a hatred of sin which 'cannot be in a reprobate.'" *Calvin and English Calvinism to 1649* (Oxford, 1979), p. 134. Hooker's understanding of the process was doubly comforting. It was at the very time when the troubled soul most despaired of its own resources that it was most ready to be "ingrafted into Christ": "Now, if the heart be once prepared and humbled, look then immediately for Christ." At the same time, the soul need not and in fact usually will not be aware of the change: "Christ is come, but thou perceivest it not." Hence, salvation occurs without a dramatic subjective sense of justification. The soul must have faith in God's promises, and, perhaps the most telling point for the troubled saint, by seeing "if we keep his commandments," for then we know that Christ is "implanted" in the soul. *Ibid.*, pp. 136–37. That some of Thomas Hooker's Essex flock suffered under the same lack of assurance that Wallington experienced is testified to by William Manning's "Confession": see George Selement and Bruce C. Woolley, eds., *Thomas Shephard's Confessions*, Pubs. of the

Colonial Society of Massachusetts Collections, vol. 58 (Boston, 1981), pp. 93–98.

129. BL, Sloane MS. 922, fos. 90r–93v. The letter describing the siege of La Rochelle is in *ibid.*, fos. 76r–77v, and in GL, MS. 204, pp. 422–23. John Bradshaw had committed some nameless "transgression" that apparently drove him to sea, although the Wallingtons, particularly John, Sr., obviously remained very fond of him. See GL, MS. 204, p. 498, and BL, Sloane MS. 922, fo. 85r–v. For Germany, see Nehemiah's prayer, GL, MS. 204, p. 502.

130. GL, MS. 204, pp. 430, 506. Lambeth Palace Library, MS. VH 95/2036; *Calendar of State Papers, Domestic, 1651*, p. 618; Charles F. Surman, ed., *The Register Book of the Fourth Classis* (Harleian Society Pubs., vols. 82 and 83; London, 1952), p. 1.

131. BL, Sloane MS. 922, fos. 118r–26r.

132. *Ibid.*, fos. 140r–41v.

133. *Ibid.*, fos. 132r–34r. For Colfe, see Richard Newcourt, *Repertorium Ecclesiasticum Parochiale Londinense* (London, 1708), vol. 1, p. 391. Colfe was forced to surrender St. Leonard's to Henry Roborough, the curate, by the Assembly of Divines.

134. BL, Sloane MS. 922, fos. 168r–70v, 165r–v. The letter to Barker, dated, April 22, 1650, is entitled "A Supposed Letter by N. W. read to Master Barker of what he would say to him concerning his sweet & pleasing preaching." The letter to Griffith is dated February 25, 1649/50.

135. *Ibid.*, fo. 166r; the quoted passage is from Ezekiel 33:7–8.

136. *Ibid.*, fos. 166r–67v; for Nathaniel Church, see Venn, *Alumni Cantabrigienses*, Part 1, vol. 1, p. 337. Church conformed at the Restoration, but by then Nehemiah was dead. Despite his strictures, Wallington did find the preaching of these ministers useful, at least to himself. In the year 1646 "I had two paper books. I did write sermons in them. . . . Some of the sermons were of Mr. Roborough, some of them Mr. Griffiths, some of Mr. Barker, and some . . . of my Cousin Church." Folger MS. V.a.436, p. 153.

137. GL, MS. 204, p. 434.

138. *Ibid.*, p. 421; see also pp. 405, 409.

139. Folger MS. V.a.436, p. 343.

140. BL, Add. MS. 40,883, fos. 172r–74r.

141. *Ibid.*, fo. 169r; Folger MS. V.a.436, p. 473.

142. Folger MS. V.a.436, p. 473.

Chapter 5

The epigraph comes from Richard Greenham's short rules sent to a gentleman troubled in mind, 1612, which Nehemiah copied into his letter book, BL, Sloane MS. 922, fo. 32r.

1. GL, MS. 204, p. 492.

2. *Ibid.*, p. 493.

3. *Ibid.*, p. 452; Folger MS. V.a.436, p. 533.

4. Folger MS. V.a.436, pp. 11–12.

5. The admissions are recorded at the back of the company's book of apprentice bindings, GL, MS. 3302/1, and the first 200 run from August 1, 1604, to June 1, 1624. The percentage gaining admission by patrimony did not change significantly after this: 8 percent entered by that means in the decade of the 1630's, 6.8 percent in the 1650's, and 6 percent in the 1680's.

6. This percentage does not change appreciably in the next generation. Between 1640 and 1644, 160 apprentices were bound, four (2.5 percent) of whom were sons of turners. Twenty years later, between 1670 and 1674, 271 apprentices were bound, ten of whom (3.7 percent) were sons of turners. The trend was rising—between 1680 and 1684, 291 apprentices were bound, 13 of whom (4.4 percent) were sons of turners—but clearly dynasties in the trade remained exceptional. GL, MS. 3302/1.

7. George Unwin, *The Gilds and Companies of London*, 4th ed. (New York, 1963), p. 68.

8. *Ibid.*, p. 370; John Stow, *A Survey of London*, ed. C. L. Kingsford (Oxford, 1908), vol. 2, pp. 190–92.

9. See the entry in the company's Court Minutes of November 11, 1614, when Thomas Fawcon [Fawken], Nehemiah's brother-in-law, was ordered to present an "armstool" at the next court day. GL, MS. 3295/1.

10. See the Company Ordinances, dated 6 James I, 1608: GL, MS. 3308, fos. 5r, 39r; Court Minutes, November 11, 1614, GL, MS. 3295/1.

11. GL, MS. 3295/1, February 20, 1615/16.

12. *Ibid.*, October 12, 1630.

13. *Ibid.*

14. GL, MS. 3800, p. 1; GL, MS. 3297/1, pp. 1, 17; GL, MS. 3308, fos. 1r–2r. For the general nature of early Stuart charters, see Unwin, *Gilds and Companies of London*, pp. 236–37.

15. GL, MS. 3308, fos. 9r, 27r–28r, 38r, 41r–42r, 18r.

16. GL, MS. 3800, p. 11; GL, MS. 3295/1, August 4, 1607. John Wallington, Sr., was himself fined 3/4 for keeping his booth too long at Bartholomew Fair, contrary to the company ordinance: GL, MS. 3295/1, September 24, 1611.

17. For the 1555 rule, see Unwin, *Gilds and Companies of London*, p. 265; for the Turners' Company rule requiring two years as a journeyman turner, see GL, MS. 3308, fo. 7r. When an attempt was made in 1627 to bind an apprentice aged only twelve, the Court of Assistants refused on the grounds of the boy's extreme youth. GL, MS. 3295/1, November 12, 1627. Clearly some flexibility was permitted, but only within reason.

18. GL, MS. 3295/1, January 18, 1619/20. He was elected master on May 6, 1619, and again on May 25, 1620.

19. *Ibid.*, January 19, 1625/26, and January 11, 1626/27.

20. GL, MS. 3295/2, October 9, 1645. For the younger John Wallington's career, see GL, MS. 3295/1, August 4, 1629; GL, MS. 3295/2, May 23, 1639, May 11, 1643, May 27, 1647.

21. GL, MS. 3295/1, April 30, 1630. In particular they ordered that fines paid by those who bound more than the allotted number of apprentices should not be remitted, a lax practice that they evidently saw as the cause of noncompliance.

22. *Ibid.*, February 1, 1629/30. Apprentices were supposed to wear collarless shirts—i.e., without bands at all. Good burghers and in fact most Englishmen wore shirts with a plain band or collar. Wearing a "lace falling band"—i.e., with the lace falling on one's chest—was dressing like a Court gallant and very unprenticelike.

23. *Ibid.*, February 3, 1630/31.

24. GL, MS. 3295/2, October 22, 1645.

25. GL, MS. 3295/1, April 15, 1630; GL, MS. 3295/2, May 8, 1651. In 1654 William Compton endowed the election sermon for twenty years. *Ibid.*, April 5, 1654.

26. GL, MS. 3295/2, October 7, 1640, June 10, 1642, August 14, 1643.

27. BL, Sloane MS. 922, fos. 146v–47r.

28. *Calendar of State Papers, Domestic, 1651*, pp. 557, 564, 584, 587. Further warrants appear in later volumes of the State Papers, the last being on September 22, 1653. How much money John made in these years is unknown, but his widow married into the gentry within a year of his death, which suggests that he left a considerable fortune. For Mary's marriage to John Ashton, Esq., see GL, MS. 17,607, fo. 16r. John Wallington, Jr., left no will: see the letter of administration issued to Mary Wallington, relict, in June 1657: Public Record Office, B 6/33, fo. 137v.

29. Lambeth Palace Library, MS. VH95/2036.

30. GL, MS. 204, pp. 428, 430.

31. Folger MS. V.a.436, p. 190. When Wallington thought in the early 1640's that he was spending too much money on newsbooks, he reminded himself that "I must one day give account before the great God as how I have improved and laid out every penny I have got; my conscience tells me I have been very remiss and unwise in some kind both in getting and spending, but I hope and trust the Lord hath forgiven me this and all other of my sins." BL, Add. MS. 40,883, fo. 15v.

32. GL, MS. 204, p. 470. It is worth noting that this is the only incident of housebreaking and theft that Wallington mentions. Wallington was well aware of the dangers of the urban environment from fire and disease, accidents with horses and carts, and accidental drownings, but urban crime figures nowhere in his catalogue of providential events or in his other writings.

33. BL, Add. MS. 40,883, fo. 37v.

34. Folger MS. V.a.436, p. 173.

35. T. C. Dale, *The Inhabitants of London in 1638* (London: published for the Society of Genealogists, 1931), vol. 1, p. 89.

36. GL, MS. 3295/2, January 21, 1636/37; the year of service ran from October 19. Evidently Nehemiah had not rushed right out to the company Hall to record the arrangement. Seeley, the son of a Birmingham panner, had been apprenticed to Wallington for nine years at Michaelmas 1626. GL, MS. 3302/1, January 11, 1626/27.

37. BL, Sloane MS. 922, fo. 159v. Yet when Wallington was negotiating for an apprentice in 1654, he noted that he expected "to have twenty pound with him." He also claimed that it cost him ten shillings a month (six pounds per annum) to keep an apprentice—a sum that evidently included food but not lodging, clothing, or wages, if any. Folger MS. V.a.436, pp. 323–24. In 1532, Walter Powell was able to apprentice one of his sons to a provincial dyer for five pounds. *The Diary of Walter Powell . . . , 1603–1654*, ed. J. A. Bradney (Bristol, 1907), p. 17. By contrast, a merchant apprenticeship in London was very much more costly. In 1632, Sir John Oglander apprenticed his son Richard to a London mercer, paying a premium of 70 pounds. *A Royalist's Notebook*, ed. Francis Bamford (London, 1936), p. 235. For merchant premiums in general, see Richard Grassby, "Social Mobility and Business Enterprise in Seventeenth-Century England," in Donald Pennington and Keith Thomas, eds., *Puritans and Revolutionaries* (Oxford, 1978), pp. 364–65.

38. BL, Add. MS. 40,883, fos. 144r, 9r.

39. *Ibid.*, fo. 12r–v. "A week earlier" had been January 4, the ill-fated day on which King Charles had attempted to arrest the five members on the floor of the House of Commons.

40. Folger MS. V.a.436, p. 401.   41. *Ibid.*, p. 353.

42. BL, Add. MS. 40,883, fo. 29r.   43. *Ibid.*, fo. 26r.

44. Folger MS. V.a.436, p. 308.   45. BL, Add. MS. 40,883, fo. 5v.

46. GL, MS. 204, p. 437.

47. BL, Add. MS. 40,883, fos. 112v, 115r.

48. *Ibid.*, fo. 144v. It is possible, as this incident suggests, that most of Nehemiah's borrowing took place within the godly community, but the evidence on this point is not conclusive.

49. *Ibid.*, fo. 148v.

50. *Ibid.*, fo. 179v. Nehemiah refused a call to the livery of the company on July 30, 1640: GL, MS. 3295/2. In 1652 John Wallington was able to lend the company twenty pounds, apparently without limit on the time of repayment: *ibid.*, July 21, 1653.

51. BL, Add. MS. 40,883, fo. 34v.   52. Folger MS. V.a.436, p. 156.

53. GL, MS. 204, pp. 39–41.   54. Folger MS. V.a.436, p. 413.

55. BL, Add. MS. 40,883, fo. 30v.   56. *Ibid.*, fo. 69r.

57. BL, Sloane MS. 922, fo. 102v; GL, MS. 204, pp. 21, 16.

58. Folger MS. V.a.436, p. 218.

59. For a recent discussion of these issues, see Laura S. O'Connell, "Anti-Entrepreneurial Attitudes in Elizabethan Sermons and Popular Literature," *Journal of British Studies*, 15 (1976), pp. 1–20; P. S. Seaver, "The Puritan Work Ethic Revisited," *Journal of British Studies*, 19 (1980), pp. 35–53; C. John Sommerville, "The Anti-Puritan Work Ethic," *Journal of British Studies*, 20 (1981), pp. 70–81; R. L. Greaves, *Society and Religion in Elizabethan England* (Minneapolis, Minn., 1981), pp. 377–95. Although these studies suggest that English Puritanism gave little encouragement to the development of what Weber rightly saw as the peculiar spirit of capitalism (Arminianism seems on Sommerville's showing a better candidate for that role), the last word has not been written on Puritanism and the Weber thesis, for no one has yet attempted the kind of sophisticated theoretical and empirical study of English data that Gordon Marshall has recently done for Scotland: see his *Presbyteries and Profits: Calvinism and the Development of Capitalism in Scotland, 1560–1707* (Oxford, 1981).

60. BL, Add. MS. 40,883, fo. 75v.

61. *Ibid.*, fo. 6v.

62. *Ibid.*, fo. 37v.

63. BL, Sloane MS. 922, fo. 103r; GL, MS. 204, p. 341.

64. GL, MS. 204, pp. 445–46.

65. Folger MS. V.a.436, pp. 292–93.

66. GL, MS. 204, p. 334.

67. *Ibid.*, pp. 51, 109.

68. *Ibid.*, p. 108.

69. *Historical Notices*, vol. 1, p. 134. Wallington had a poor box in his chamber into which he placed the odd farthing or penny he fined himself when he broke one of his many self-imposed rules of conduct. GL, MS. 204, p. 35.

70. BL, Sloane MS. 922, fo. 175v.

71. Folger MS. V.a.436, p. 404.

72. GL, MS. 204, p. 440.

73. *Ibid.*, p. 479; BL, Sloane MS. 922, fo. 175v.

74. GL, MS. 204, p. 454; Wallington is here quoting without attribution from Arthur Dent, *The Plaine Mans Path-Way to Heaven* (London, 1601), p. 123.

75. BL, Sloane MS. 922, fo. 32r; Wallington is here quoting from a letter by the Rev. Richard Greenham, dated 1612, which he had copied into his letter book.

76. GL, MS. 204, pp. 487, 12.

77. *Ibid.*, p. 452.

78. BL, Add. MS. 40,883, fos. 5r, 187r.

79. For Wallington's service on the grand jury, see GL, MS. 3461/1, Bridge Ward Within: Wardmote Inquests, etc., under dates 1644, 1645, 1655. For his participation as a member of the Fourth London Classis, see *The Register Book of the Fourth Classis in the Province of London, 1646–59*, transcribed and intro-

duced by Charles E. Surman (London, 1953; Harleian Society Pubs., vols. 82–83).

80. The classic study is E. H. Phelps Brown and Sheila V. Hopkins, "Seven Centuries of Building Wages," *Economica* (1955), reprinted in E. M. Carus-Wilson, ed., *Essays in Economic History* (New York, 1966), vol. 2, pp. 168–96. The consequences of inflation on traditional patterns of work have been analyzed in Ian Blanchard, "Labour Productivity and Work Psychology in the English Mining Industry, 1400–1600," *Economic History Review*, 31 (1978), pp. 1–24.

81. GL, MS. 3295/1, January 11, 1626/27. It is worth noting that the company sought to appease the one dissenter, a Mrs. Lewis, by including her among the 1627 group.

82. For the acreage of St. Leonard's, see Roger Finlay, *Population and Metropolis: The Demography of London, 1580–1650* (Cambridge, Eng., 1981), p. 170. The number of butchers has been compiled from the parish register, 1602–11, GL, MS. 17,607.

83. BL, Add. MS. 40,883, fos. 8v, 167v.

84. *Ibid.*, fo. 29v.   85. BL, Sloane MS. 922, fo. 56r.

86. BL, Add. MS. 40,883, fo. 9r.   87. *Ibid.*, fo. 7r–v.

88. GL, MS. 17,607, fos. 25r, 20r; for his lectureship at St. Leonard's and at neighboring St. Clement's, see Lambeth Palace Library MS. 942, no. 14; see also Benjamin Brook, *Lives of the Puritans* (London, 1813), vol. 3, pp. 530–32; John and J. A. Venn, *Alumni Cantabrigienses* (Cambridge, Eng., 1922), Part 1, vol. 3, p. 476.

89. A. G. Matthews, *Calamy Revised* (Oxford, 1934), pp. 28–29; *Biographical Dictionary of British Radicals in the Seventeenth Century*, ed. R. L. Greaves and Robert Zaller (London, 1982), vol. 1, pp. 38–39.

90. BL, Sloane MS. 922, fo. 169r–v.

91. It is notoriously difficult to be precise about level of income or wealth. The survey conducted in 1638 for the "Settlement of Tithes" (see *The Inhabitants of London in 1638* [2 vols., ed. T. C. Dale, for the Society of Genealogists, London, 1931]) shows Wallington's house as having a rental value (not the actual rent) of 20 pounds per annum at a "moderated" rent (i.e., 75 percent of actual market value); his brother John's house was assessed at 24 pounds. These rents might be compared to those of the City elite: Alderman Backhouse's house at 60 pounds, Alderman Andrewes's at 60 pounds, Alderman Gurney's at 70 pounds, and Sheriff Atkins's at 80 pounds. A mere 24 houses in the City were assessed at higher than 100 pounds. Only 26 percent of the houses were assessed at a higher rate than Nehemiah's (21 to 40 pounds) and 24 percent were assessed at 10 pounds or under. The average rental in St. Leonard's Eastcheap was 17 pounds, but the average for the City as a whole was under 15 pounds. In other words, by this measure (and it is hard to know what this assessment measured precisely) Nehemiah fell within the middling group within his own parish but well above the median in the City

as a whole. Further, this assessment, since based on households, did not measure the wealth of servants or lodgers renting rooms. For attempts to come to grips with the social structure of London in this period, see Finlay, *Population and Metropolis*, pp. 70–82; Emrys Jones, "London in the Early Seventeenth Century: An Ecological Approach," *London Journal*, 6 (1980), pp. 123–33; and Valerie Pearl, "Change and Stability in Seventeenth-Century London," *London Journal*, 5 (1979), pp. 3–34. For the process of social differentiation that separated the respectable members of a parish from those on whom social discipline was exercised, see Keith Wrightson and David Levine, *Poverty and Piety in an English Village: Terling, 1525–1700* (New York, 1979), esp. pp. 110–41.

92. For examples of the casuists' art, see William Perkins, *Epieikeia*, in *The Work of William Perkins*, ed. Ian Breward (Abingdon, Berks., 1970), pp. 489–91, and William Ames, *Conscience with the Power of Cases Thereof* (n.p., 1639), Bk. 4, ch. 42 "Of Contracts."

93. Ames, *Conscience*, Bk. 4, p. 248.

94. *The Work of William Perkins*, p. 449.

95. Dent, *Plaine Mans Path-Way*, p. 99. Wallington incorporated substantial portions of pp. 122–29 into his journal "The Mercies of God," GL, MS. 204, pp. 453–56.

96. Dent, *Plaine Mans Path-Way*, pp. 35, 197.

97. *Ibid.*, pp. 125–26.

98. *Ibid.*, pp. 77, 80–81, 99.

99. *Ibid.*, p. 192.

100. Hill, *The Pathway to Prayer and Pietie* (London, 1613), pp. 77–78, 81–82. These distinctions were not, of course, peculiarly Puritan nor unique to the dominant orders. As mentioned, the Turners' Company was still trying to maintain sumptuary regulations as late as 1631.

101. *Ibid.*, pp. 80–83.

102. *Ibid.*, pp. 254, 239.

103. John Ball, *The Power of Godliness* (London, 1657), pp. 446–48, 452, 456–57.

104. George makes this point in an undeservedly neglected article, "The Making of the English Bourgeoisie," *Science and Society*, 35 (1971), p. 409.

105. BL, Sloane MS. 922, fos. 117r–v, 120r, 127r, 128v. See also Lucy Hutchinson, *Memoirs of the Life of Colonel Hutchinson*, ed. James Sutherland (Oxford, 1973), pp. 78–115, for the events of 1643 as seen by the wife of the Parliamentary governor of Nottingham Castle.

106. Folger MS. V.a.436, pp. 299, 323–24.

107. *Ibid.*, pp. 334, 336, 459. For the binding of Heacock (called Lecocke in the records) and William Knight, Wallington's last apprentice, see GL, MS. 3302/1, November 1, 1654; February 1, 1654/55.

108. BL, Add. MS. 40,883, fo. 9r–v.

109. *Ibid.*, fo. 167v.

110. *Ibid.*, fo. 170r–v.

111. Folger MS. V.a.436, pp. 351, 491–92, 503.

112. *Ibid.*, pp. 426–28. The only sanctioned coinage in lead, tin, and copper were tokens of small denominations intended for local markets. Brass (normally an alloy of tin and copper in this period) shillings and half crowns seem more likely to have been counterfeits, the base metal being silver-plated to enable it to pass. See C. E. Challis, *The Tudor Coinage* (New York, 1978), pp. 208–10, 284–90.

113. Folger MS. V.a.436, pp. 327–28.

Chapter 6

The epigraph is from Folger MS. V.a.436, p. 277.

1. BL, Add. MS. 21,935, fo. 173v; GL, MS. 204, pp. 424, 448, 449.

2. BL, Add. MS, 21,935, fo. 91v; *Historical Notices*, vol. 1, p. 61.

3. BL, Add. MS. 21,935, fo. 93v. Compare Wallington's letter to James Cole in Hartford, Connecticut, dated 1642, where in describing the same incident he refers to "not one company taken." BL, Sloane MS. 922, fo. 105v.

4. GL, MS. 204, p. 424.

5. Wallington talks about being delivered into the hands of the Midianites in *ibid.*, p. 449. Wallington uses "papists" for Roman Catholics throughout his writings. "Prelates" and "prelatical," rather than the neutral "bishops" and "episcopal," are the terms used throughout BL, Add. MS. 21,935. The earliest use seems to be in a section titled "1633 A Woeful Profaning of the Lord's Day," in which Wallington asks the reader: "Oh, now consider the woeful and miserable sinful days we are fallen into, for, Oh, how have the prelates and their chancellors put down preaching in divers countries and stopped and silenced many of God's faithful servants. And so they caused the abominable sin of profanation of the Lord's day to abound with the book which they did get of the King's Declaration for Sports and May games on the Lord's Day (in 1633), which book must be read in all public congregations" (fo. 26v; see also fos. 12r, 39v, 40r, 45v, 66r). However, the evidence of usage is ambiguous, since the bulk of Add. MS. 21,935 is based on a compilation of notebooks begun in 1640 (notebook no. 16, "Three paper books of the weekly passages of Parliament, 1640, 1641," and later volumes), although some early parts may come from his notebook no. 10 "The Complaint of a Sinner admiring at the mercies of God," which dates from 1635. See Folger MS. V.a.436, "To the Reader," and the Appendix.

6. For Wallington's participation in the Presbyterian classical system, see *The Register Book of the Fourth Classis in the Province of London, 1646–59*, ed. and intro. by Charles E. Surman, Harleian Society Pubs., vols. 82–83 (London, 1953). Contrast Wallington's attitudes with those of his contemporary Thomas Edwards, whose *Gangraena: or a Catalogue and Discovery of many of*

the Errors, Heresies, Blasphemies and pernicious Practices of the Sectaries of this time was published in London in 1646.

7. BL, Sloane MS. 922, fos. 145v–46r.

8. GL, MS. 204, pp. 495, 497, 502.

9. From *Some Christian Letters of Master Paul Bains* (London, 1620), as quoted in BL, Sloane MS. 922, fo. 56r.

10. *Ibid.*, fos. 119v, 120r.

11. Sir Thomas Smith, *De Republica Anglorum*, ed. L. Alston (Cambridge, Eng., 1906), pp. 30, 46.

12. The evolving government of London in Wallington's lifetime is sketched both in Frank Freeman Foster, *The Politics of Stability: A Portrait of Elizabethan London* (London, 1977), pp. 29–53, and in Valerie Pearl, *London and the Outbreak of the Puritan Revolution* (Oxford, 1961), pp. 45–68.

13. GL, MS. 17,607, The Register Book of St. Leonard's Eastcheap. John Wallington appears as one of the churchwardens on the title page, which is dated December 17, 1599.

14. Wallington was elected constable for two years on December 21, 1637, and found this office "very troublesome." Folger MS. V.a.436, p. 60; cf. Joan Kent, "The English Village Constable, 1580–1642: The Nature and Dilemmas of the Office," *Journal of British Studies*, 20, no. 2 (1981), pp. 26–49; GL, MS. 3461/1, Bridge Ward Within, Wardmote Inquests.

15. BL, Sloane MS. 922, fos. 134v–36v; Wallington accompanied his letter to Waddington with "two little books: one called *Helps to Humiliation*, the other . . . *A Sermon of Repentance*." *Ibid.*, fo. 137v.

16. BL, Add. MS. 21,935, fos. 8r, 9r, 10r, 1r; BL, Sloane MS. 922, fo. 147v.

17. For the creation of the Parliamentary church settlement in 1646, see Claire Cross, "The Church in England 1646–1660," in G. E. Aylmer, ed., *The Interregnum* (London, 1972), pp. 99–120; Lawrence Kaplan, *Politics and Religion During the English Revolution: The Scots and the Long Parliament, 1643–1645* (New York, 1976); Rosemary D. Bradley, "The Failure of Accommodation: Religious Conflicts Between Presbyterians and Independents in the Westminster Assembly, 1643–1646," *Journal of Religious History*, 12 (1982), pp. 23–47; and Michael Mahoney, "Presbyterianism in the City of London, 1645–1647," *Historical Journal*, 22 (1979), pp. 93–114.

18. For Wallington's letter to Player, see BL, Sloane MS. 922, fos. 153r–54r; for those initially elected, see *The Register Book of the Fourth Classis*, pp. 2–3; for Captain Player, the future Chamberlain of London, see the entry for Sir Thomas Player in the *Dictionary of National Biography*. Wallington wrote a book, his thirty-second, about his becoming an elder in 1646. Folger MS. V.a.436, p. 160.

19. *Register Book of the Fourth Classis*, pp. 16–18.

20. *Ibid.*, pp. 59–60, 64, 77–78.

21. *Ibid.*, pp. 157, 159.

22. *Ibid.*, pp. 6–7, 40. On July 17, 1648, the Classis drew up orders on the conditions governing the admission of "strangers" to the Sacrament: *ibid.*, p. 57; see also p. 63. The ready movement of parishioners from one parish to another when seeking congenial religious exercises had clearly created unanticipated problems for parochial discipline.

23. *Ibid.*, p. 67.

24. *Ibid.*, pp. 9–16, 49.

25. *Ibid.*, pp. 60–61, xvii.

26. BL, Sloane MS. 922, fo. 169r–v.

27. *Register Book of the Fourth Classis*, pp. 99, 89; for Roborough's burial, see GL, MS. 17,697, fo. 25r.

28. BL, Sloane MS. 922, fo. 169r; Folger MS. V.a.436, p. 160; *Register Book of the Fourth Classis*, p. 124. For Barker, see. A. G. Matthews, *Calamy Revised* (Oxford, 1934), pp. 28–29; *Biographical Dictionary of British Radicals in the Seventeenth Century*, ed. Richard L. Greaves and Robert Zaller (London, 1982), vol. 1, pp. 38–39. Barker had previously had another London living between 1643 and 1648: see the vestry minutes of St. James' Garlickhithe, GL, MS. 4813/1, fos. 67r, 70r.

29. All were inhabitants of St. Leonard's; see GL, MS. 3461/1, precinct lists. The story of Thomas Adams's wife appears in BL, Add. MS. 21,935, fo. 162v; both Adams and Estwick are mentioned in Pearl, *London and the Outbreak of the Puritan Revolution*, pp. 292–93, 315.

30. GL, MS. 204, p. 472; *Historical Notices*, vol. 1, p. 137. The green bay or laurel is the emblem for fame and victory, and rosemary is, of course, for remembrance.

31. *Historical Notices*, vol. 1, pp. 244, 241. For an account of the various demonstrations on behalf of Strafford's trial and later attainder, see Brian Manning, *The English People and the English Revolution* (London, 1976), pp. 8–18.

32. *Historical Notices*, vol. 1, p. 259.

33. BL, Add. MS. 40,883, fo. 12r.

34. *Historical Notices*, vol. 2, pp. 9, 13.

35. BL, Add. MS. 40,883, fo. 49r.

36. *Ibid.*, fos. 142v–43r.

37. GL, MS. 204 was begun in 1619, according to Folger MS. V.a.436, p. 11. R. Webb, the Victorian editor whose two-volume edition of BL, Add. MS. 21,935 was published in 1869 as *Historical Notices*, supposed that both were begun in 1630, but she was wrong on both counts. Add. MS. 21,935 includes material from the 1630's and earlier, but the earliest volume in Wallington's own catalogue of notebooks that bears any resemblance to it was begun in 1640. Add. MS. 21,935 in fact appears to be a later compilation of a number of notebooks he kept in the 1640's, which he numbered 16, 17, 21, 23, and 26 in his catalogue, plus some prefatory material, perhaps from notebook no. 10: see Folger MS. V.a.436, "To the Christian Reader." R. Webb in the published *Historical Notices* rearranged the material in Add. MS. 21,935 and

omits much of Wallington's personal reflection, as well as matter regarded as tasteless by the "altered manners of the age" (p. xxvi). For example, Wallington's graphic description of how Attorney General Noy died horribly "pissing blood" is omitted. Compare *Historical Notices*, vol. 1, p. 68, with Add. MS. 21,935, fo. 45r.

38. See the prefatory "To the Christian Reader" in each volume, but particularly in GL, MS. 204.

39. GL, MS. 204, pp. 444–45.

40. *Historical Notices*, vol. 1, 7.

41. BL, Add. MS. 21,935, fos. 8r–10r, 1r; GL, MS. 204, p. 498, misnumbered p. 483. The initial section of Add. MS. 21,935 is titled "A Bundle of Mercies," and the argument is that after the defeat of the Armada and the discovery of the Gunpowder Plot, the enemies of God "went more cunningly and politically to work . . . bringing in by little and little their corruptions and abominations . . . , so that the Church and commonwealth were both of them infected and sick together, and if God of his great goodness and mercy had not an instant . . . helped us, they had perished together." The catalogue of sins begins with idolatry and breach of covenant, contempt of the Gospel, and "marrying of strange wives," proceeds to swearing and cursing, the breach of the Sabbath, whoredom, gluttony, and drunkenness, and continues to stage plays. Chronologically the mercies begin with the defeat of the Armada, and the judgments with the plague of 1625; but the first specific mention of "sins and abominations" (as opposed to the general sins catalogued at the beginning of the section) occurs in 1633, when Wallington describes how Dr. Collins maintains transubstantiation, how Perne, "the popish master of Peterhouse . . . preacheth many popish points," and how "a writing came to my hand" that maintained that the baptized are truly regenerate, etc., "among other grievous things." In short, although Wallington sees a long sweep of history stretching back to Elizabeth's reign during which the Catholics and crypto-Catholics have attempted to destroy the godly and the English state, his actual awareness of specific "sins and abominations" seems to date from the year William Laud became archbishop. BL, Add. MS. 21,935, fos. 1r, 2r–3r, 10r.

42. *Historical Notices*, vol. 1, p. 17.

43. *Ibid.*, vol. 1, p. 20.

44. Wallington warns against being a "vain beholder" and in fact draws a specific parallel to the sermonic use: "the good Lord teach us . . . that we may all make such use of this and all other His judgments . . . as He requireth in His word we should do. . . ." *Ibid.* Compare GL, MS. 204, p. 483.

45. *Historical Notices*, vol. 1, pp. 61–62; GL, MS. 204, pp. 448–50. Cf. Lady Brilliana Harley, who wrote on April 9, 1641: "We must all say, if the Lord does not appear in His almighty power to overrule the actions of men, we may fear woeful days. If such days should befall us, the woe would light on

those that have not walked with God, and God's children should only taste of the sorrow of them." *Letters of Lady Brilliana Harley*, ed. Thomas Taylor Lewis (Camden Society, old series, vol. 58; London, 1854), p. 123.

46. GL, MS. 204, pp. 457, 450. Cf. Lady Brilliana Harley, who wrote: "And for our comforts, I think never any laid plots to rout out all God's children at once, but that the Lord did shew Himself mighty in saving His servants and confounding His enemies, as He did Pharaoh. . . ." *Letters of Lady Brilliana Harley*, pp. 180–81.

47. BL, Add. MS. 21,935, fo. 80v.

48. *Historical Notices*, vol. 1, p. 8. On February 19, 1640/41, Lady Brilliana Harley wrote that "I have always believed that the Lord would purge His Church from all these things and persons that have been such a hindrance to the free passage of His glorious Gospel, and I trust now is the time." A month later she added: "I am glad the bishops begin to fall, and I hope it will be with them, as it was with Haman: when he began to fall, he fell indeed." *Letters of Lady Brilliana Harley*, pp. 115, 119.

49. BL, Add. MS. 21,935, fo. 173; *Historical Notices*, vol. 2, pp. 13–14.

50. *Historical Notices*, vol. 1, p. xxv.

51. BL, Add. MS. 40,883, fos. 15v–16r.

52. *Ibid.*, fo. 16r.

53. BL, Add. MS. 21,935, fos. 5r–7r. The mercies were all the more note-worthy because, in Wallington's view, quite undeserved. The pages preced-ing the Bundle of Mercies contain an exact catalogue of the 27 sins of the English, ranging from idolatry to lying. None of this material is contained in the published *Historical Notices*.

54. BL, Add. MS. 21,935, fos. 194r, 193v.

55. BL, Sloane MS. 922, fo. 145v.

56. *Ibid.*, fo. 176r.

57. GL, MS. 204, p. 43; BL, Sloane MS. 922, fo. 105r.

58. BL, Sloane MS. 922, fo. 105r.

59. BL, Add. MS. 21,935, fo. 9r–v; fos. 20r–38v contain a long account, including many stories from Thomas Beard's *Theatre of Gods Iudgements* (London, 1597, 1612, 1632), about the divine punishment of Sabbath break-ers. For Wallington, "they are blind who see not this, the finger of God," in the punishments. What is perhaps more evident to the modern reader in these stories is the degree to which the promulgation of the Book of Sports brought into the open for the first time the division in many communities between the godly and their neighbors.

60. BL, Add. MS. 21,935, fo. 10r.

61. *Ibid.*, fos. 53r–65v. The twelfth of Wallington's 50 notebooks was "A book wherein I did write the cruel sufferings of Mr. Burton, Mr. Prynne, and Doctor Bastwick under the prelates in 1637." Folger MS. V.a.436, "To the Christian Reader." The art of Protestant martyrology did not cease with John Foxe.

62. BL, Add. MS. 21,935, fo. 60v.

63. *Calendar of State Papers, Domestic, 1633–34*, p. 579; *1634–35*, pp. 50, 108, 110, 117.

64. GL, MS. 204, pp. 469–75. Wallington had indeed correspondents in the country; in 1639 his friend Francis Wilsmore thanked him for sending a copy of one of Thomas Hooker's books to him in Nottingham. BL, Sloane MS. 922, fo. 116v. Wallington was served a second writ on May 22 but did not appear, the cost of four pounds for counsel and for a copy of the interrogatories being beyond his means when money was so short. GL, MS. 204, p. 476. For the trials of Burton, Bastwick, and Prynne and the clandestine book trade, see Stephen Foster, *Notes from the Caroline Underground* (Hamden, Conn., 1978), esp. pp. 40–65.

65. BL, Add. MS. 21,935, fos. 80r–81r.

66. *Ibid.*, fos. 74r–77r, 80v–81v.

67. *Ibid.*, fo. 86v. In 1639 hope even in King Charles was still possible: "Oh, then how did I with tears pour out my enlarged heart unto the Lord my God that he would be pleased of his great mercy to spare us one year longer, and to try us once more and to send us our king in peace again." Folger MS. V.a.436, p. 75. Nevertheless, that hope, such as it was, was soon falsified by events. "Now when the king was come back again from Scotland . . . still there was oppression in paying of money for new corporations. . . . So still there was oppression for ship money, and they that would not pay, some had their best of their kine or horses driven out of their ground, or their goods attached and taken away, or else themselves sent to prison to their much damage, if not to their undoing." BL, MS. 21,935, fo. 88r–v.

68. BL, Sloane MS. 922, fo. 105r; he called it "another and grievous monstrous abominable sin among us," only too likely to "provoke God to throw down judgments," and he copied a lengthy excerpt from a tract, *A Short View of the Prelaticall Church of England*, published anonymously in 1640, which dissected both the Canons and the policies of the Laudian Church from the "godly" point of view. BL, Add. MS. 21,935, fos. 66r–73v.

69. See GL, MS. 204, p. 495, for Wallington's 1632 prayer that neither the one nor the other would affect the king's judgment. In Wallington's circle monarchy may always have been viewed with a certain amount of skepticism. In a letter of October 30, 1628, Livewell Rampaigne had written to Nehemiah that not the least of the disasters that had overtaken the French Huguenots at La Rochelle was to have "fallen under the power of a king that hath been taxed for promise-breaking, in whose eyes it may seem a small thing to deprive them of lives and liberties at once." GL, MS. 204, p. 424. Nevertheless, Wallington was slow to see the king as actively evil. On the one hand, he could celebrate the king's signing of the early Long Parliament acts: "Oh, how hath God heard our prayers in giving our royal King Charles a heart to sign and seal to those acts that concern the Church of God." On the other hand, when Charles told the House of Lords on May 1, 1641, that

his "tender conscience" would not permit Strafford's execution, Wallington noted that "these words made our hearts heavy and sad." Wallington was evidently prepared to believe the truth of a letter that came to light early in January 1641/42 in which a "papist" plotter wrote that "the king's heart is a Protestant, but our friends can persuade him and make him believe anything; he hates the Puritan party and is made irreconcilable to that side." But on the whole, as late as 1642 Wallington saw the king less as a man actively bent on wickedness than as one who would not do the good he could do. "You may see our king (as it were, the midwife) stand by (or gets afar off) and may come and help and (for all so many petitions) yet he will not." The role of active evil was left to the "wicked papist," who "like the great red dragon (Rev. 12:3–4) stands by that as soon as any good motion, as it were the child, coming forth, is ready to devour it, and, if not with overpowering it, yet with their devilish plots to destroy it." BL, MS. 21,935, fos. 156r, 138v, 188r, 193r. This vision of the king would only change when Wallington came to believe that Charles had actively encouraged the rebellious Catholics in Ireland.

70. BL, Add. MS. 21,935, fo. 12r.

71. BL, Sloane MS. 922, fos. 92v–93r.

72. BL, Add. MS. 21,935, fo. 86v; cf. fo. 87r–v, for Wallington's account of the defeat of the Spanish fleet, a second Armada, by the Dutch, while the power of England was away in the north, arrayed against Scotland. "The Lord hath graciously frustrated their purposes and delivered his Church and children by a miraculous way," was Wallington's conclusion.

73. *Ibid.*, fo. 88r.

74. *Ibid.*, fos. 91v–92v.

75. *Ibid.*, fos. 93v–94r.

76. BL, Add. MS. 40,883, fos. 5r, 7r; Add. MS. 21,935, fo. 133r.

77. BL, Add. MS. 21,935, fo. 157r.

78. *Ibid.*, fos. 99v, 110r, 111r.

79. BL, Sloane MS. 922, fo. 126v.

80. BL, Add. MS. 21,935, fos. 157v–58r.

81. *Ibid.*, fos. 160v, 162v.

82. *Ibid.*, fos. 180r–81v; cf. fo. 189v.

83. *Ibid.*, fos. 168v–69r. It is worth noting that Zachariah was also the name of Wallington's brother-in-law, who was murdered in the early weeks of the Irish Rebellion.

84. *Ibid.*, fos. 187r–88r. According to Wallington's notes, this letter was addressed to Orlando Bridgeman, M.P., and was read in the House of Commons on January 10 and 11, 1641/42.

85. *Ibid.*, fos. 199r, 200r.

86. *Ibid.*, fos. 204r, 199r.

87. BL, Add. MS. 40,883, fo. 118r.

88. BL, Add. MS. 21,935, fo. 194r.

89. BL, Sloane MS. 922, fo. 133v.

90. BL, Add. MS. 21,935, fo. 204v.

91. *Ibid.*, fos. 202r, 214r, 220r.

92. *Ibid.*, fo. 229r–v.

93. *Ibid.*, fos. 280v–81r.

94. BL, Sloane MS. 922, fo. 146r.

95. BL, Add. MS. 40,883, fos. 128v–29r.

96. *Ibid.*, fo. 133v.

97. *Ibid.*, fo. 143r–v.

98. *Ibid.*, fo. 142r–v.

99. *Ibid.*, fo. 154r–v.

100. BL, Sloane MS. 922, fo. 146v. For all his discouragement over the divisions within the ranks of the godly, Wallington did acknowledge that "God did hear and answer the prayers of his children for the land in general" in 1645, and in consequence wrote "another book of particular mercies of God in hearing the prayers of his children which I called An encouragement to Faithful Prayer." Folger MS. V.a.436, p. 135. Nevertheless, on reflection it became evident that the victories of 1645 were ephemeral, because Parliamentary reforms proved so superficial: "But as if deliverance did come too soon, and as we made show of a Reformation, so God made show of our deliverance, so that before the old war had ended, new sins begat a new war." *Ibid.*, p. 175. The "new war," which Wallington in his disillusionment dubbed "the hypocritical war," was the Second Civil War in 1648.

101. BL, Sloane MS. 922, fo. 140r.

102. Folger MS. V.a.436, pp. 177, 449. Not that Wallington thought that there had been no error abroad in the land until the victories of the New Model Army made possible a de facto toleration. As early as April 1643 Wallington had had a very unsatisfactory argument with an Antinomian whose views "opened a very wide gap of liberty to sin." Nevertheless, although Wallington knew that his opponent's views were in error, "yet he was too hard for me in reasoning and did puzzle me in so much that it did distemper me on the Lord's day." Fortunately, and not for the first time, "God . . . did send his servant Mr. Roborough to refresh my distempered mind." BL, Add. MS. 40,883, fo. 94v.

103. BL, Add. MS. 40,883. Wallington went to Henry Burton's church, St. Matthew's Friday Street, about half a mile west of St. Leonard's, on several occasions in 1643: *ibid.*, fos. 95v, 105v, 154v. Burton was an Independent. Wallington also heard Simeon Ash at Lazarus Seaman's Church of All Hallows' Bread Street, which was next to St. Matthew's Friday Street: *ibid.*, fo. 33r. Ash and Seaman were both Presbyterians.

104. BL, Sloane MS. 922, fo. 173v.

105. *Ibid.*

106. *Ibid.*, fos. 173v–74r.

107. BL, Sloane MS. 1457, fos. 88r–94r; Sloane MS. 922, fo. 176r.

108. BL, Add. MS. 40,883, fo. 186v.

109. BL, Sloane MS. 1457, fos. 99r–101v. See Wallington's letter to Colfe for a picture of his high expectations of the ministry. BL, Sloane MS. 922, fo. 132r–v.

110. For the role of Puritanism in the creation of the active citizen, see Michael Walzer, *The Revolution of the Saints* (Cambridge, Mass., 1965).

111. BL, Add. MS. 21,935, fo. 193v. Wallington acknowledges that he is here paraphrasing Richard Sibbes's *The Bruised Reed*.

112. BL, Add. MS. 21,935, fos. 180v–81r. This long passage on the inevitability of conflict between the wicked and the godly is omitted from the printed *Historical Notices*. However much the forces of Antichrist might be fated for ultimate defeat, Wallington was in no doubt that where the "well affected" were too few, the forces of Antichrist might triumph at least temporarily. Hence, "in Ireland, which was farther off, they had [enough] time to prepare their work that they [would have] possessed themselves of the whole kingdom, totally subverted the government of it, rooted out religion and destroyed all the Protestants . . . if by God's wonderful providence their main enterprise upon the City and Castle of Dublin had not been detected and prevented." *Ibid.*, fo. 181r.

113. BL, Add. MS. 40,883, fo. 186v.

114. *Historical Notices*, vol. 2, p. 14.

115. Folger MS. V.a.436, pp. 375, 388. Success was never the proper or only measure of political action. Just as wealth might not follow from the diligent pursuit of one's vocation, so godly initiatives in politics might seem to fall on stony ground. Nonetheless, Wallington was convinced that the saint would ultimately have his just reward: "And when I think it is anything that concerns God's glory, I never think much of any pains and charge, being assured I shall have a thousandfold for it again, and so I find it at this present. Since I have bought and spread these books, God hath blessed me the better in my Calling." *Ibid.*, p. 376.

116. BL, Sloane MS. 922, fo. 132r–v.

117. BL, Add. MS. 21,935, fo. 162v.

118. GL, MS. 204, p. 43.

119. Folger MS. V.a.436, p. 75.

120. BL, Add. MS. 40,883, fo. 118r.

121. Folger MS. V.a.436, p. 144.

122. *Ibid.*, p. 305.

123. *Ibid.*, p. 143. Lady Brilliana Harley's understanding of the efficacy of prayer was similar: "I persuade myself, the enemies of God's Church will lay their plots deep, but our God is above them, and to Him do we look that never yet deserted Her in the time of trouble. Nay, this is our comfort, that the time of trouble is a special time in which the Lord has commanded His children to seek unto Him, and the Lord does not bid us to seek Him in vain. I pray God preserve the Parliament and guide them in the good way, that they may counsel for the good of His Church." *Letters of Lady Brilliana Harley*, p. 102. Nonetheless, cold and dead prayers were without efficacy. In early April 1641 Wallington feared that his own backwardness in prayer was the cause of the political stalemate. "Insomuch that I think the whole Church of God fared the worse for me, but now more especially in this time of Parliament, when the wicked wretch, the Deputy of Ireland, caused to be a fort-

night's time in trial and yet justice not to take place and proceed against him. Surely my deadness and backwardness in duty is some cause." BL, Add. MS. 40,883, fo. 6v.

124. *Historical Notices*, vol. 1, p. 280.

125. BL, Add. MS. 21,935, fo. 169r. This passage is omitted in *Historical Notices*.

126. GL, MS. 204, p. 458.

127. *Historical Notices*, vol. 1, pp. 134–35.

128. BL, Sloane MS. 922, fos. 146r, 105v–6r. See also Add. MS. 40,883, fo. 7r, where he writes that "the king send that the Deputy should not die. . . . And at the last God did hear us, for on the xii of May the Deputy was beheaded to the joy of the Church of God." This view was by no means unique to Wallington. Thomas Goodwin wrote that "through which Spirit of Prayer and Supplications thus poured forth, believers come to be at once anointed to the fellowship, and execution of those three glorious offices of Christ their Head, not only of Priests, by offering up their prayers, as Spiritual sacrifices, acceptable to God through Jesus Christ, but of Kings, to rule with God. Hosea 11:12. Being hereby made of Privy Counsel to the King of Kings, so as their counsels and desires expressed in their petitions are said to be fulfilled, and their decrees in their prayers made, ratified, and established. Nay further, by virtue of this privilege, advanced to such height of favor as by their strength in prayer alone, to have power with God himself, and not only with him but also over him, and in their wrestlings to prevail, yea to command: Himself hath said it, 'Thus saith the Lord, the Holy one of Israel and his maker, Ask of me of things to come concerning my sons, and concerning the work of my hands, command ye me,' Isaiah 45:11, which so transcendent privilege of power is . . . universally extended unto all transactions of this lower part of his dominions, whether ecclesiastical . . . , or what ever other . . . that appertain to common providence." *The Returne of Prayers* (London, 1643), Epistle Dedicatory.

129. GL, MS. 204, p. 457.

130. BL, Sloane MS. 922, fos. 173r–74r.

131. BL, Sloane MS. 1457, fos. 99r–101v.

132. Wallington quoted this saying both in GL, MS. 204, pp. 116, 406, and 457, and in a 1642 letter to James Cole: BL, Sloane MS. 922, fo. 105r.

133. GL, MS. 204, pp. 449–50.

134. Folger MS. V.a.436, p. 177.

135. *The Returne of Prayers*, pp. 6–7.

136. *Ibid.*, p. 140.

137. Folger MS. V.a.436, p. 177.

138. See J. A. W. Gunn, "'Interest Will Not Lie': A Seventeenth-century Political Maxim," *Journal of the History of Ideas*, 29 (1968), pp. 551–64.

139. John Wallington, Sr., to John Allen, March 31, 1635, "setting forth the high calling of the ministry of God." BL, Sloane MS. 922, fo. 108r.

140. "Master Wells" [Thomas Weld's] letter from New England to his people at Terling, Essex, 1633. *Ibid.*, fo. 92v.

141. Nehemiah Wallington to Henry Roborough, December 25, 1638. *Ibid.*, fos. 119r, 120r.

Chapter 7

The epigraph is from Folger MS. V.a.436, p. 1.

1. *Ibid.*, p. 516.

2. Quoted by Gordon Craig in a review of *Thomas Mann: Diaries 1918–1939*, in *The New York Review of Books*, December 2, 1982, p. 32.

3. *The Diary of Roger Lowe of Ashton-in-Makerfield, Lancashire, 1663–74*, ed. William L. Sachse (New Haven, Conn., 1938); *Remarkable Passages in the Life of William Kiffin*, ed. William Orme (London, 1823).

4. *Remarkable Passages in the Life of William Kiffin*, p. 1; see also the memoirs of John Dane, the Stortford tailor: John Dane, "A Declaration of the Remarkable Providences in the Course of My Life," in *New England Historical and Genealogical Register*, 8 (1854), pp. 149–56.

5. Joseph Hall, *The Shaking of the Olive Tree*, in *The Remaining Works of . . . Joseph Hall, D.D.* (London, 1660), p. 1.

6. *Letters of Lady Brilliana Harley*, ed. Thomas Taylor Lewis (Camden Society, old series, vol. 58; London, 1854), p. 69.

7. See *Two Elizabethan Puritan Diaries*, ed. M. M. Knappen (Chicago, 1933; reprinted Gloucester, Mass., 1966), pp. 53–55. By December 1587 Rogers was already writing a daily "direction of life for to guide us by," which was eventually to be published as his famous *Seven Treatises* (1603): *ibid.*, pp. 71, 7.

8. Quoted in Peter Clark, "Thomas Scott and the Growth of Urban Opposition to the Early Stuart Regime," *Historical Journal*, 21 (1978), p. 5.

9. *The Diary of Ralph Josselin, 1616–1683*, ed. Alan Macfarlane (London, 1976), p. 19; see also p. 17, entry of August 26, 1644.

10. Folger MS. V.a.436, p. 1; Oliver Heywood, *His Autobiography*, ed. J. H. Turner (Brighouse, Yorks., 1882), vol. 1, pp. 153–54.

11. *Letters of Lady Brilliana Harley*, p. 69.

12. BL, Sloane MS. 922, fo. 122v.

13. GL, MS. 204, p. 47.

14. BL, Add. MS. 40,883, fos. 9v, 83v, 104r.

15. *The Elizabethan Nation* (New York, 1967), p. 95.

16. Folger MS. V.a.436, p. 399.

17. P. S. Seaver, *The Puritan Lectureships* (Stanford, Calif., 1970), p. 127.

18. *A Compendius Form and Sum of Christian Doctrine . . . Meet for Well-Disposed Families* (London, 1579), B1ʳ. I owe this and the subsequent quotation from Gifford to Dr. Patricia Hutchinson.

19. As quoted in Richard L. Greaves, *Society and Religion in Elizabethan England* (Minneapolis, Minn., 1981), p. 292.

20. Arthur Dent, *The Plaine Mans Path-Way to Heaven* (London, 1601), pp. 348–49.

21. "The True Report of Our Examination and Conference . . . ," reprinted in H. C. Porter, ed., *Puritanism in Tudor England* (Columbia, S.C., 1971), p. 91.

22. *Catechism: Containing the Sum of Christian Religion* (London, 1583), D1^r–D2^r; cf. Robert Sherrard, *The Countryman with His Household* (London, 1620), pp. 206, 208.

23. Folger MS. V.a.436, p. 71.

24. "A Declaration of Remarkable Providence in the Course of My Life," in *The New England Historical and Genealogical Register*, 8 (1854), p. 153.

25. For the Barringtons and their role in the godly community, see William Hunt, *The Puritan Moment: The Coming of Revolution in an English County* (Cambridge, Mass., 1983), pp. 219–33; *Barrington Family Letters, 1628–1632*, ed. Arthur Searle (Camden Society, 4th series, vol. 28 [1983]), Introduction. The godly laity themselves seem to have had the means to find their coreligionists, even in distant communities. Nehemiah's first apprentice was James Weld, son of Edmund Weld of Sudbury, Suffolk, a linen draper and brother of the preacher Thomas Weld: see GL, MS. 3302/1, under date March 20, 1620/21, for the record of James Weld's indenture (Edmund is here noted as a mercer, defunct) and John and J. A. Venn, *Alumni Cantabrigienses*, Part I (Cambridge, 1922–27), vol. 4, p. 360. Thomas Weld, the vicar of Terling and later pastor of Roxbury, Massachusetts, must have been some ten years older than James. Although James may have come to Nehemiah by chance, it seems more likely that some connection existed between Edmund Weld and John Wallington, Sr., if only their membership within the godly community. Again, there appears to have been much passing around of manuscripts within the godly community. Nehemiah had a copy of Thomas Weld's letter written to his former congregation at Terling, Essex, in 1633 after he had emigrated to Massachusetts (BL, Sloane MS. 922, fos. 90r–93v), and in 1635 Wallington copied a manuscript of a work compiled by Nathaniel Bacon, the Recorder of Ipswich, and published three years later as *A Relation of the Fearefull Estate of Francis Spira, in the year, 1548* (London, 1638); for Wallington's copying of this manuscript, see Folger MS. V.a.436, fo. 46v.

26. For letters of a former apprentice and Puritan to his former master, a London merchant, see "Letters from a Subaltern Officer of the Earl of Essex's Army, written in the Summer and Autumn of 1642," ed. Sir Henry Ellis, *Archaeologia*, 35 (1853), pp. 310–34. Nehemiah Wharton, the former apprentice, refers at one point to the events of the army's march to the West as "the passages of my pilgrimage" (p. 317). Wharton's letters give some sense of his wonder at Worcester, "the very emblem of Gomorrah," and at

the Herefordshire countryside, where "the inhabitants are totally ignorant in the ways of God" (pp. 330, 332). Clearly, this young officer, accustomed to a city rich in preachers and possessing godly communities already two generations old, was amazed to discover an England populated by "Baalists" who prayed for king and bishops.

27. Thomas Hooker, *Writings in England and Holland, 1626–1633*, ed. George H. Williams et al. (Cambridge, Mass., 1975), pp. 245–46.

28. See Keith Wrightson and David Levine, *Poverty and Piety in an English Village: Terling, 1525–1700* (New York, 1979), esp. Chapter 6; Hunt, *The Puritan Moment*, pp. 79, 130–55.

29. GL, MS. 204, pp. 505–10.

30. Folger MS. V.a.436, pp. 164, 187–88.

31. *Ibid.*, pp. 474, 482.

32. *Ibid.*, pp. 537–38. John Crook, some twenty years younger than Wallington, had an analogous experience of certainty followed by recurring doubts. As a child of ten or eleven tempted by the devil, Crook found that "on a sudden, there came around me a Power and Life that did oppose and gainsay the Enemy, making my spirit say within me with much boldness and courage, I will not serve thee, O Satan, but I will serve the Lord God. . . ." Shortly afterward, he went to school in London, where he "was not without much trouble and exercises in [his] mind." Later, as an apprentice in the 1630's, he concluded that he was "but an Hypocrite, and did not belong to the Election of Grace," despite his frequenting of "Puritan" sermons and lectures. Several years later he heard a sermon on the text from Isaiah, "He that walketh in darkness, and hath no light, let him trust in the Name of the Lord, and stay upon his God." Crook thought that the preacher spoke "as if he had known my condition," but found little relief from his misery until "on a sudden, there sprang in me a Voice, saying, Fear not, O thou tossed, as with a Tempest, . . . I will help thee; and although I have hid my face from thee for a moment, yet with everlasting Kindness will I visit thee, and thou shalt be mine." The "peace and joy" that followed was soon over, and Crook soon "perceived an abatement of the Glory." Nevertheless, despite continued worldly temptations, "this continued Cry and Sound in my Ears inwardly called for watchfulness over my ways and obedience unto what was made manifest to be the will of God in my conscience." Like a number of young Puritans of his generation, Crook became an army officer, a Baptist, and eventually a Quaker. However, Quaker preaching "did not make void my former Experiences of the Love and Mercy of God to my poor Soul, nor in the least beget my Mind unto Contempt of his sweet Refreshings in my wearied Pilgrimage." John Crook, *A Short History of John Crook* (London, 1706), pp. 4, 6, 8, 11, 14–16, 22.

33. BL, Sloane MS. 1457, fo. 2v.

Index